Policy and practice in primary education

The so-called 'Alexander Report' on primary education in Leeds, published in 1991, provoked a nation-wide controversy. It has been hailed as 'seminal', 'the most important document since Plowden', but it has also been quoted – and misquoted – in support of widely-opposed political and professional agendas, thus underlining the need for a new kind of debate about the purposes and practice of primary education, one in which ideology and sloganizing are replaced by analysis, evidence and argument.

This book allows the general reader to see what Robin Alexander's report actually said. It includes the report itself, re-edited and expanded for a national readership, together with three additional chapters on some of the wider issues raised by the report and the attendant furore. Beyond the rhetoric are serious questions about how young children should be educated, and it is these which are the book's basic concern.

This is a major contribution to the debate about primary education. Everyone involved in the education of young children, at whatever level, will need to engage with its arguments.

Robin Alexander is Professor of Primary Education at the University of Leeds. He has worked in primary schools and teacher education, is past Chair of the Association for the Study of Primary Education, and is a member of the Council for the Accreditation of Teacher Education. His past books include *Primary Teaching, Changing Primary Practice, The Self-Evaluating Institution*, and *Change in Teacher Education*.

Policy and practice in primary education

Robin Alexander

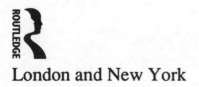
London and New York

First published 1992
by Routledge
11 New Fetter Lane, London EC4P 4EE

Simultaneously published in the USA and Canada
by Routledge
a division of Routledge, Chapman and Hall, Inc.
29 West 35th Street, New York, NY 10001

Typeset by Laserscript Limited, Mitcham, Surrey
Printed and bound in Great Britain by Mackays of Chatham PLC, Chatham, Kent

British Library Cataloguing in Publication Data
A catalogue record for this book is available from the British Library.

ISBN 0-415-08007–X
      0-415-08008–8 (pbk)

Library of Congress Cataloging in Publication Data
has been applied for.

Contents

Figures

Tables

Acknowledgements

Leeds City Council commissioned and funded the evaluation of which the first part of this book gives an account. They deserve not merely the conventional thanks but also credit for joining with Leeds University in making public the findings of what was, after all, a purely internal affair – especially in view of the way sections of the national press so cynically distorted some of the report's main findings.

This double acknowledgement – for taking part and for suffering the media fallout – must extend to the staff of the 230 or so primary schools involved in the Leeds Primary Needs Programme who participated so willingly in the evaluation. All schools were involved at the minimum level of completing annual questionnaires, but many submitted to a much more searching and time-consuming programme of observation, interviews and other fieldwork.

The evaluation was undertaken by a team, the individual and collective contributions of whose members I would like to acknowledge with considerable gratitude. For part of each of the four years of data collection we were supported by a succession of teachers seconded by Leeds LEA: Gwyneth Christie, Elizabeth Emery, Keith Goulding, Adrianne Harker, Jill Herron, Denise Nathan, Maggie Robson, Veronica Sawyer, Bob Shelton, Brian Taylor, Colleen Torcasio and Kevin Walker. The Leeds University members of the team included, besides myself as director, Steve Conway, Martin Ripley and Val Carroll, who succeeded each other as research assistants; Kay Kinder, who served for three years as research fellow; and John Willcocks, who as senior research fellow/coordinator stayed with the project from beginning to end. We also had support in the project's closing stages from Elizabeth Willcocks.

It was a complex, sensitive and difficult project and thanks are due to all of these for helping to make it work. Especially I would like to thank Kay and John, whose analytical perspectives are very evident in many of the project reports, not least the final one on which this book's first part is based. John's role in the preparation of the final report was critical, and he made significant contributions to what have become Chapters 2, 4, 5 and 7 of this book.

Abbreviations

CATE	Council for the Accreditation of Teacher Education
DES	Department of Education and Science
EESA	Early Education Support Agency
EPFAS	Educational Psychology and Family Advisory Service
ERA	Education Reform Act
ESG	Educational Support Grant
GEST	Grants for Education, Support and Training
GRIST	Grant-Related In-Service Training
HE	higher education
HMI	Her Majesty's Inspectorate of Schools
HSLO	Home–School Liaison Officer
INRS	Individual Needs Recording System
INSET	in-service education of teachers
ITT	initial teacher-training
LEA	local education authority
LEATGS	Local Education Authority Training Grants Scheme
LISSEN	Leeds In-Service for Special Educational Needs
LMS	local management of schools
MPG	main professional grade
NCC	National Curriculum Council
NFER	National Foundation for Education Research in England and Wales
PGCE	Post Graduate Certificate in Education
PNP	Primary Needs Programme
PrIME	Primary Initiatives in Mathematics Education
PRINDEP	Primary Needs Independent Evaluation Project
SATs	Standard Assessment Tasks
SD	standard deviation
SEAC	School Examinations and Assessment Council
SEN	special educational needs
SOA	Statement of Attainment
TA	Teacher Assessment
TTT	Teachers Teaching Together

Introduction

This book has two distinct purposes. The first is to make more generally available the evaluation report *Primary Education in Leeds*, which when it was first published attracted considerable publicity and provoked a great deal of comment. Much of that comment was ill-informed, since it was made on the basis of press accounts which ranged from the merely selective to the blatantly distorted. Although *Primary Education in Leeds* was prepared as a document for local use, the fact that it rapidly acquired national standing (or notoriety) made it essential that the media version of the report be ousted as soon as possible by the real thing.

The second and more ambitious purpose is to use the Leeds material as the basis for reflecting more globally on policy and practice in primary education, on the relationship – at both local and national levels – between the two, and on ways that both need to change in order to ensure that young children are given the quality of education they deserve.

This then, is a book within a book. The Leeds material provides both a study in its own right and case material for a more general appraisal of what primary education is about and where it is going.

In the first capacity, it also serves as a companion volume to the edited collections of interim project reports contained in Alexander *et al.* (1989) and Alexander and Willcocks (1992).

Turning *Primary Education in Leeds* into Part I of the present book has called for substantial modifications. The outward trappings of the report – numbering of every paragraph, extensive numbered cross-references, generous use of bullets to mark significant points – have mostly been removed to enable the chapters in question to flow. The style of these nine chapters, however, remains that of a document prepared for a particular audience – in this case, teachers, advisers, and LEA officers and members. It is direct, to the point, avoids an excess of technical detail, and is only occasionally discursive. This should be borne in mind by the minority of readers from the research community who may be expecting something more like a research report. At the same time, the latter should note that much of the fine detail of methodology and data appears in the project's interim reports, most of which are in the two companion collections referred to above, and that there is a complete list of instruments and sources of evidence in this book's appendix.

It should also be noted – in case any readers wish to compare Part I with the original report – that there have been many revisions and additions throughout, including a major expansion and rewriting of Chapter 4.

The background to the evaluation (described in detail in Alexander *et al.* (1989)) is, briefly, as follows.

Leeds City Council initiated its Primary Needs Programme (PNP) in 1985 and a year later commissioned an independent evaluation from a team at Leeds University directed by myself.

The evaluation was to be both formative and summative. In a series of eleven interim reports published between October 1986 and May 1990 (PRINDEP 1986a–1990) we charted the progress of the Council's programme of reform for primary education, describing emerging practice and commenting on a wide range of issues. These documents were intended to stimulate and support the processes of review and modification to which we assumed those involved in the initiative would be committed. Dissemination of these reports was extensive: multiple copies were sent to every primary school and its governing body, to advisers, officers and members of the LEA, and to public libraries.

The final report, in draft, was delivered for comment to LEA officers and the Chair of Education in March 1991. There followed a period of negotiation, much of it paragraph by paragraph, before, on 30 July 1991, the agreed final version (Alexander 1991) was presented to the City Council. The Council accepted the report and its recommendations in full and adopted an action plan. A joint Leeds University/Leeds City Council press release was issued, and the report was then distributed to schools, governing bodies and other interested parties.

All reporting was open: we were not prepared to participate in the essentially divisive process of producing reports for one group about the activities of another. We saw the whole educational community as our client: teachers and parents as much as LEA officers and members.

The programme for the evaluation was both negotiated and independent: that is to say, we consulted widely at the start of the project and sought to include concerns identified by the various constituents, but we also reserved the right to include our own. In the event, we identified six evaluation themes. The first four of them – *children's needs, curriculum, teaching strategies* and *home–school links* – were derived from the four aims of the Primary Needs Programme; the other two – *management* and *professional development and support* – were concerned with the strategies adopted by the LEA and its schools for making the aims a reality. Part I takes each of these themes in turn.

The focus was therefore very broad. It was broad, too, in the way it included the three levels of the local system: LEA, school and classroom. We were aware of an expectation that the evaluation should focus on schools and classrooms alone, commenting on how successful they had been in implementing LEA policy. This seemed to us to be entirely unacceptable. The success of the programme depended not only on what heads and teachers did with the resources they were given, but also on the LEA's own strategies. More fundamentally, success depended in part on the character and quality of the policies themselves.

To have focused on schools and classrooms alone would have been to absolve the LEA of its responsibilities and to deny us access to important areas of insight and explanation about the programme's strengths and weaknesses. In the event, as this book shows, the relationship between the three levels – classroom, school and LEA – was a powerful one, and the study was able to show the considerable extent to which the individual classroom teacher can be both enabled and constrained by the actions and policies of school and LEA.

The scope of the evaluation was broad in a third sense. It examined ideas as well as action. It did so not out of academic self-indulgence but for the very practical reason that the quality of educational action depends critically on the quality of thinking which informs it. Pursuing this notion has not been easy. There is a strong anti-intellectual streak in the English education system, as indeed there is in English culture generally, which manifests itself in extreme dismissiveness towards theory and speculation. Yet all teaching is theoretically grounded in the sense that it is informed and shaped by teachers' ideas and assumptions about children, knowledge, society, curriculum and pedagogy. For teaching to improve, therefore, not only must practices become more efficient but the ideas and assumptions which inform practice must be brought into the open and critically examined.

Thus in Part I we move freely between the practices as observed or described and the ideas by which they are sustained.

In Part II, which takes the Leeds 'case' as the basis for a wider discussion, we maintain the concern with both ideas and practices but place them more firmly in a cultural context. We look at the way different versions of primary education have been propelled into the political arena. We explore the relationship between the prevailing ideas about primary education and the professional culture of primary teaching. We attempt to demystify that ultimate article of professional faith, 'good primary practice'. We argue that progress in primary education depends partly on substantial changes in policy and resourcing, and partly on liberation from the two dominant influences in primary thinking: the pauper legacy of nineteenth-century education which has become consolidated into the class-teacher system and the ways of thinking by which that system has been elevated from cheap expedient into unquestioned educational ideal.

As this book goes to press, a major debate about primary education appears to be under way. Those of us who have made it our business to work to raise the profile and standing of this most vital yet undervalued phase of education will be pleased that it is at last getting the scale of attention it deserves. The quality of that attention, however, is another matter, and it is to be hoped that both the profession and the public will insist that in place of trial by tabloid we achieve a level of debate which reflects the true seriousness and complexity of the issues which confront us.

Note: Although the interim reports were intended for distribution within Leeds, most are now available in published form. Reports 4–10 appear in Alexander *et al.* (1989), while Reports 10 and 11 (the classroom practice study) are published as Alexander and Willcocks (1992).

Part I

Primary education in Leeds: the Report

1 The Primary Needs Programme: overview

ORIGINS

Since the 1974 local government reorganization, Leeds has been the third largest city, by population, in England. To many this is a surprising statistic, since Leeds has far less of the appearance or feel of a big city than, say, Liverpool or Manchester: but while these two cities lost population to the satellite towns of Merseyside and Greater Manchester, Leeds gained a substantial part of the old West Riding county. For the new LEA, the result was a mixture both of educational traditions – under Alec Clegg, the West Riding had been a showcase for progressive primary education – and of patterns of school organization. At the start of Leeds City Council's Primary Needs Programme (PNP) – the initiative which forms the subject of this study – the 230 Leeds primary schools ranged in size from village schools with a handful of children to large inner-city schools with up to 600 on roll. Their pupil age-spans included 5–7, 5–8, 5–9, 5–11, 5–12 and 7–11. By 1988, the average primary school size in Leeds was 191, with a population of 48,000 pupils and 2,400 teachers.

For many years before the inception of the Primary Needs Programme, Leeds was consistently low in national league tables of primary school per capita educational spending and pupil–teacher ratios. The Authority operated a 'ring-fence' policy on new primary teacher appointments, and advisory and support services were, by comparison with many other LEAs, very thin. These factors, combined with a relatively low rate of teacher mobility, generated a primary schooling system which by 1985 was perceived by those who inherited it to be stagnant and old-fashioned, though it also had, as do all LEAs, its pockets of excellence.

The Primary Needs Programme originated against this background, and should be seen first and foremost as a serious attempt to shift resources on a large scale towards the city's primary sector in order to reverse years of decline. Primary education, at last, was deemed to be an area of high priority. (For a more detailed discussion of the background to PNP, see Alexander *et al.* 1989: 1–7).

In 1984, the Department of Education and Science invited bids from LEAs, under its Education Support Grant (ESG) scheme, for funding to improve the quality of education provided in primary schools in urban areas. Leeds LEA made a successful application for a five-year project which started in April 1985 (Leeds City Council 1984a). Though the ESG project was rapidly overtaken and indeed submerged by PNP, it served as the latter's prototype and provided a legitimation, if one was needed, for the Authority's 1985 decision to increase its own resources for inner-city primary education. The goals and strategy for the ESG programme, as proposed to DES, were very similar to those which emerged a few months later as the Primary Needs Programme (Lawler 1988).

The inception of PNP was complicated by the fact that there were four competing (to some extent) views of the nature of the 'primary needs' which were to be addressed. These are mentioned here because their persistence generated ambiguities in policy and confusion in teachers' understandings of PNP which caused serious difficulties at first, especially in Phase 1 schools, and indeed continued to generate tensions for the entire four-year period of our evaluation. The competing priorities were:

• provision for children with special educational needs in mainstream primary schools;
• provision for children in inner-city primary schools suffering social and/or material disadvantage;
• the improvement of standards of literacy and numeracy (especially reading) among inner-city children;
• the improvement of the quality of of primary education across the city as a whole.

These priorities were not in themselves incompatible but, because they had different points of origin in the LEA and reflected competing territorial ambitions, teachers found themselves being offered varying and sometimes conflicting versions of PNP's nature and purposes.

AIMS

The aims of PNP, as they were published by the City Council in 1985, sought to reconcile these views. There was one overarching aim:

• to meet the educational needs of all children, and in particular those children experiencing learning difficulties;

and three specific goals by which this aim would be realized:

• developing a curriculum which is broadly based, with a stimulating and challenging learning environment;
• developing flexible teaching strategies to meet the identified needs of individual pupils, including specific practical help for individuals and small groups, within the context of general classroom provision;
• developing productive links with parents and the community.

(Leeds City Council 1985a)

Three problems have been provoked by these frequently quoted statements. First, the problem of ambiguity: from the outset, and for much of the programme's duration, many school staff were uncertain whether PNP was about the special educational needs of certain children or the provision of 'good primary practice' for all. Second, the problem of amorphousness: even assuming the first matter was clarified, few of the phrases in the three enabling or subsidiary goals conveyed any clearly defined meaning. Finally, the problem of application: it was difficult to see what practical function, if any, aims expressed in this way could usefully fulfil.

Despite such difficulties, these remained the Primary Needs Programme's officially endorsed goals. They featured in numerous documents, job-specifications, courses and other LEA statements, and provided the framework within which heads and teachers were expected to work. Necessarily, of course, they were also the starting point and continuing point of reference for the evaluation which the Council commissioned from Leeds University in 1986 and which provides the focus for this book, its companion volumes (Alexander *et al.* 1989, and Alexander and Willcocks 1992), the eleven interim reports (PRINDEP 1986a–1990) and the final report (Alexander 1991).

Whatever its subsequent achievements, the lack of carefully worked-out, clearly expressed and seriously regarded aims must be held to be a weakness of the Primary Needs Programme as educational policy. The programme lacked the precision of focus and direction which would have enabled the substantial resourcing to be exactly targeted. Our data show that, as a consequence, in some schools these resources, especially the PNP coordinators, were channelled into activities which bore little relation to the programme's goals as officially interpreted, yet which could nevertheless be justified in terms of these goals as stated because of their ambiguity.

The problem of amorphous language in the Authority's policy statements on primary education was not limited to the PNP aims, as we show in both our interim reports and this book: indeed if this had been a feature of the aims alone its consequences would have been considerably less serious, since aims by their nature tend to be somewhat broad and sweeping, and need to be given operational meaning through objectives and strategies. Nor is this a problem peculiar to Leeds. It is in fact a characteristic of much of the professional discourse in English primary education which goes by the name of 'progressive', and the case for many of the ideas and practices under that banner is often weakened by the way they are expressed and discussed. Equally, meaningful professional dialogue of the kind required to improve practice is made extremely difficult because of the absence of shared or precise meanings (Alexander 1984, 1988). There is no reason, however, why an LEA cannot give a lead in its own documents and courses in promoting greater clarity and precision about the purposes and processes of primary education.

The tension between the 'special needs' and 'good primary practice' views of PNP persisted partly because of an institutional separation and indeed rivalry between the departments responsible within the Authority for primary education and children with special educational needs. Moreover, major components of PNP, like the 7+ and 9+ reading tests used to determine PNP phasing and levels of resourcing, were administered from outside the Primary Education Division. Such separation is common in English LEAs and has been criticized by HMI as likely to frustrate the integrative goals of the 1981 Education Act (DES 1989a). The LEA took note of our earlier comments on this matter (in the seventh interim report) and from May 1990 the integration of the Authority's advisory services had began to produce much more effective inter-divisional consultation.

Many of these problems stemmed from the speed with which PNP was conceived and introduced. To achieve such a radical shift in policy and resources in so short a time was impressive, but against this should be set the confusion referred to above and the professional disaffection discussed in later chapters. The Authority itself recognized and acknowledged the latter and in subsequent policy matters was more scrupulous in consulting interested parties.

PHASES AND CRITERIA

PNP was introduced in three phases. The seventy-one Phase 1 schools were identified by reference to two criteria: educational need and social need. The measure of educational need was an analysis of each school's scores on the Authority's 7+ and 9+ reading screening tests. The extent of social need was determined by the proportion of children in each school qualifying for free school meals. The process was designed to ensure that those schools with the greatest need received the earliest and most substantial resourcing, starting in September 1985. The fifty-six Phase 2 schools were introduced on a similar basis in January 1987, and the remaining 103 schools entered the programme, with a rather smaller budget spread more thinly, in September 1988.

Crude though the phasing measures may seem, our analysis shows them to have been, by and large, reasonably accurate indicators of schools' needs in respect of the two criteria in question. However, there were a number of anomalies, among which the most notable and contentious were the several small Phase 1 schools in affluent areas where low pupil numbers produced distortion in the reading score analysis. This generated a certain amount of resentment among staff in other schools, partly because they felt they had manifestly greater 'problems' than some of the schools selected for Phase 1, and partly because they felt that some of the anomalies were tantamount to a reward for professional inadequacy, or that, conversely, they themselves were being penalized for professional competence.

In a sector as resource-starved as primary education, especially given the particular situation in Leeds referred to above, such reactions are inevitable. The important issue here would seem to be that at least the Council was prepared to commit substantial additional funds to primary education and to seek to devise a fair scheme for ensuring that these were targeted in accordance with policy. However, it is worth noting that such crude measures for selective targeting are bound to produce anomalies, and the government's scheme for the local management of schools (LMS) may well, on a much larger and more complex scale, introduce similar difficulties and reactions since the approved LMS formula for Leeds includes weightings for needs derived directly from those used in the Primary Needs Programme (Leeds City Council 1989c).

RESOURCES

Between 1985 and 1989, the Council invested nearly £14 million in its Primary Needs Programme. The main areas for expenditure were:

* additional staff;
* increased capitation;
* refurbished buildings;
* in-service support.

The 530 additional staff appointed between 1985 and 1989 under PNP, at a cost of £11,428,000, comprised the following:

* 103 PNP Coordinators (Scale II/III, main professional grade (MPG) with/without allowance after 1988);
* 213 PNP Support Teachers (Scale I, MPG after 1988);
* 54 Probationers;
* 21 Nursery Nurses;
* 12 Home–School Liaison Assistants (later called Liaison Officers);
* 120 Ancillary Assistants;
* 1 Coordinator of the Primary Needs Programme;
* 1 Head of the Primary Schools Centre;
* 1 Primary Support Teacher (Equal Opportunities);
* 1 Teacher in Charge of the Multicultural Resource Centre;
* 3 Administrative Staff.

The year-by-year breakdown is shown in Table 1.1.

The senior and most innovative of the PNP school-based appointments were the PNP coordinators, most of whom had a general, cross-school developmental brief, but a small number of whom were appointed with a multicultural brief only. The assimilation of pre-1988 coordinator appointees to the 1988 salary scales gave rise to difficulties in some schools in terms of each school's quota of above-MPG allowances. Similarly, the later appointees could find themselves undertaking a job defined as senior and responsible but being paid the same as ostensibly junior colleagues. This problem was not of the Authority's making, and it did its best to resolve it equitably. The role of PNP coordinator is discussed in Chapter 6, and in greater detail in our fifth interim report (Alexander *et al.* 1989: Ch. 5).

Each PNP appointee worked to a job specification. At first, the brief for the PNP coordinator was unrealistic in terms of the time available and the wide range of expertise required: it was subsequently modified by the Authority.

Table 1.1 Appointments to the Primary Needs Programme, 1985–9

	1985–6	1986–7	1987–8	1988–9	Total
School-based staff					
Coordinators	53	28	18	4	103
Scale 1/MPG	54	36a	35	88[b]	213
Probationers	6	29	5	14	54
Nursery Nurses	17	4	–	–	21
Home–School Liaison Officers	–	10	–	2	12
Ancillary Assistants	–	–	120	–	120
Support Staff					
Coordinator	1[c]	–	–	–	1
Head of Primary Schools Centre	–	1[d]	–	–	1
Equal Opportunities Support Teacher	–	1	–	–	1
Teacher in charge of Multi-cultural Resource Centre	1	–	–	–	1
Administrative Staff	2[d]	1[d]	–	–	3
Total					530

Notes: [a] Includes five half-time appointments
[b] Includes twenty-eight half-time appointments
[c] For one year only
[d] Until 1987–8, when absorbed into central administration

The appointments of the 120 ancillary assistants in 1987–8 were anomalous in the sense that they were mainly of staff redeployed from other Council departments as a result of financial cuts rather than part of the original conception of PNP; they were none the less useful for that.

Between 1985 and 1989 the Council allocated a total of £461,000 to enhance schools' existing capitation. Schools prepared bids specifying and costing their requirements which were then vetted by advisers before being forwarded to the Special Programmes Steering Group for formal approval. A detailed analysis of this spending is contained in our eighth interim report (Alexander *et al.* 1989: Ch. 4) and is referred to in later chapters.

PNP incorporated a £1.9 million Minor Works Programme of refurbishment to some of the least satisfactory buildings – other than those whose state was such as to warrant replacement – in each phase. Each school was tackled differently, but the refurbishment could include some or all of the following:

- new furniture;
- provision of display boards and curtains;
- repainting;
- carpeting;

- lowering ceilings;
- removing walls and changing layout.

The number of refurbished schools in each PNP phase, to 1989, was as follows:

- Phase 1: 16
- Phase 2: 6
- Phase 3: 3

The fourth major area of investment under PNP was in the in-service education of teachers (INSET). Because of the separate funding arrangements for LEA in-service activities, the way these changed even during the short lifetime of PNP, and the fact that the distinction between PNP courses and ordinary courses for primary teachers became increasingly blurred after the first year of PNP, it is not possible to cost them as a PNP expenditure item. The important statistics in this regard concern the types of courses and the attendances they achieved, and these are discussed in Chapter 7. However, it should be noted that centralized courses for primary teachers expanded dramatically with the arrival of PNP and that they became a most important tool in the Authority's strategy for transmitting and fostering its versions of good primary practice.

The venue for the majority of LEA courses for primary teachers was the Primary Centre, established as part of PNP, first on the upper floor of St Charles RC Primary School and later in the redundant Elmete Middle School. Since its inception, the Centre has diversified to include a range of other activities besides courses, and without doubt came to represent a most valuable additional resource for the Authority and its primary teachers.

The year-by-year breakdown of PNP expenditure between 1985 and 1989 is shown in Table 1.2.

Table 1.2 Summary of expenditure on the Primary Needs Programme, 1985–9

	1985–6	1986–7	1987–8	1988–9	Total
Extra school staff	1,217,000	2,301,000	3,109,000	4,623,000	11,250,000
Extra support staff	52,000	53,000	35,000	38,000	178,000
Increased capitation	119,023	125,704	97,762	79,120	421,609
Refurbishment/minor works		600,000	650,000	650,000	1,900,000
Major works			8,200	17,200	25,400
Total	1,388,023	3,079,704	3,899,962	5,407,320	13,775,009

This, then, is the background to the initiative whose development, impact and implications are considered in the chapters which follow. The particular package of goals, philosophy, strategies and resources provided the framework and starting point for our evaluation. We needed to establish how the goals were being interpreted, how far the philosophy was sustainable and in practice viable, the way the resources were deployed, and the impact on children and teachers of the various strategies commended and adopted. We now take each PNP goal in turn, starting with the overarching commitment to address the needs of all the city's primary children, especially those seen as meriting particular attention.

2 Defining and meeting children's needs

POLICY

The notion of needs is central to any educational activity or programme, a fact which the Primary Needs Programme underlined not only in its name but also in its resource investment. To be complete and useful, a policy directed at meeting children's needs should specify:

- the nature of the needs in question;
- the means of identifying the children who have them;
- the procedures for diagnosing these children's specific requirements;
- the appropriate forms of educational provision.

Thus, it should include, at the very least, matters of *definition, identification, diagnosis* and *provision*.

A brief treatment of the needs which all children might be thought to share appears in the Authority's *Primary Education: A Policy Statement* (Leeds City Council 1988: 3, sect. b). However, this document is of limited relevance to the present evaluation since it was not issued until three years after PNP began. In any case, the section in question is couched in terms too general to meet the criteria listed above or to offer specific guidance for practice.

Indeed, needs were never defined or discussed at length in any statement of PNP policy, although certain assumptions can reasonably be made from the wording of the PNP aims. For example, the flexible teaching strategies of the third aim were *'to meet the identified needs of individual pupils'*, and this clearly implies some kind of identification process, however informal. It may also be inferred that such needs as were identified were to be tackled by the provision of a broadly based curriculum, a stimulating and challenging learning environment, the flexible teaching strategies already mentioned, and specific practical help for individuals and small groups.

In the field of Special Educational Needs and 'statementing', the Authority's policy was implicit in the detailed system devised by the Special Services Division for the recording of individual needs.

In the early days of PNP, the Authority's policy in relation to the particular needs of other specific groups or categories tended to be piecemeal and reactive, and had to be inferred from memoranda, minutes, job descriptions and daily practice – a task which we undertook, and summarized in our seventh report. The Education Committee approved policy statements on equal opportunities and anti-racist education soon after the start of PNP, and followed these with more specific primary guidelines (Leeds City Council 1986, 1987a, 1989f).

PRACTICE

Children with special educational needs

At both LEA and individual school levels, needs policies were more comprehensive in the area of special educational needs than in any other. Against the background of the national working definitions laid down by the 1981 Education Act and Circular 1/83 (DES/DHSS 1983), the Special Services Division of the LEA developed a local procedure for teachers to identify children who might fall into the various categories of special need, and to begin the process of more precise diagnosis. This Individual Needs Recording System (INRS) (Leeds City Council 1984b) was a comprehensive instrument whose application introduced rigour and thoroughness into the identification and diagnosis stages, and went considerably further than the reading screening tests on which some other LEAs have relied (Gipps, *et al.* 1987).

To train teachers in the use of INRS and help them devise educational programmes and evaluate children's progress, the Authority mounted a highly successful and very popular in-service programme, Leeds In-service for Special Educational Needs (LISSEN) (Leeds City Council 1985b). In addition, the Educational Psychology and Family Advisory Service (EPFAS) provided specialist guidance and support, and centrally monitored both general trends and individual cases. 'Statementing' then introduced a wider array of medical and social expertise. The procedures themselves were subjected to internal evaluation and have acquired national recognition, not least because the Leeds initiative stands in marked contrast to the known failure of a number of other LEAs to implement the 1981 Act in full (Wolfendale 1987).

The number of statemented children in our representative sample of schools was, at 0.5 per cent, very much lower than would have been predicted on the basis of Warnock's figure of 2 per cent of the school population (DES 1978a), and this low proportion remained fairly constant across the PNP phases. It might be supposed that the discrepancy arose from the efficiency of the INRS procedures in preventing children from reaching a stage where statementing became necessary. However, such an interpretation would be convincing only if large numbers of children were subjected to the earlier stages of INRS, and if their educational needs were subsequently met without recourse to formal statementing. The relevant figures do not support such a notion.

The overall proportion of children who were not statemented but who were nevertheless perceived as having special needs of some kind was only 11 per cent as against Warnock's notional 20 per cent of the school population. As would be expected from the way in which schools were selected for the first two phases of PNP, the proportions were systematically related to PNP Phases, being highest in Phase 1 and lowest in Phase 3.

The INRS package earned a high reputation in the areas of definition, identification and diagnosis, but our evidence suggests that many teachers did not use the system to the full, possibly because it carried no guarantees about educational provision. By July 1988, three years into PNP, heads were reporting that their requests for extra staffing to implement agreed programmes for state-mented children were being met by the response that this was the job of PNP coordinators and that no further support was available. Such a trend would seem to represent a return on the part of the Authority to a very early model of PNP – PNP coordinators as *special needs* coordinators – which it had later taken pains to modify: an apparent shift of attitude which we charted in our fifth report and which is illustrated in the comments of a Phase 1 coordinator quoted among others in that report:

> The information I received with the application form and the style of inter-views led me to believe I would be dealing with special needs. This emphasis changed between my appointment in May and my taking up the post in September.

By 1989, our annual surveys of heads and PNP coordinators were finding that the apparent return to the special needs role had become even more marked, and subsequently some heads expressed anxiety that despite its good intentions in this regard the Authority's LMS formula might erode further the ability of schools to deploy staff with the flexibility required for children's special educational needs to be fully met. Clearly, this is a problem which will need careful monitoring during the period of transition to full delegation under LMS in 1994 (DES 1991d).

There can be no doubt that over the years the lack of both clarity and consistency in coordinators' terms of reference led to a certain amount of confusion as they and their colleagues sensed an uncomfortable discrepancy between, on the one hand, the advisory team's messages about the 'broadly-based curriculum' with its emphasis on first-hand experience and outside visits, and, on the other hand, the precision teaching strategies which are normally associated with special educational needs (SEN) provision and which were part and parcel of the INRS procedures.

From the beginning, only a few coordinators (usually those in larger schools with several PNP appointments) defined their role solely in terms of special educational needs. Indeed, throughout the history of the programme it was unusual for coordinators to have only a single role of any kind, most of them undertaking three or four simultaneously. Many PNP coordinators combined work in the area of special educational needs with other responsibilities, and a few also supported the work of their schools' existing SEN coordinators, perhaps taking responsibility for children on Stage One of INRS, or for those with learning difficulties in a particular age group.

From year to year, the involvement of PNP coordinators in the area of special educational needs steadily declined as they increasingly undertook senior managerial roles or found themselves used as class teachers. This trend, and other aspects of the PNP Coordinator role, are discussed more fully in Chapter 6. During the same period fewer and fewer heads deployed their PNP staff on special educational needs. It should be noted, however, that even in 1989 about a half of PNP Coordinators were still involved in this work, and responses to our survey of all local primary heads in the summer of that year indicated that the major perceived impact of PNP on special educational needs had been at the level of provision rather than at the levels of definition, identification or diagnosis. Extra PNP staffing and resources brought about a significant increase in the amount of individual and small group work in this area.

Thus, in relation to special educational needs, the requirement we set out under 'Policy' above seems to have been met. Leeds LEA made available the mechanisms and resources for SEN *definition*, *identification* and *diagnosis*, and increased staffing – backed by INSET and central support services – offered appropriate *provision*. However, more recent events, and notably the impact of LMS on school staffing, should caution us against complacency here. By 1990, schools were claiming increasing difficulties in continuing the extent of SEN provision which had been possible from 1985–8.

Children from ethnic minority groups

Leeds City Council developed policies at various levels, not only for education, in an attempt to meet the aspirations and needs of ethnic minorities and to improve relationships between all groups in the wider community. A policy on anti-racist education was approved by the City Council in 1987 (Leeds City Council 1987a) and distributed to schools along with guidelines on *Combating Racist Behaviour in Educational Institutions*. All schools, not merely those with children from ethnic minority groups, were instructed to produce their own policy statements on anti-racism for discussion and adoption by their respective governing bodies.

For its part, the Authority launched a number of initiatives in relation to the particular social and linguistic needs of children from ethnic minority groups, who tended to be concentrated in certain areas of the city and hence in certain schools where they might form anything from a substantial minority to well over 90 per cent of the children on roll. Among these initiatives were:

- a multicultural centre;
- in-service courses to enhance professional skills and understanding;
- a primary adviser with multicultural responsibilities;
- advisory teachers;
- multicultural coordinators;
- second language teachers;
- home–school liaison officers;
- bilingual and cultural development assistants.

The help and support most frequently mentioned to us in relation to children from ethnic minorities came in the form of courses offered jointly by the multicultural advisory teacher and the equal opportunities support teacher. These courses were challenging in content and highly interactive in their style, and hence made heavy personal demands on organizers and participants alike. However, courses on racial issues during the evaluation period accounted for only 39.5 teacher-days a year on average, an allocation of time which, if shared equally among the primary teachers of Leeds, would have given them only about six minutes a year each. In their responses to our 1989 survey of all primary heads, respondents also made frequent mention of extra language support, and the provision of role models (in the form of teachers, nursery nurses and bilingual assistants who were appointed as a direct result of PNP and who were themselves members of ethnic minority groups).

Quantitatively, however, the level of support for professional development in this area during the Primary Needs Programme remained inadequate to the task. Our evidence showed the extent of the ground to be covered, in terms of the frustrations of some heads and teachers who wished but were unable to do more, and the persistently ethnocentric attitudes of others.

Part of the problem, in Leeds as – even more markedly – elsewhere, was that in many primary schools the education of children from ethnic minority groups is simply not part of everyday experience. That being so, some of these schools, adopting the common fallacy of equating *multicultural* and *multi-ethnic* (Lynch 1983), asserted that in their schools multicultural education was not on the agenda because it did not need to be. At the same time, other all-white schools articulated policies and introduced innovative practices in multicultural education, recognizing that this is quite a separate thing from ethnic minority provision, and that although they have no need for the latter, the former is relevant and important whatever the ethnic composition of their own catchment area. However, even where there was a good deal of sympathetic awareness in matters of definition, identification and diagnosis, and even where long-term goals were relatively clear, there was often vagueness about the practicalities of provision.

If this matter is one of an Authority's priorities, substantial changes in the amount, content and balance of current guidance and support to schools may be necessary. As a start, and as a simple minimum, these matters could and should be openly and seriously discussed in schools. The extra staffing which PNP brought in its wake could have greatly facilitated such discussion, but its use for such purposes, like multicultural provision generally, was extremely patchy.

Generally, it has to be said, the task in the area of multicultural education in primary schools remained a long way from completion, despite well-publicized policies and a generous allocation of resources. It is not just that provision on the ground was uneven and in some schools inadequate. For schools to take seriously their responsibilities in this regard, attitudes and perceptions at the level of individual teachers have to change, sometimes radically, and for this to happen the teachers concerned have to become much more knowledgeable about societal and cultural matters and about the nature and causes of prejudice. This, for the time being, is where the main thrust of initiatives must continue to be concentrated.

At the same time, the initiatives taken in many of the schools that chose to confront this issue directly were both imaginative and greatly facilitated by the PNP staffing enhancement.

Girls, equal opportunities and gender

In relation to gender issues, as in multicultural education, teachers are confronted with a matter which does not seem to all of them to be directly related to their traditional task of handing on acquired skills or information, but which depends on their own understanding of, and sympathy for, a major contemporary issue and the ways in which they can do something positive about it. Well over a quarter of our respondents completely rejected the idea of special gender-related provision in their schools. One head commented, 'I don't understand what all the fuss is about,' and a very common response was, 'We treat everybody equally here' – an assertion which was hard to reconcile with our own systematic observation of teachers and children, reported in detail in our tenth and eleventh interim reports, and summarized in Chapter 4 below.

This discrepancy between stated beliefs and observed behaviour may be easier to understand in the light of the manifest, yet widely ignored, gender-related inequality of opportunity which runs through our society as a whole. Within this context, primary teachers' own opportunities for both promotion and subject specialization are very closely related to their gender, the relatively small number of men in the profession occupying a disproportionately large number of headships, deputy headships and posts of special responsibility in specific, high-status curricular areas. In this matter, as we illustrated with a detailed analysis of local data in our eighth report, Leeds was no exception to the national trend. The educational and professional implications of the gender discrepancies in school and curriculum management are also discussed in Chapter 3 of the present volume.

In situations of such widespread and generalized discrimination, two quite separate factors impede change. The first is the tendency for what is very common to seem normal or natural, so that many people remain genuinely unaware of the extent of the discrimination. The second is the fact that among the comparatively few people who are alert to the problem, those who are in the most favourable position to implement change are nearly always those who are deriving benefit from the discrimination in question. Against this background it is scarcely surprising that some of the heads and class teachers with whom we spoke were blandly dismissive of gender issues.

Those of our respondents who were sympathetic to the topic mentioned only one source of help or support in their attempts to clarify their ideas about gender issues or to make appropriate provision for the particular needs of girls, and this was the primary support teacher seconded by the Authority. All the respondents who mentioned her work spoke with unreserved enthusiasm of her visits to their schools, the books she had lent and the courses she had run both on her own and in conjunction with the multicultural advisory teacher. Because of her other commitments, these courses were necessarily few in number, accounting for only sixty-nine teacher-days a year on average, the equivalent of about ten minutes per teacher per year throughout Leeds as a whole.

Mainly through the efforts of this teacher, the major gender-related impact of PNP reported by heads in the 1989 survey was increased awareness of the issues involved and the formulation of school policy documents. It should be added that a substantial minority of heads reported no change, making such comments as, 'It's never been a problem. We've always had strong feelings and positive policies in this area.'

As with multicultural education, however, we have to report that in gender matters policy and school practice remained a long way apart throughout the period under review. This was partly a matter of resources as we have shown, and it was encouraging to be able to note that by 1990 the Authority had extended and rationalized these so that there would be not only an increase in support staff dealing with gender issues but also a new Equal Opportunities Unit could develop a coherent and coordinated approach to the whole field of equal opportunities, of which gender is only one part. But resources alone, even on this increased scale, will make limited headway in an area like this where gender-related ways of thinking, seeing and acting are so deeply embedded in the consciousness of individuals and groups. This is a long-term problem, not resolvable simply by spending money. The main thrust of initiatives, in gender as in multiculturalism, has to be in the area of the professional education of teachers.

Social and material disadvantage

In a sense, by far the largest proportion of PNP funding was dedicated to the needs of socially and materially disadvantaged children, since extra staffing and refurbishment, which together accounted for 97 per cent of the total cost of the programme, had their greatest concentration in schools with very large numbers of children in this category.

However, the root causes of social and material disadvantage are, both in their scale and their nature, such as to place much of the problem beyond the range of practical competence of teachers. If we ask what a child from a family which is poor, hungry, homeless and ill-clad needs, the list of answers is obvious, but no class teacher can hope to meet those requirements in her role as a teacher. It was perhaps for this reason that the Authority issued no policy statement, no formal definition of its term 'social need', and no practical guidelines on procedures for the identification of individual cases, ways of diagnosing their specific educational needs, or appropriate provision.

This was in marked contrast with its strategy in relation to special educational needs, where teachers could reasonably be expected to tackle problems with some hope of success and where consequently it was a realistic proposition to devise systematic procedures for identification and diagnosis, backed by clear guidance on the classroom provision to be made in individual cases.

In relation to social and material disadvantage, the strategy was extremely basic. It was not to single out particular disadvantaged children for special or different treatment, but simply to give to the schools in which most of them were located the first and largest share of a package of resources which was intended in the long run to benefit everybody. In this way, if PNP succeeded in raising educational standards and helping children throughout the city's primary schools as a whole, the chances were that it would help the socially and materially disadvantaged more (and more quickly) than anyone else.

This policy might seem to be the only one possible in the circumstances, but as with several other aspects of PNP it is open to question on the grounds of its diffuseness and lack of precise targeting or follow-up. Thus, schools had little choice other than to employ mainly rule-of-thumb methods for identifying socially and materially disadvantaged children, and to use some of their PNP resources to make what provision they could in the light of the advisory team's general advocacy of a stimulating and challenging learning environment. No guidance of a more exact kind was available.

This emphasis on milieu is in marked contrast to strategies adopted elsewhere, not only through the community curriculum which was such an important part of the Educational Priority programme of the 1970s (DES 1972) but more straight-forwardly through a direct, sustained emphasis on the basic skills of literacy and numeracy, on the grounds that in the end these skills are what school-leavers seeking jobs are judged by, and that without them they are far more dis-advantaged than they would be if they had missed other kinds of experience at the primary stage. This quite widely held view is implicit in the comment from a Leeds primary teacher which we have quoted elsewhere:

> If a child leaves my class and can't paint, that's a pity; if he leaves and can't read, that's a problem.

> (Alexander *et al.* 1989: 284)

These are admittedly contentious issues, but for that very reason they may be thought to have merited a fuller and more balanced public discussion under the umbrella of PNP. Whatever the achievements of the Programme may have been in terms of improved working conditions, the fact remains that after an additional expenditure of nearly £14 million in four years to identify and tackle the educa-tional needs of the city's primary school children and to regenerate schools in socially disadvantaged areas, not only did overall reading standards fail to rise by so much as a single point on either of the two measures used annually by the Authority, but the very wide discrepancy between the standards of reading in inner-city and suburban schools did not diminish in the smallest degree (see Chapter 3).

The central problem here, as will become increasingly apparent in this volume, is that curriculum was a major and persistent point of weakness in the

Primary Needs Programme as a whole. Where the Authority took the lead in identifying socially and materially disadvantaged children as deserving positive discrimination, primary professional staff failed to address the question of precisely what, in curricular terms, these children needed from schools in order to give them the best possible chance of surmounting the adverse social, educational and occupational consequences of their situation. Instead it was assumed – though never demonstrated – that an upgraded learning environment would somehow deliver what was required. The rhetoric of the 'broadly-based curriculum' and the constant reiteration of 1960s-style exhortations about 'good' classroom practice were a poor substitute for the close analysis of curriculum provision which was needed. In this respect, by failing to consider more radical solutions, the Authority may risk being accused of simply 'throwing money' at the problem, and of confirming in some schools the very 'curriculum for disadvantage' so heavily criticized in the 1960s and 1970s.

At the time of going to press, we note that the government's programme of Grants for Education Support and Training (GEST) for 1992–3 includes 'a major new initiative for the inner cities . . . to raise standards in identified schools facing severe problems' (DES 1991e). If Leeds LEA bids for funding under this scheme, we trust that it will heed our commentary on this particular aspect of PNP. Equally, we hope that DES, in considering LEA bids, will look carefully at the proposals on *curriculum* which they contain.

Children with very high ability

A final category of need must be mentioned before we turn to other matters. We occasionally encountered a particular concern with the needs of children of very high ability. It seems clear from all the written evidence that this topic did not feature at all in the thinking which led to the setting up of PNP, and we found no examples of schools with systematic procedures for identifying such pupils or diagnosing their individual needs.

This is a disturbing situation since even gross underachievement in exceptionally able children can all too easily go undetected. Work which by no means reflects the full extent of their abilities may still be well up to the standard of their fellow pupils.

A major difficulty in formulating guidelines for practice is that discussion of high ability often becomes bogged down with talk of élitism and privilege. However, it is decidedly and demonstrably not the case that exceptional ability is to be found only in the children of highly educated and well-off parents, although such an assumption is still widely held. Yet some teachers also hold extremely low expectations of children from materially less advantaged backgrounds, a situation which actively encourages underachievement (Tizard *et al.* 1988; Maltby 1984).

The full range of human potential is, of course, to be found in every social context. Therefore we have to ask whether Leeds LEA gave sufficiently broad attention in its policies to the full range of ability-related needs. There is surely a strong case for concentrating quite specific attention on other levels of ability and attainment in addition to the lowest.

CONCLUSION

There are two quite distinct ways to evaluate a policy and its related programmes and practices. One is in its own terms – to accept the policy as it stands and then consider how successful it has been. The other is to stand back from the policy as such and ask questions about its validity as well as about its success in practice.

So far we have concentrated mainly on the first of these. Though PNP was a programme nominally concerned with the needs of every child, its resourcing and support were directed at particular categories of need and at children identified as coming into those categories. In terms of the four-part framework described in detail in our seventh report (Alexander *et al.* 1989: 68–9) and referred to briefly at the start of this chapter, we found that as a category of need, SEN was the most comprehensively served. That is to say, there were clear *definitions* of the needs in question, explicit procedures for the *identification* of children having the needs so defined, procedures (INRS) for the *diagnosis* of what those needs might be, and a range of *provision* at the level of both LEA and school.

The other three categories in the programme were rather less comprehensively covered. The disentangling of ethnic minority needs from the multicultural needs of all children – an essential preliminary to defining needs in this area – happened rather belatedly, and some schools persisted in confusing the two. In this they were perhaps reinforced by the way provision concentrated more on the minority needs aspect than on the broader task of multicultural education, and in any case questions of diagnosis and provision overall were not tackled with anything like the same rigour that obtained in the area of special needs. Gender presented a similar picture, with a comparable confusion for many between the specific challenge of giving girls and boys equal opportunities and the broader task of developing gender awareness among all children and their teachers. In these cases, the paucity and unevenness in provision were exacerbated by the rather modest level of resourcing.

Finally, when we came to socially disadvantaged children we found that while provision was in one sense very generous, it may well have been in many cases inappropriately used and thus wasted, since there was a general tendency to avoid addressing afresh the question of what precisely the educational needs of these children are, and how in curriculum terms they can best be met.

Heads viewed staffing enhancement as the most valuable resource for meeting the designated categories of need. However, such a global view takes us only so far. In fact, the 'needs' part of PNP had highly variable and in some cases rather limited impact. This was due partly to resource limitations (in the cases of multicultural education and equal opportunities); partly to a failure to give sufficient attention to all four components of each policy, from clear definitions through to carefully devised and precisely targeted provision; partly to a neglect of the curriculum questions which must lie at the heart of all educational provision, of whatever kind, for whatever children; and partly to the way that most if not all of the needs in question require a substantial increase in teachers' professional knowledge and understanding, coupled in some cases with a major shift in attitudes: such attributes are not easily developed.

At the same time, there are considerable strengths in the Leeds approach. The policy of discriminating positively in favour of particular categories of need and of those children who are identified as being in them represented a dramatic change in policy, particularly as the Authority was prepared to go well beyond mere words and back its commitments with a substantial resource investment. Where the resources were located in schools with committed staff having an intelligent and sensitive grasp of the issues and possibilities, the impact of the resources and central support could be considerable, as our interim reports showed.

However, basic questions remain, and here we move to the other dimension of policy evaluation mentioned above. The policy was essentially grounded in a deficit view of children's needs. That is to say, it concentrated more on what children could *not* do than on what they were capable of. The most obvious casualties of this approach were those children defined as socially disadvantaged and children who were very able. In the former case, the tendency was to seek to make good a perceived social or material deficit in social or material rather than in educational or curricular terms. In the latter case, able children simply did not feature.

Relatedly, it was also very much a problem-centred view of needs. That is to say, although it was asserted that all children have needs which it is the obligation of primary schools to meet, only when those needs presented schools with some kind of problem were they defined with anything approaching precision, or allocated resources in anything like a specific way. For the rest, in other words for the majority of primary school children, it was enough to assert that teachers could meet their needs simply by purveying a partly updated version of the post-Plowden model of 'good primary practice'.

Such a basis for policy is both pessimistic and highly selective. In this sense it ran contrary to the claim that PNP was about the needs of *all* children, since no attempt was made to help teachers to discover what this potentially limitless diversity of needs and talents might be.

Moreover, the policy had its counterpart in classroom practice. As we show in Chapter 4, some consciously adopted teacher strategies of giving certain groups of children – classically defined by one respondent as 'the undemanding ones' – less attention in order to concentrate on others. At any given point in time, selectivity of teacher attention is an essential response to the demands of the task. However, if it leads to the persistent neglect of some children then the consequences are likely to be serious, and the strategy must be called into question, especially if, as we found, there is a tendency for 'undemanding' children to be given undemanding work.

The failure to engage properly with needs was coupled with a failure to grasp the essential connection between a teacher's ability to diagnose a child's needs and the educational opportunities with which that child is provided – in other words, the curriculum. Children will begin to show what they are capable of if they are offered curricular tasks which absorb and challenge them, and if their teachers hold, and make it clear that they hold, high expectations of them. As we have seen, such questions were not really addressed in the Primary Needs Programme, though there were many individual schools and teachers who understood these matters very well. But elsewhere, as we showed in our discussion of needs in the seventh report and in our accounts of curriculum and classroom practice in Reports 8, 10 and 11, low expectations might be combined with curriculum experiences and teaching strategies which demanded relatively little, or which frustrated rather than enabled children to pursue the questions they wanted and needed to answer. Thus, while PNP policy on needs was in general terms an enabling one, in so far as diagnosing and meeting needs are bound up with the child's curriculum experiences and the teacher's curriculum understanding, it could also be somewhat debilitating.

Now that the National Curriculum and National Curriculum Assessment are in place, many of these problems have to be looked at in a different light. There are grounds for optimism in the way the formal assessment requirements (SEAC 1991) have enabled LEAs and schools systematically to confront questions about children's difficulties and achievements, and to develop procedures for recording and building on their diagnoses and assessments. In this area, Leeds may have progressed faster and further than some other LEAs in its setting up of an assessment unit and its production of documentary and other support (Leeds City Council 1990b). Similarly, the attainment targets, statements of attainment, programmes of study and non-statutory guidance present curriculum possibilities of which many primary teachers may have been unaware – especially in areas like science and technology, but also perhaps in fields like speaking, listening and writing.

However, though the National Curriculum opens up possibilities and provides the spur for teachers to develop new kinds of professional skill and understanding, these consequences are by no means inevitable. Increased curriculum understanding does not come from reading the National Curriculum statutory orders alone, nor does increased diagnostic skill come merely from having to keep records. Each of these attributes requires a positive programme of professional development.

We have argued that it is only when the staff of a school individually and collectively confront their assumptions about children – their identities, their needs and their potential – and it is only when the question of needs-related provision is tackled in day-to-day curricular terms, that an LEA's commitment to meeting each child's needs can become a reality. The professional climate of primary schools – in Leeds partly because of PNP and generally as a necessary response to the National Curriculum – seems more conducive to such exploration than it used to be. Where schools commit themselves to such reassessment and realignment, they can be greatly aided by national and local policies of school-devolved INSET. However, where attitudes are entrenched, knowledge is limited, or commitment to change is low, devolved INSET may do nothing to overcome the problem, and children will suffer. Indeed, devolved INSET in such circumstances could well reinforce a school's inadequacies. It seems essential, therefore, that LEAs maintain a significant stake in centralized INSET and support, and the power to intervene in those schools which show signs of becoming locked into a cycle of self-reinforcing inadequacy. But in doing so, the LEAs must also examine the same assumptions about children, their learning and the curriculum to which teachers need to attend, and which lie behind the consistently-noted pattern of underexpectation and underachievement in primary schools (for example, Sharp and Green 1975; Nash 1976; Tizard *et al.* 1988; King 1989; DES 1978b, 1982, 1989g, 1990e, 1991a). This, it should be noted, is a matter as much for central government as for LEAs and schools.

It is interesting to note that the DES Education Support Grant Urban Primary Schools Scheme to which we referred at the beginning of the first chapter and which in some respects served as a prototype for PNP, had a very explicit emphasis on raising teachers' expectations, grounded in over a decade of concern flagged fairly persistently by HMI and successive governments. Somehow that goal, to which the Authority's successful ESG application also subscribed, became dissipated, and indeed PNP itself may have encouraged this. Where the Authority's ESG proposal sought 'to raise pupil performance and levels of expectation' (Leeds City Council 1984a) the PNP aims and subsequent documents referred merely to meeting pupils' 'identified needs'. Thus, where the Authority's ESG statement implied that we should re-think what children's needs and capabilities are, the PNP rationale seemed to suggest that we already know, and that the problem is simply one of provision. The initial emphasis was more apposite and should perhaps have been pursued further.

We argued above that future initiatives concerned with inner-city education ought to give close attention to curriculum issues. These, in turn, are inseparable from the even more fundamental matter of teachers' expectations of their pupils, by common consent much more likely to be pitched too low than too high. It is to be hoped that the government's 1992–3 inner-city GEST initiative referred to earlier (DES 1991e) will seek to ensure that the rhetoric of raising expectations and standards is translated into kinds of policy and INSET which probe the vital relationship between teacher expectations and classroom provision much more searchingly than has been the case hitherto.

Beyond these issues is a more fundamental question. To what extent are some of the problems we have identified here intrinsic to the primary class teacher system and thus capable of redress to only a limited degree? It is one thing to argue that primary teachers need skill and support in order to identify and address the wide range of individual needs and potentialities with which they are daily confronted. It is another to demonstrate convincingly that one person can achieve the level of knowledge and skill required to do this.

We have suggested here, and in greater detail elsewhere (Alexander 1984: Ch. 2), that although the class-teacher system is frequently justified on the grounds that it provides the teacher with a deeper understanding of the child than is possible under the secondary specialist model, this argument is in certain respects flawed.

For a start, to know someone in any meaningful sense demands far more of the knower than of the setting, and merely being with a person over a long period of time does not of itself generate such insight. Moreover, much depends on the conditions within which that most elusive yet overworked of educational notions, human potential, is evoked. Here there would seem to be a necessary link between the teacher's own level of knowledge or skill and his or her capacity to recognize such knowledge or skill, or its potential, in the child.

How, for example, can one identify a child's potential in mathematics if one's own mathematical understanding is limited? Or in music? Or in any other area of human learning? Each of these acts of recognition or diagnosis surely requires appropriate knowledge on the part of the teacher. To recognize something you need to know it.

Similarly, can a child's potential, or needs, be manifested with anything approaching precision unless the teacher provides the kinds of educational tasks which will challenge the child to the extent required? Without appropriate *opportunities* the child's potential may remain undiscovered; and without appropriate *curriculum knowledge* providing such opportunities will be beyond the teacher's competence.

How far, therefore, is it useful to constantly stress the need for primary teachers to have higher expectations of the children they teach without also addressing the need for such expectations to be specifically focused rather than generalized?

There are two missing ingredients in conventional discussion of the relationship between teacher expectations and pupil performance: the curriculum experiences the teacher provides, and the knowledge and skill the teacher needs in order to do so. To this extent children's needs and teacher expertise are linked, for in the end it is the teacher, and not the child, who defines what those needs are (Alexander 1984: Ch. 2).

For as long as these ingredients are neglected we shall continue to encounter a model of educational needs couched, as it was in Leeds, more in terms of children's manifested problems than their latent potential. Yet as soon as we address the curricular and pedagogical issues with any seriousness we shall have to confront the question, unpalatable to many in primary education, of the extent to which the generalist class-teacher system is capable of delivering either the professional expertise or the classroom experiences which are required if children's needs and potentialities are to be identified and addressed. Far from vouchsafing special insights into what children are capable of, as is usually claimed, the class-teacher system may sometimes do the exact opposite.

3 The curriculum

THE LEA AND THE CURRICULUM

The curriculum was treated prominently from the outset of the Primary Needs Programme: a 'broadly-based curriculum, with a stimulating and challenging learning environment' was to be both a major aim in its own right and one of the three routes to achieving the programme's goal of meeting the needs of every child in the city's primary schools.

LEA curriculum policies, some of them specific to PNP but most intended to apply across the board, were contained in various documents, notably the Education Committee papers of 1985 and 1986, the job specifications for PNP appointees, and the draft and final versions of *Primary Education: A Policy Statement* (Leeds City Council 1988) and *The Curriculum 5–16: A Statement of Policy* (Leeds City Council 1990a). Another source, providing not so much formally approved curriculum policy as preferred curriculum sentiments or interpretations, were the various talks given by members of the advisory team at the Authority's in-service courses, and the important compendium of such interpretations contained in the Autumn 1989 *PNP Conference Report* (Leeds City Council 1989a). The LEA also produced a number of subject documents, though most of them post-dated the period in question.

Our content analysis of all this material shows that it tends to focus on the broad purposes and character of curriculum rather than its operational detail. At first sight it is also fairly eclectic, drawing on a variety of (mainly official) sources; in fact, these appear to have been selected not so much to present alternatives as to buttress or legitimate a particular value-position. Moreover, justifications for the particular views and practices espoused are rare: the documents are essentially vehicles for the transmission of beliefs and values, with the implicit message that they are incontrovertible by virtue of their source rather than their substance.

In fact, the curriculum statements most influential in the Primary Needs Programme espoused values of a particular persuasion – that of post-Plowden progressivism (CACE 1967; Cunningham 1988) – whose defensibility as educational principles and viability as educational practice had begun seriously to be challenged long before the start of PNP (for example, Dearden 1968, 1976; Peters

1969; Entwistle 1970; Bennett 1976; Galton and Simon 1980; Alexander 1984). Given the quasi- legal status of such statements in the eyes of many of our teacher respondents, therefore, it is a matter for some concern that while curriculum and classroom practice were prescribed in terms which were manifestly in need of debate, no such debate was initiated or encouraged.

The authority of the LEA's curriculum statements, and the dangers inherent in their lacking any explicit justification, were somewhat blunted by their tendency to impreciseness and ambiguity. Thus, as was shown in interim reports 6, 8 and 10 (Alexander *et al.* 1989: Chs 2, 3 and 5), schools were confronted by the dilemma (or opportunity) of being required to implement policies whose exact meaning they could not always grasp. Nowhere was this problem more acute than in respect of the PNP goal of 'the broadly-based curriculum', as originally set out and as subsequently elaborated in a variety of contexts.

Within certain limits, therefore, centrally devised curriculum statements meant what schools wanted them to mean. The limits in question were those set by the basic 'progressive' tenets of thematic enquiry, curriculum integration, a learning environment strong on visual impact, an 'exploratory' pedagogy, group work, and the other patterns of classroom organization discussed in Reports 6, 10 and 11 and in our next chapter. These, at least, were viewed by many teachers as non-negotiable. This is an important distinction – vagueness on curriculum and precision on pedagogy. We argue later that perhaps it should have been the other way round, and it is worth noting that in specifying curriculum content and leaving the manner of classroom implementation to heads and teachers, the government appeared to endorse this alternative principle in respect of the National Curriculum. (This statement of the 1988 legal position may well be overtaken by events. As we go to press ministers are preparing the ground for a major initiative in primary education by mounting an assault on the state of primary classroom practice, using, as it happens, material from the Leeds report. The government would seem to have recognized that the success of the National Curriculum depends more on the quality of its delivery in the classroom than on the manner of its specification on paper. Perhaps – an unpalatable truth, maybe – the success of a central curriculum initiative requires attention to both content and method.)

PNP has now been superseded by the requirements of the 1988 Education Reform Act in respect of curriculum and delegated school budgets, yet although from 1988–9 Leeds, like other LEAs, paid increasing and substantial attention to the INSET implications of the National Curriculum subject and assessment requirements, there was also a general tendency to attempt to accommodate these to the mainstream primary ideology referred to above. Thus, while some saw the 1988 Act as a vehicle for radical transformation of the school curriculum, others offered the reassurance of continuity, encouraging primary teachers in the belief that 'we do all this already' and that the once-condemned subject framework is now acceptable in so far as it is no more than a relabelling of 'good primary practice'.

Although the urge to reassure is understandable, longer-term problems may be generated by this short-term strategy if at the same time two points are not grasped and addressed. First, that the foundations upon which the National Curriculum is to be constructed – established primary philosophy and practice – are at the very least somewhat problematic; second, that the new edifice and these foundations, far from providing a comfortable continuity, are in certain important respects in conflict. In particular, the systematisation of subject knowledge in the National Curriculum (DES 1989b, 1989c, 1990a, 1990b, 1991b, 1991c, 1991k, 1991l, 1991m) represents a version of curriculum sharply at variance with that espoused in the primary mainstream during the last three decades (Kelly 1990).

To evade these two realities is in the best interests of neither primary children nor their teachers. But to confront them will require a much more rigorous approach to curriculum discourse in the primary sector than has been evident to date.

As noted elsewhere, the Authority's primary education support services expanded dramatically as a direct consequence of PNP. In the case of curriculum, we witnessed a shift from an exclusively generalist advisory brief to a partly specialist one, mirroring the development of curriculum consultancy in schools. Simultaneously, as our analysis of primary INSET in the Authority will show, curriculum became an increasingly prominent INSET focus, with courses related to the National Curriculum showing the sharpest increase of all after 1987.

Alongside LEA curriculum policy and INSET were several specific initiatives bearing directly on curriculum. These included commitments in the fields of special needs, gender and multiculturalism, discussed in Chapter 2 under 'needs' but all with a necessary (though not always manifest) curriculum dimension; and participation in two national curriculum initiatives, in science and mathematics. The first of these drew on DES Education Support Grant (ESG) funding; the second was funded by the LEA, but in association with the national PrIME project. Feedback from schools testifies to the perceived positive impact on curriculum of all these initiatives, particularly PrIME.

CURRICULUM IN THE SCHOOL: RESPONDING TO POLICY

PNP straddled the old and new dispensation in respect of curriculum control. Before the 1988 Act, the head was the main arbiter of the content and character of a primary school's curriculum, subject to LEA policy. Since 1988, the content of the larger part of this curriculum has been determined by central government and specified in statutory instruments, though in addition schools and LEAs have needed their own curriculum policies and development plans.

Despite this change, there were two constants throughout the PNP era: the existence and force of views on the curriculum emanating from the LEA and/or its officers, and the pivotal role of the primary school head in interpreting and acting on such views.

We found considerable variation in the latter. Heads interpreted LEA statements on curriculum in widely differing ways, partly – as we have already suggested – as a result of those statements' inherent ambiguities. Moreover, heads' attitudes to Authority curriculum statements ranged from acceptance to opposition, with a variety of uncertain or non-committal reactions in between.

Opposition in turn divided into what we termed 'traditionalist' and 'modernist'. 'Traditionalists' reacted to LEA curriculum policy as an encroachment on their autonomy, while the 'modernists' felt that it was they rather than the Authority who set the pace on curriculum thinking and practice and that the Authority's own prescriptions were in certain respects inadequate. 'Modernist' heads also valued dialogue and rigour in professional discourse and asserted the need for such discourse to be centred on the staff of the school, rather than conducted elsewhere and imposed on them.

Thus, the question of the character and interpretation of curriculum statements leads to the equally pressing issues of how these were evolved and of professional structures and relationships both within the school and between the school and LEA. Three matters became clear. First, heads had been needlessly antagonized by the LEA's failure to involve them in the development of policies, such as those on PNP and the curriculum, which intimately concerned them and their staff. Second, the LEA's ideas and recommendations on curriculum could have benefited greatly from open dialogue with primary heads, and in this sense the latter were an undervalued resource within PNP. Third, policies stand a better chance of being understood and implemented if those most affected are involved in their formulation. This is a lesson which the LEA was keen to transmit in respect of schools' internal decision-making: the lesson should perhaps have been applied to the LEA's own practices. We note, however, that subsequent – post-PNP – curriculum initiatives (for example, Leeds City Council 1990b, 1990d) involved a greater measure of teacher participation.

Class teachers displayed similar diversity to heads in their interpretations of the 'broadly-based curriculum', coupled with considerable consensus on what we termed earlier its 'non-negotiable' aspects like curriculum integration, experiential learning and group work. They felt themselves under a clear obligation to enact such policy, nevertheless.

The exclusion of class teachers from curriculum policy and decision-making is at least as counterproductive as the exclusion of heads. It has the added consequence of inducing dependence on others in respect of those vital aspects of professional life where teachers need to think for themselves. There is, indeed, clear evidence of a strong 'dependency culture' in the primary sector in Leeds, as elsewhere.

However, there were three countervailing influences. One was enhanced staffing under PNP, which, when coupled with a properly worked-out structure for curriculum leadership, considerably increased professional discussion within many schools. The second was the National Curriculum, which teachers acknowledged to have shifted the climate of schools towards collective policy development, especially where curriculum and assessment were concerned. The third was the change in the balance of power, over matters like finance and staff appointments, from the LEA to school governing bodies and heads. The net result was a wider involvement of heads and teachers in the discussion of those issues and policies which concerned them, together with membership of the various working groups – for example, on science, technology, history, geography and assessment – set up in the context of the National Curriculum. This was a welcome trend in view of the severity of the problems directly attributable to a failure to consult and involve teachers during the PNP period. However, membership by a small minority of teachers on LEA working groups neither proves nor secures the necessary democratization of professional discourse for the majority. There remain major challenges here for schools and LEAs.

CURRICULUM IN THE SCHOOL: EXPLOITING PNP ENHANCED STAFFING FOR CURRICULUM REVIEW AND DEVELOPMENT

Our annual surveys of primary heads reinforced the view that of the various PNP resources, enhanced staffing had a particularly important impact on the curriculum. It enabled schools, as we have said, to rationalize curriculum responsibilities, often moving away from a situation where curriculum review and development were undertaken on the basis of 'one subject per year' (and perhaps, in small schools, 'four subjects per teacher') to one where several major areas could be kept under review simultaneously, each the responsibility of a specialist committed to building on his or her existing knowledge by studying the professional literature and attending courses.

PNP coordinators became especially prominent in curriculum review and development. Our annual coordinator surveys showed curriculum moving into first place among coordinator responsibilities after 1987, overtaking special needs.

In our fifth report (Alexander *et al.* 1989: 169–73), we identified four distinct ways in which PNP coordinators were undertaking their curriculum responsibilities:

- as *Curriculum Managers* involved in overall school curriculum policy as part of a senior management team;
- as *Curriculum Consultants* responsible for the school-wide review and development of a specific subject or subjects (in our fifth report we termed these 'specialists');
- as *Curriculum Enhancers* working collaboratively with other staff in a class or year group to support development, inject new ideas, and serve as a catalyst for change;
- as *Curriculum Facilitators* having no direct engagement in curriculum development processes themselves but releasing other staff to undertake this work.

Each of these is a valid strategy for curriculum improvement – and there could well be others. It is important, however, that schools recognize both that such alternatives are not only possible but that they can coexist in any one school. In some schools only one such role might be taken, and where, for example, it was that of Curriculum Facilitator, this might seem a waste of the curriculum expertise of the coordinator.

Another powerful device for promoting curriculum improvement, also directly attributable to PNP resourcing, was collaborative teaching, or what we termed Teachers Teaching Together (abbreviated to TTT). A fuller discussion of TTT appears elsewhere in this volume (see Chapter 4), but we can note here certain points about its potential within the arena of curriculum review and development.

Our fourth report analysed and discussed four key aspects of each TTT arrangement, based on observation and interviews in PNP classrooms:

* participants;
* purposes;
* collaborative style;
* pupil organization.

Of the various *purposes* which TTT could serve, we identified three which were widespread:

* special educational needs;
* curriculum enhancement;
* professional development.

It is the second such purpose, curriculum enhancement, which concerns us here.

As defined on the basis of the first stage of our study of TTT the term 'curriculum enhancement' referred particularly to those activities where teachers shared and exploited each other's curriculum strengths, often, though not exclusively, in the context of thematic enquiry. The follow-up studies (hitherto unpublished) showed such enhancement to be taking a number of forms beyond this specific focus.

First, a team of teachers would work together for the *shared delivery of the whole curriculum*. In larger schools these might be members of a year-group; in smaller schools they could be most or even all of the staff. Enhanced staffing under PNP would then enable flexibility in staff deployment to allow for the disposition of curriculum expertise where at any one time it was most needed. The essential prerequisite in such arrangements, which could be logistically quite complex, was collaborative *planning*: this arrangement was essentially about the open pooling of individual ideas and strengths for the benefit of all.

Second, PNP support staff might be deployed to provide (or to enable others to provide) regular tuition, usually in language or mathematics, for particular groups of children, often though not necessarily the less able. Such teaching often utilized a structured scheme or programme, and its purpose is best described as *curriculum intensification*.

Third, PNP support staff might be used to facilitate *curriculum invigoration*. Where the focus in curriculum intensification was on the curriculum needs of specific groups of *children*, curriculum invigoration was designed to meet the needs of their *teachers*. It is thus best seen as a device for the remediation of curriculum deficiency. Characteristically, the curriculum areas concentrated on tended to be other than those of the 'basics' of mathematics and language: areas like art or environmental studies which, under solo teaching arrangements and in the context of the very unequal distribution of curriculum resources within the Authority and its primary schools, were more commonly left to fend for themselves, with adverse consequences which are now well documented in HMI surveys and elsewhere.

Finally, the simplest form of curriculum enhancement was one where PNP support staff were used merely to release a class teacher to undertake curriculum-related work elsewhere within the school. We have already termed this *curriculum facilitation*.

Each of these arrangements presented challenges for those concerned – team dynamics, problems of status, problems of ownership and difficulties in planning.

However, our TTT follow-up studies confirmed and strengthened two views we set out in our earlier reports. First, that TTT was one of the most significant consequences of PNP resourcing, with the potential in this case to provide a major corrective to the inconsistencies in curriculum expertise and delivery which are such a widespread and unsatisfactory feature of the primary school class-teacher system. Second, that the realization of this potential was by no means an inevitable consequence of enhanced staffing (or, to put it another way, there were many schools where enhanced staffing, in respect of its TTT potential at least, was wasted).

It will be seen that our studies of the work of PNP coordinators and of TTT combine to produce a repertoire of roles and strategies for using teacher collaboration to promote curriculum improvement:

- the curriculum manager;
- the curriculum consultant;
- the curriculum enhancer:
  (a) shared delivery of the whole curriculum;
  (b) curriculum intensification;
  (c) curriculum invigoration;
- the curriculum facilitator.

Of these, the first two are school-wide roles while the last two are classroom-based roles involving TTT. The most productive and successful use of PNP staff resources occurred in those schools which realized and exploited all of these. In contrast, some schools failed to grasp that enhanced staffing provided a chance to go well beyond the two established ways of using extra staff: for 'remedial' attention to certain children (one, but only one, aspect of curriculum intensification); and for providing cover for staff needed elsewhere (possibly for curriculum facilitation, but sometimes for more mundane purposes).

With the familiar exceptions of music and physical education (where, unlike subjects like mathematics, English and art, primary teachers have always found it acceptable to admit to insecurity or ignorance), we came across no examples of PNP coordinators serving as fully specialist subject teachers, despite the fact that the level of staffing enhancement frequently permitted this. The strength of professional loyalty to the class-teacher system seems to have prevented this from even being considered. However, as we go to press, the specialist option is very much under discussion, partly as a consequence of issues raised in the Leeds report. Its discussion is arousing, as one might predict, fierce passions and a strenuous defence along the lines that the generalist class teacher system is without question best for the child. We return to this matter in Chapter 12.

CURRICULUM IN THE SCHOOL: EXPLOITING THE PNP DEVELOPMENT FUND AND INSET FOR CURRICULUM REVIEW AND DEVELOPMENT

The PNP development fund of just under £500,000 between 1985 and 1989 was a useful device for extending curriculum resources. Of the many and varied bids coming through the LEA's Special Programmes Committee during this period, the largest proportion by far were for mathematics and language resources, followed some way behind by computing and science. The lowest call on the fund was made for design and technology, PE, art and craft, humanities and drama, though of these, design and technology's share increased throughout the period in question, in line with its emergence as an important curriculum area, confirmed in the National Curriculum subject hierarchy from 1988.

Chapter 7 contains an analysis of LEA-mounted INSET in support of PNP from 1985–9, though in focusing on courses mounted at the Primary Schools Centre it does not claim to cover the full range of INSET on offer during that period. Overall, 31 per cent of these courses dealt with curriculum. In terms of our formula for calculating INSET teacher-days, mathematics again predominated, taking 44 per cent of the curriculum time, with English receiving 30 per cent, science 13 per cent, and all other curriculum areas sharing the remaining 13 per cent.

Given the needs of the National Curriculum core subjects, the considerable maths/English/science discrepancy might seem unsatisfactory. However, two points should be noted. First, PNP preceded the National Curriculum and thus the confirmation of science's status as a new 'basic'. Second, analysis of changing INSET priorities shows a sharp increase in INSET teacher-days devoted to English from 1987–8. However, during the same period the increased science INSET commitment was not maintained.

There were clearly anomalies in schools' use of the very full and varied INSET curriculum support programme provided centrally. However, it should be noted that though the Authority mounted these courses, heads and teachers decided whether or not to attend them. The issue, then, is one of *take-up* rather than *provision*, and indeed to some extent take-up in one year determines provision the next. In any case, Leeds LEA has for several years asked teachers to identify their INSET preferences and the programme has been constructed partly by reference to their views.

Global analysis of courses and attendances provides only part of the picture of how school curriculum development was supported by LEA INSET. Our analysis showed considerable variation between schools in the extent of their use of such courses, with, as a general tendency, large inner-city schools making most use, and small outlying schools least. Heads and staff identified a number of factors; frequently cited were the lack of sufficient staff in small schools to cope with cover problems and the time taken to travel to the Primary Centre. However, our comparison of schools having similar staffing levels and access shows that this, too, is not the whole story. Clearly, some schools which could make use of curriculum courses were not doing so, as a consequence of deliberate choice rather than accidental circumstance. In such cases, the attitudes and management styles of heads were crucial factors: these are discussed in Chapter 6.

Alongside centrally provided courses on aspects of the curriculum, schools undertook their own INSET. The process of school-led INSET was boosted by the arrival of Grant-Related In-Service Training (GRIST) in 1987 (to which Leeds LEA responded with a pilot scheme of devolved INSET budgets for 30 per cent of primary schools) and its successors, the LEA Training Grant Scheme (LEATGS), and Grants for Education, Support and Training (GEST). Since then, budgetary devolution for INSET in Leeds primary schools has been greatly extended.

The limited resources made available to our evaluation project and the requirements of its existing programme made it impossible to include all these school-led INSET developments in the evaluation of PNP. However, we understand that the Authority undertook its own evaluation of the GRIST pilot scheme, and to gain a more complete picture of schools' use of INSET to enhance curriculum provision and development it would be useful to juxtapose the LEA study and our own.

CURRICULUM IN THE SCHOOL: OTHER DEVELOPMENT STRATEGIES

Review and development are both essential aspects of curriculum improvement. In the period immediately prior to the introduction of the National Curriculum, we gathered data on these processes from our sample schools. The lists of subjects under review in the two years in question were dominated by mathematics and language, with science increasing in prominence though still some way behind. This closely mirrors the use of INSET and the PNP development fund discussed above. The list of reviewed subjects across all the schools covers the full gamut of the primary curriculum, which indicates that schools, regardless of external pressures, were identifying and attempting to remedy their particular curricular needs.

However, such league tables are less significant than study of the review processes themselves. Here, clear subject-related discrepancies emerged. Thus, school-based review of mathematics was strongly supported by the advisory service, both in person at the schools in question and through central courses. As a consequence the review process tended to be carefully thought out, and treated as a long-term programme of development rather than a one-off discussion. In contrast, external support for language review was rare, and for the first two years of PNP the INSET alternative was negligible, with no courses at all on reading.

Science was even more patchy and homespun, despite the existence of the ESG team. For all other curriculum areas, the situation was even worse.

Many schools have considerable staff strengths in particular curriculum areas, and their capacity to engage in curriculum review and development can be independent of the availability of external support. However, because curriculum expertise is as yet disposed in such a random way across primary schools, particularly the smaller ones, it seems essential that an LEA provides some kind of development safety-net for those schools without the expertise or resources for independent curriculum development. The gross discrepancies between the 'basics' of mathematics, English, and now science, and the rest of the curriculum, though scarcely defensible in educational terms, is at least understandable as a consequence of societal values. The discrepancy between mathematics and English is not so easy to understand, and may have an important negative bearing on the state of this subject in Leeds as discussed towards the end of the present chapter.

Although curriculum consultants/coordinators/postholders/leaders (the terms are still used interchangeably) were not specific to PNP, they were an important contingent aspect of the Authority's primary policy. Indeed, schools were expected to ensure that all teachers, other than probationers, had school-wide responsibility for a curriculum area, and it was a reasonable assumption that the enhanced staffing under PNP would enable this particular aspect of policy to be fulfilled.

We have seen that between 1985 and 1989 PNP coordinators themselves gave an increasing lead in curriculum development both within the classroom and across the school. Our annual returns made it clear that during the same period the numbers of curriculum leaders and curriculum areas covered also rose steadily. Curriculum consultancy in primary schools, at first resisted within some parts of the teaching profession, is now part of the normal fabric of school management, and PNP certainly helped to accelerate its institutionalization in Leeds. The next stage – an even higher hurdle for the collective professional psyche – is an acknowledgement of the potential of specialist teaching in primary schools.

Despite the general acceptance of curriculum consultancy, a detailed study of such posts in the evaluation project's sample schools once again reinforces the picture of anomaly and discrepancy in respect of curriculum review, support and development which emerged from our earlier discussion. A simple head count of subjects covered by curriculum posts suggests a reasonably satisfactory situation, in that mathematics, English, science, music, art and craft were all attended to in most schools. Leadership in computers, environmental studies, history, geography, drama and other subjects was more patchy. With these it was less a question of ensuring that they were covered as a matter of policy than of responding if people happened to express an interest in taking them on. With the Orders for history and geography now published (DES 1991b, 1991c) schools will need to look urgently at the level of support these subjects are given, especially in the light of recent HMI criticism of the quality of history and geography teaching in primary schools (DES 1989f). The same argument applies to the remaining National Curriculum foundation subjects of art, music and physical education, the Orders for which are due to be implemented in September 1992 (DES 1991k, 1991l, 1991m).

Matters are made even more problematic by the tendency for clear links to emerge between curriculum leadership, status and gender. Thus, to take status, mathematics had the highest concentration of senior staff involved in curriculum leadership, then language (though with far fewer heads and deputies than mathematics). At the other end of the scale, art and music were mainly led by main professional grade (MPG) staff. Similar patterns emerged with gender: in relation to the overall male/female ratio in primary schools, mathematics, computing and environmental studies were disproportionately covered by men, while language, art, music and science were mainly covered by women.

There are two reasons why these patterns should give pause for thought. First, the linking of particular subjects to status and gender conveys, whether we like it or not, clear and questionable messages to children and their teachers about what subjects are most and least important, about where career advancement lies, and about which are 'male' and 'female'. Second, though there is no necessary connection between professional status and quality of work, there is certainly a connection between such status and the *opportunity* to undertake the kinds of work involved in curriculum leadership. Curriculum leadership requires time, and it requires access to classrooms and staff throughout the school: the MPG teacher with a full-time class-teaching commitment will have little of either. This last point is also strongly supported by the evidence from the AMMA study of teacher-time at Key Stage One (Campbell and Neill 1990).

Thus, in a fairly subtle way, the disposition of curriculum posts among a school's staff may reinforce other discrepancies in curriculum provision and development of the kind that we have already noted. Equally, it can convey messages to children and their teachers which may be wholly inconsistent with the policies on gender and equal opportunities to which LEAs like Leeds are committed. But, it must be stressed, this is a complex matter and we are not saying that any of these consequences is inevitable: rather, that the whole question of status and gender in school and curriculum management deserves further attention.

Overall, schools used a wide range of strategies for curriculum development, of which the following emerged most frequently:

- Defining school and teacher needs:
    staff meetings;
    GRIDS (McMahon *et al.* 1984);
    appraisal interviews.
- Delegating responsibility:
    establishing coordinating teams or working parties;
    drafting of guidelines or policy statement by staff member.
- Extending expertise:
    attending courses;

  requesting support from the advisory service;
  visiting other schools;
  inviting outside experts to talk to/work with staff.
- Staff discussion:
  staff meetings;
  workshops;
  training days;
  informal discussion;
  structured small group discussion;
  collective formulation of guidelines or policy statements.
- Classroom activity:
  collaborative teaching (TTT);
  year-group planning.

No school used all of these strategies. However, they (and others) constitute a *repertoire* for curriculum development of which heads and staff need to understand the potential. A systematic exploration of all of these can provide a useful focus for both school-based INSET and the Authority's courses on management and curriculum leadership, and by the time our final report was published this had begun to happen.

Meetings – whether involving all the staff of a school, or a subset like a year-group – were and are a universal device in connection with curriculum review and development. They have an even more critical function in the context of the National Curriculum now that schools have to respond to external initiatives at such great speed and with so little warning.

Though informal exchanges between staff are, and will remain, vital to the fabric of professional life in primary schools, staff are finding it increasingly necessary to operate within the framework of formal meetings. At the start of PNP these were a rarity in many schools; by the end of PNP they had become much more common, partly as a consequence of the opening up of professional discourse and decision-making which enhanced staffing and the PNP coordinator role permitted but mainly in response to the arrival of the National Curriculum.

Running meetings is a considerable skill, especially against the background of low professional morale and rapid change. The most successful meetings we observed were those with the following characteristics:

- a clearly understood and stated purpose;
- an agreed focus and/or agenda;
- a clear structure, moving from analysis of a problem or need through to conclusion and decision;
- support from the head, though the meeting was not necessarily led by him/her;
- on complex issues, some kind of prepared oral or written input – if the latter, then preferably in advance;
- someone, not necessarily the head, taking a chairing or leading role;
- genuine rather than token involvement of all those attending, with particular

attention paid to staff reluctant to press their case and those inclined to view the proceedings with suspicion or disdain;
* individual preparedness to submit to the disciplines of
  (a) sticking to the point;
  (b) decentring from one's own particular preoccupations and situation to the wider issue at hand;
  (c) resisting the urge to hog the proceedings;
* a recognizable outcome in the form of decisions or documentation.

CURRICULUM IN THE CLASSROOM: THE PHYSICAL SETTING

Roles and strategies for curriculum review, development and management have little point unless they exert a positive influence on the quality of the curriculum experienced by the child in the classroom. Our evaluation of PNP culminated in a large-scale study of classroom practice in sixty (over a quarter) of the city's primary schools. This study, conducted at three levels, each one more concentrated than the last, is described in full in Reports 10 and 11 which in turn are used as the main basis for the present book's next chapter, 'Teaching Strategies'. Taking this study together with those described in Reports 4, 7 and 8, however, we encounter certain issues to do with curriculum in the classroom which can usefully be isolated at this point.

The first such issue is the relationship between curriculum and the physical appearance and layout of the classroom. The Leeds advisory team's views on classoom layout and appearance were a prominent aspect of its work, consistently purveyed to teachers through in-service courses, documents, and the work of individual advisers and advisory teachers. The physical character and arrangement of a classroom, it was asserted, should be a reflection and embodiment of two basic principles. One was that children learn best in what the second PNP aim terms 'a stimulating and challenging learning environment', hence the very strong emphasis on display and the visual appearance of the classroom. The other was that a thematically-dominated integrated curriculum is best achieved through an 'integrated' arrangement of furniture. The advisory service went as far as to set up a model classroom to serve as the centrepiece of a number of its in-service courses and to project the image of what advisory staff called the 'quality learning environment' to which teachers were expected to aspire (for example, Leeds City Council 1988, 1989a, 1989d, 1989e, 1990a, 1990c).

Without doubt, the quality of classroom display in primary schools improved over the period of our evaluation of PNP. When such improvements were undertaken in the context of school refurbishment and the upgrading of furniture, the visual transformation of the physical context for learning could be dramatic.

The layout commended by advisory staff, and perceived by our interview and questionnaire respondents as being less a suggestion than a requirement, had work bays for each major area of the curriculum. These were intended to facilitate the patterns of curriculum provision generally denoted by terms like the 'flexible day' or 'integrated day', in which at any one time a classroom will contain children working on quite disparate tasks in different areas of the curriculum. Since some such tasks might involve children standing or working on the floor, advisory staff also encouraged teachers to make flexible use of furniture, some commending what was termed 'the concept of fewer chairs than children': the argument being that since the nature of the activity did not require one chair per child, more space for those activities could be created by dispensing with superfluous chairs.

In practice, we found a tendency for PNP classrooms to cluster round four layout types ranging from what in Report 10 we termed 'Type 1' classrooms with no work bays, through Types 2 and 3 with a limited number of work bays for certain activities, to Type 4 with a comprehensive arrangement of work bays for each curriculum area, as in the model classroom set up in connection with the primary INSET programme. Since the majority of classrooms were Types 2 or 3, with half of the total observed having just one curriculum-specific work bay (invariably a reading corner and/or class library), this particular message would seem to have had limited impact, in its pure form at least, though teachers were widely aware of what was preferred. At the same time, if we compare Leeds with, say, inner London at the time of Mortimore's study (Mortimore *et al.* 1988), the message was clearly influential. In Leeds, some degree of curriculum-specificity in layout was a feature of most classrooms we visited, while in the London study it occurred in only a minority of classrooms. (We develop this point in the next chapter, where, in Figures 4.1–4.4, the four layout types are illustrated.)

Where there were several work bays, these were most commonly for reading, other language work, art/craft and mathematics. Science areas were less common, and our evidence from this and other studies suggested that the messages about the growing importance of science were taking some time to filter through into the classroom. The National Curriculum, clearly, will change this.

Teachers were similarly reluctant to adopt the 'fewer chairs than children' suggestion, on the grounds that it made for less rather than more flexibility.

These findings raise a number of issues. First, despite the high profile given to classroom appearance and layout in the Authority's courses and documents, the message was only selectively and partially responded to.

Second, both teachers and evaluation team members gained the strong impression that the concern with the visual dimension of primary teaching was sometimes pursued as an end in itself, rather than as a means to an end: what we call elsewhere 'surface rather than substance'.

Third, the classroom arrangements and curriculum patterns recommended, though arguable in terms of progressive ideology, have come in for increasing criticism as to their capacity to promote children's concentration and learning, and the effective management, interaction, diagnosis and assessment on which learning and progress depend (for example, Galton and Simon 1980; Bennett *et al.* 1984; Alexander 1984; Delamont 1987; Mortimore *et al.* 1988; Galton 1989; DES 1990c).

Fourth, despite the existence of well-documented evidence of this kind, such arrangements continued to be commended as constituting 'good primary practice'.

Finally, far from promoting the 'flexibility' in teaching and learning espoused in the PNP goals and claimed for such arrangements on PNP courses and elsewhere, they may actually have had the opposite effect, since many teachers found that their practice was constrained or compromised, rather than facilitated, by their attempting to conform to what they took to be official requirements on such matters as layout, display, furniture and grouping. (The paradox of 'inflexible flexibility' in primary teaching is explored in Alexander 1988 and Alexander *et al.* 1989, Ch. 8.)

CURRICULUM IN THE CLASSROOM: PLANNING AND RECORD-KEEPING

That curriculum planning is a prerequisite to effective teaching is not, publicly at least, disputed. We found that teachers' planning had three main dimensions:

- Time-scale:
  short/medium/long term;
  daily/weekly/half-termly/termly/yearly.
- Formality:
  elaborate and schematic written documents;
  brief written notes;
  planning 'in the head'.
- Structure:
  comprehensive planning of an entire programme;
  incremental planning, each stage building on the last;
  ad hoc planning according to circumstances and needs.

To a large extent, these dimensions operated independently of each other, different circumstances and needs dictating different approaches or combinations of approaches. Thus, even comprehensive and long-term planners were also at times *ad hoc* planners – out of necessity if not choice.

The majority of teachers made written plans of some kind. A sizeable minority appeared to undertake little written planning and to leave more than was defensible to the last minute. Such a response to the demands of teaching was sometimes defended on the grounds of 'flexibility', and indeed there is still a body of opinion in primary education which sees written planning as by definition the product of inflexible thinking and practice. However, the failure to engage in forward planning seemed to reflect anything but favourably on the commitment and capacities of some of the teachers concerned, and reinforces our view that 'flexibility' is a much abused word in primary education.

Similar variation marked teachers' approaches to record-keeping, though here school policy was as likely as individual preference to be a determining factor. Most teachers kept records of some kind, though many were fairly rudimentary.

Further, there is a clear distinction to be made in record-keeping systems between a record of what a child has *encountered* and what he or she has *learned*. In many cases, records purporting to be the latter were in fact no more than lists of tasks undertaken.

The National Curriculum spurred schools to review policy and practice in both planning and record-keeping. The existence of age-related key stages and the amount and complexity of what had to be covered dictated a long-term approach to planning. The challenge of mapping subjects and attainment targets, statements of attainment and programmes of study on to themes and topics, required an approach which was comprehensive rather than incremental, and certainly not *ad hoc*; and planning on the scale required could no longer be held in the head.

Some schools were reviewing their approaches to record-keeping before the National Curriculum. Its arrival, coupled with the statutory requirements in respect of the provision of information to parents, accelerated the review process in these schools and encouraged its initiation in others. In these matters, the Authority's considerable investment since 1989 in subject-specific INSET and in support for assessment may have helped many teachers.

CURRICULUM IN THE CLASSROOM: CONTENT

We discussed earlier the many ways in which heads and teachers understood and interpreted statements and policies on the scope and character of the primary curriculum, while noting the pervasiveness of certain commitments: to holism, to integration, to thematic rather than subject-based activity, to different aspects of the curriculum being pursued at any one time, and so on.

In studying classroom practice in PNP classrooms, we found teachers using the term *curriculum* in three rather different ways. For some the term connoted the conventional *subjects* of mathematics, language, science, art, and so on. A second group had in view not so much these familiar labels as particular *generic activities* like writing, reading, drawing, play, investigating and making which are not necessarily specific to a particular curriculum area as defined in subject terms. Others defined as curriculum areas what can only be described as *organizational strategies*: 'choosing', a term much favoured in this region from West Riding days, is a prime example, since what is indicated is neither an area of learning and understanding nor a specific activity, but the teacher's particular approach to these.

Such ambiguity about defining the curriculum, from broad policy down to everyday discourse and practice, has been a recurrent feature of recent primary education in this country, certainly not confined to Leeds alone. In the present case it provided the evaluation project with both difficulties and opportunities. The difficulties emerged when we attempted to calculate the proportions of time children and teachers were spending on different aspects of the curriculum: teachers used different labels for the same area and frequently one area subsumed another. The opportunities had to do with shedding new light on the nature and scope of primary children's classroom experiences.

The detailed figures on the time spent by children and teachers on different areas of the curriculum are contained in Report 11 (Alexander and Willcocks 1992) and discussed, within the context of classroom practice as a whole, in the next chapter. At this point, however, it is pertinent to make three general observations.

First, our figures for time spent within the curriculum are remarkably similar to those from other studies undertaken before the arrival of the National Curriculum – for example, DES 1978b; Galton *et al.* 1980. Despite the terminological confusion, there appears to be a fairly consistent national pattern. The league table in Leeds, as elsewhere, was dominated by language, which accounted for about a third of pupils' time, and mathematics, which accounted for a fifth. All other subjects came a long way behind: science (8.5 per cent), art (6.1 per cent), PE (5.4 per cent), topic (4.5 per cent), environmental studies (1.7 per cent), computing (under 1 per cent), and so on. It should be noted that since the arrival of the National Curriculum the overall picture has remained much as here; the notable exception is science, now a core subject, which has moved up the league table, thus squeezing still further the other subjects (Campbell and Neill 1990).

Second, the large amounts of time allocated to language and mathematics were the least efficiently used, since children spent less of their time working and more of their time distracted in these subjects than in other areas given far less time. This somewhat undermines the conventional allocations of curriculum time in primary classrooms, and indeed the assumption (now embedded in official thinking about the National Curriculum as well as in teacher consciousness) that the quality of curriculum delivery depends directly on the amount of time allocated.

Third, we gained evidence of a tendency for some teachers to use certain aspects of the curriculum, notably art, craft and topic work, as a means of creating time for them to concentrate their attention on language and mathematics. The work set in art, craft and topic was sometimes of a very undemanding nature, and only spasmodically monitored. This is one of many ways in which in practice the lie is given to the rhetoric about curriculum breadth and balance. We return to this issue below.

We have noted that many teachers defined curriculum in action in terms of activities rather than the familiar subject labels. Detailed observation of children at work showed this to be a more valid alternative perception than perhaps even they realized, since it became clear that regardless of the task set and the subject labels used, children invariably tended to be undertaking one or more of a limited number of *generic activities*. Analysed in these terms, their curriculum was dominated by writing, with reading, the use of apparatus, and listening/looking also paramount, though some way behind. The list then tailed off through drawing and painting, collaborative activities with other children, and movement, to talking with the teacher and talking to the class as activities on which children were engaged for a very small proportion of their time. Thus, children were required to spend far more time writing than undertaking any other activity, and over half their time on reading and writing together.

These figures are shown in Table 3.1, which also indicates the value of juxtaposing two of the versions or definitions of curriculum we referred to above: teachers' own subject labels and the observed 'generic activities'. The result is not only a league table of such activities in terms of time spent by children overall, but also a profile of each subject showing the particular mix and proportion of generic activities which each contained. We stress that the curriculum labels were teachers' own.

These figures prompt questions about the proper balance of activities both within the curriculum as a whole and within each of its constituent areas to which we return below. They also suggest the need for a reassessment of the whole thrust of the 'activity-based learning' movement which has been so prominent in recent primary education. Was it really only the activities of writing and reading that the Hadow Committee of 1931 had in mind when it argued for the curriculum 'to be thought of in terms of activity and experience rather than knowledge to be acquired and facts to be stored'? (Board of Education 1931).

CURRICULUM IN THE CLASSROOM: CHILDREN'S NEEDS AND CURRICULUM DIFFERENTIATION

In Chapter 2 we set out a four-stage framework for investigating LEA policy and school practice in respect of the various categories of specific need given priority in the Primary Needs Programme and in related policies of the Authority. The fourth stage, 'provision', is to some extent a synonym for curriculum, our concern here. We therefore remind readers briefly of certain salient points from that analysis.

We noted how, in general terms, provision for children with special educational needs was relatively well-supported and resourced, though school staff believed that provision had been squeezed during the later stages of PNP and again under LMS. In contrast, we expressed concern that apart from well-publicized schemes like second language support, provision in respect of ethnic minority groups seemed rather more patchy, and we were particularly concerned at the numbers of heads and teachers who appeared to assume that meeting the educational needs of ethnic minority groups and multicultural education were synonymous. We found an even greater discrepancy between policy and curriculum when we examined gender-related needs, once again underscored by inadequate understanding or dismissive attitudes by some heads and teachers. As far as socially and materially disadvantaged children were concerned – a major focus of PNP, it must be remembered – we found that the generosity of resourcing for the schools in which many of them were concentrated (Phase One of PNP) had not been followed through into careful analysis of their curriculum needs. Instead, there was a widespread assumption that the problem was less a curricular than an affective or behavioural one, with emotional security the prime concern. Finally, we noted the absence of policy in relation to other definable categories of need – for example, very able children.

As we indicated in Chapter 2, the Authority subsequently extended some of its

Table 3.1 Percentage of time spent by pupils on ten generic activities in different areas of the curriculum

	Write	Apparatus	Read	Listen/Look	Draw/Paint	Collaborate	Move about	Talk to teacher	Construct	Talk to class
Language	56	4	39	24	17	9	5	9	0	1
Maths	55	37	42	7	21	14	4	2	0	0
Science	16	39	5	27	25	20	5	18	11	2
Admin	0	2	9	82	0	9	29	30	0	0
Art	0	57	3	3	55	7	4	0	6	0
PE	0	18	0	18	0	27	100	0	0	0
Topic	41	0	19	12	47	15	3	8	0	4
Play	0	87	2	0	0	42	47	4	21	0
CDT	5	84	5	0	0	56	0	0	95	0
Choosing	10	49	19	19	29	44	28	0	0	0
Music	0	12	10	21	0	88	12	0	0	0
Environmental Studies	44	0	0	44	33	0	0	22	0	0
Sewing	0	100	0	0	0	0	0	0	0	0
Table games	0	100	0	0	0	63	0	0	0	0
Computer	53	47	53	23	0	30	0	23	0	0
Cooking	0	100	0	0	0	0	100	0	0	0
Television	0	0	0	100	0	0	0	0	0	0
All curriculum areas %	33	28	24	20	19	18	14	8	6	1

Note: The values in this table are percentages of the total time spent in each curriculum area. The rows generally sum to considerably more than 100 because the listed activities are not mutually exclusive.

needs-related policies. However, our study of classroom practice showed that curriculum provision in respect of these children requires continued attention at every level of the system. There were significant differences in the work of certain groups of children: older and younger, girls and boys, and those perceived by their teachers to be of average, above average, and below average ability. These differences concerned the amount of time such children spent on various kinds of task-related behaviour – working, performing routine activities, awaiting attention, being distracted – both overall and in relation to each area of the curriculum. Our eleventh report provides full details.

We suggested that while some of these discrepancies may be attributable to the many individual pupil differences which are wholly independent of the teacher, others may well be related directly to a teacher's assumptions and expectations about the children in question, in as far as there is an established relationship between a teacher's view of a child and that child's characteristic responses.

Given the kinds of assumptions and expectations about particular groups of children which emerged from our other studies, the concern expressed here remains a valid one. Teachers need both opportunities and procedures for ensuring that the evidence about children on which their diagnoses, curriculum provision and assessments are based is as secure and reliable as possible. This matter was given little attention within PNP, despite the rhetoric of individual needs and provision which was so prominent a feature of that programme. More recently, the National Curriculum has dictated a concern with assessment to which the Authority has responded through courses and documents and by setting up an assessment unit.

Yet assessment is not merely, or even mainly, about procedures. The quality of an assessment depends vitally upon the quality of the evidence on which it is based; in turn, such evidence depends on the knowledge and skills of the teacher and the nature and duration of the interactions with children and their work through which the evidence about their needs and attainments is obtained. However, since the central pupil–teacher and pupil–pupil interactions of which teaching is constituted were somewhat peripheral to the messages of the Primary Needs Programme, and the emphasis was more on aspects like display, resources, classroom layout and organization, we can anticipate continuing problems of misdiagnosis and inaccurate assessment among those teachers whose view of their task has been unduly influenced by this emphasis.

In the context of the National Curriculum, the Standard Assessment Tasks (SATs) provide a check on the teacher's judgements. However, SATs are used only twice in a child's primary schooling, at the ages of 7 and 11, and even then they provide only a small proportion of the evidence on which assessments are based, the majority coming from Teacher Assessment (TA). In any event, after the 1990 pilot for Key Stage One National Curriculum Assessment the government began a severe pruning exercise, cutting back first the number of attainment targets covered by the SATs and then, after the 1991 assessment run, the scope of the SATs themselves.

Thus, a national system of assessment notwithstanding, most decisions about children's learning and progress will be based, as they always have been, on *informal* assessments by their teachers. In no more than a limited sense, therefore, does National Curriculum Assessment resolve this problem. Though it is encouraging to note the Authority's investment in assessment policy, training and support (Leeds City Council 1990b) as a consequence of the 1988 legislation, it is important that what we have termed 'informal' assessment receives no less attention than the statutory requirements. Just as there is now a trend to defining 'generic' skills in management (DES 1990f), so there are generic skills in classroom assessment, and in turn these are vitally dependent upon classroom strategies which maximize teachers' opportunities for careful observation of and interaction with their pupils.

THE QUALITY OF THE PRIMARY CURRICULUM

In this final section of the present chapter we return to the 'broadly-based curriculum' – the goal of both PNP and the 1988 Education Reform Act. How far was it a reality in Leeds primary schools during the period in question? The first problem we encounter, rehearsed at several points in this and other chapters, was that the concept of curriculum breadth was ill-defined in Authority policy and multifariously interpreted in schools. Until the arrival of the National Curriculum, indeed, Leeds LEA had no meaningful conception of the primary curriculum as a whole. The eight contrasting versions of the Leeds 'broadly-based curriculum' in Alexander *et al.* (1989: 123–6) illustrate the extent of this problem.

Thus, whole curriculum thinking in the schools was highly variable in quality and widely divergent in emphasis. All too frequently, the ritual genuflection to 'wholeness' barely concealed an absence of hard thinking and planning in relation to whole curriculum matters, or discrepancies in provision across subjects which were so substantial and deeply ingrained that they invalidated even the vaguest of 'broadly-based curriculum' claims, let alone those involving contingent principles like balance, coherence, continuity and differentiation. In disentangling themselves from this legacy, it must be said, schools had little help from elsewhere.

Thus, at each level of the system we found claims to breadth and balance undermined by countervailing policies and practices: in Authority special projects; in central INSET provision; in PNP development fund allocations; in the allocation of posts of responsibility in schools; in school-based INSET programmes; in the status of postholders and the time and support available to them to undertake their responsibilities; in the range of curriculum areas subjected to review and development and the time and support given to each; in teacher expertise; and above all, and as a consequence of all this, in the quality of children's curriculum experiences in the classroom.

Equally, it must be stressed, for every school which neglected a given subject or treated it indifferently, there was another whose staff taught it with commitment, flair and challenge. The variables, then, were not merely LEA policy and support, but also school policy and priorities, and – always a critical factor – the availability and extent of staff curriculum expertise.

At the same time, our data tended to lead inexorably towards confirmation of Alexander's (1984) 'two curricula' thesis – the idea that the primary world's claims to curricular wholeness, balance and integration are frequently invalidated by a sharp divide, both quantitative (in terms of time spent and resources allocated) and qualitative (in terms of professional expertise, thinking and practice) between 'the basics' and the rest, or 'Curriculum I' and 'Curriculum II'. In this matter, the proposition that different aspects of the curriculum should receive different proportions of time in the classroom is not contested: a complete curriculum is necessarily one in which priorities have been clearly identified. What is not acceptable educationally, let alone compatible with ideas of curriculum breadth and balance, is that there should be such variation in the actual *quality* of what teachers offer and children experience in the classroom as between the different curriculum areas. Put another way, however much or little time the various subjects are allocated, each of them should be fully staffed and resourced, carefully planned, seriously treated, and delivered in the classroom in a convincing, stimulating and challenging manner.

The National Curriculum, far from eliminating this historical tendency, could well reinforce it, unless positive steps are taken by both LEAs and schools (and indeed by central government) to enhance the quality of support, expertise and provision in *every* subject, regardless of its status.

Putting together our data on policy, INSET, school management and classroom practice, we can present the following brief summary of the overall position in relation to five contrasting areas of the curriculum as they stood immediately prior to the introduction of the National Curriculum, always emphasizing that there were many notable exceptions to each general trend. The areas are listed in the order of their apparent importance in the classroom as signalled by the proportion of overall curriculum time spent by pupils on the subject or area in question.

English

In the classrooms we observed, the average pupil-time spent on English as a specific area of the curriculum was 31.5 per cent. English had some 30 per cent of the central LEA INSET teacher-days devoted to curriculum from 1985–9. There were no special LEA support programmes, except in relation to second language learners. English had the second largest share of the PNP development fund. Curriculum leadership posts were allocated in most schools. These postholders were mostly female; a relatively small proportion were senior staff. English was a high priority area for curriculum review in schools, but not as high as mathematics.

The priority accorded to English in the school was frequently reflected in classroom layout, with reading and/or language bays common, though less so for the 7–11 age group than for the 5–7. Pupils spent a lower proportion of time working and a higher proportion distracted than in most other subjects: English had the highest time allocation of all subjects, but the time was not always economically used. Girls spent more time on task than did boys. Older children spent more time on task than did younger. Pupils rated as above average by their teachers worked less hard and were much more likely to be distracted than those rated average or below.

Classroom activities were dominated by writing (56 per cent) and reading (39 per cent), with very little time devoted to the systematic fostering of children's speaking and listening. The quality of teacher-initiated classroom talk was not, in general, high. (For a more detailed discussion of trends in this subject across the Authority, see pp. 50–7.)

Mathematics

The average pupil time spent on mathematics in the classrooms we observed was 20.2 per cent. From 1985–9, mathematics had by far the largest share – 44 per cent – of the central LEA INSET teacher-days devoted to curriculum. Mathematics had considerable LEA support through the advisory service and PrIME, and the largest share of the PNP development fund. Curriculum leadership posts were allocated in nearly all schools – more than for English. These postholders were, in terms of the overall staff gender balance in primary schools, disproportionately male; mathematics also had the highest proportion of senior staff in leadership roles. The subject was top of the list of priorities for curriculum review.

In the classroom, mathematics workbays were common, equally so for ages 5–7 and 7–11, but less common than in English and art. As in English, pupils spent a lower proportion of their time working and a higher proportion distracted than in most other subjects: mathematics had the second highest time allocation, but the time was not always economically used. Girls and boys appeared to work equally hard. Older children spent more time on task than did younger. Pupils rated as above average ability spent more time working and less distracted or awaiting attention than those rated average or below.

Mathematics was more commonly taught as a separate subject than any other in the curriculum. Classroom activities were dominated by writing (55 per cent) and reading (42 per cent), with substantial amounts of time using apparatus (37 per cent) and drawing or other graphic activity (21 per cent). There was little collaborative activity between pupils, and little discussion with the teacher.

Science

In the classrooms we observed, the average pupil-time spent on science was 8.5 per cent. Of the central LEA INSET teacher-days devoted to curriculum from

1985–9, science had 13 per cent, though this figure fluctuated from one year to the next. Over the years in question, LEA support for primary science, from the advisory service and through programmes like ESG Science and collaborative projects with the University of Leeds, expanded considerably, yet it had a much smaller share of the PNP development fund than mathematics or English. Curriculum leadership posts were allocated in most schools. Postholders were predominantly female and of low (that is, main professional grade) status. Science became a review priority in many schools, especially after its designation as a National Curriculum core subject.

Science workbays were not common, especially where older children were concerned. Children spent a significantly higher proportion of their time on task in science than in mathematics or English, though of course a much smaller proportion of their overall time was devoted to the subject. However, girls worked for more of the time than did boys and the latter spent a disproportionate amount of time awaiting the teacher's attention. Children of all ages worked equally hard. Pupils rated as above average by their teachers worked considerably harder and were much less likely to be distracted than those rated as below average.

During the period in question, the subject was in a state of transition from being treated as an aspect of environmental studies-based topic work, with a predominantly biological emphasis, to being identified as a specific curriculum area. Classroom activities were a mixture of working with apparatus, drawing and other graphic activity. They were much more collaborative and interactive than language or mathematics, but with little writing and hardly any reading.

Humanities/environmental studies

In the classrooms we observed, the average pupil time spent on humanities and/or environmental studies (the labels were used interchangeably) was 6.2 per cent. There was very little LEA INSET commitment in terms of teacher-days from 1985–9, no specific support programmes, and the area had a very insignificant share of the PNP development fund (less even than art and craft). A minority of schools surveyed had curriculum leadership posts in this area, though the number was rising. The designation was often for environmental studies and might be combined with another area, notably science or PE. In terms of gender-bias in curriculum posts, the area contrasted dramatically with art/craft, having a larger proportion of male postholders than any other subject, with a significant number of these being senior staff. It was not given priority in review, however.

Classroom activities in this area were usually delivered through the medium of the topic, an approach in which children spent a fairly low proportion of their time actually on task (55 per cent – the same as in English). Against the general trend, girls spent *less* time than boys on task. In topic work generally, pupils perceived by their teachers as above average worked hard, but in environmental studies (that is, a specific content area usually delivered through topics) those rated above average worked much less hard and were much more frequently distracted than those rated average or below.

This area of the curriculum was dominated by writing, drawing and painting, with some collaborative activity, though considerably less so in topic-based approaches than advocates tend to claim. There was evidence of relatively undemanding work, sometimes used to free the teacher (as, sometimes, was art) to concentrate on other curriculum areas. Since the area in question nearly always subsumes the two National Curriculum subjects history and geography, schools and the LEA will need to attend carefully to ways of rationalizing it and giving it greater rigour and challenge in the classroom (DES 1989f).

Art

In the classrooms we observed, pupil-time devoted to art was 6.1 per cent. There was very little central LEA INSET commitment to art in terms of teacher-days during the period 1985–9, and no specific LEA support programmes, though plenty of advisory encouragement to teachers to improve the quality of the visual environment of schools and classrooms. Art had an insignificant share of the PNP development fund. There were curriculum leadership posts for art/craft in just over half of the schools surveyed. Of all areas of the primary curriculum, art had by far the highest proportion of female postholders (followed by music), and by far the lowest proportion of senior staff involved in such roles. It was rarely the subject of curriculum review: curriculum leadership tended to have more to do with resources and display than with curriculum content and progression.

Children spent a fairly high proportion of time on task, though girls much more so than boys, who were rather more frequently distracted, and younger children tended to be more absorbed by their art activities than older. Pupils rated as above average spent less time working and more time distracted than did those rated average or below, and this confirms the other observational evidence of the lack of real challenge or interest in many tasks in art/craft. The activities were a combination of two- and three-dimensional work, with a predominance of the former, and little collaboration or discussion. Activities defined as art were frequently used to extend or round off other work ('Now do a picture.') and in this respect were sometimes little more than a time-filler. Moreover, some teachers consciously adopted the strategy of using art as an unsupervised activity which freed them to concentrate on groups undertaking mathematics and language tasks.

In this and various other respects, our evidence indicates that, primary rhetoric and the visual emphasis of PNP notwithstanding, art frequently lacked seriousness, integrity or challenge. The emergence of Design and Technology in the National Curriculum (DES 1990b, Leeds City Council 1990d) has led to a re-examination of aspects of art/craft. The two are clearly not synonymous, though there is an increasing tendency to treat them as such, thus quite erroneously implying that aesthetic judgement is a kind of technical problem-solving.

These five summaries indicate general trends, though of course they cannot do justice to significant variations between individual classrooms and schools. It will be noted that they represent the situation as it was in the last few months before the introduction of the National Curriculum. With that in mind, we can reasonably anticipate that the character of each area will begin to change as teachers adjust their practice to meet the statutory requirements. The most obvious change will be in time allocations, especially in the newer subjects like science. How much deeper change will penetrate is at present an open question, and one which a number of projects are beginning to address, including one based at Leeds University. For the moment we can note that the national evidence points to the long-term persistence of certain fundamental problems in the teaching of language, mathematics, science, history and geography (DES 1989d, 1989e, 1989f, 1990d). In any case, many of the tendencies we have noted are unrelated to the attainment target specifics of the National Curriculum. For all these reasons, we believe that the longer-term significance of the character-izations is considerable, and that they repay careful study.

THE QUALITY OF THE PRIMARY CURRICULUM: THE PARTICULAR CASE OF ENGLISH

The anomalous character of English in policy, school management and classroom practice will be readily apparent from the above comparisons. It is clear that during the PNP period the Authority, and in many cases schools, did not provide support commensurate with the subject's central place in the curriculum. Further grounds for concern about English emerged from two rather more specific studies which we undertook. One of these, dealing with teacher–pupil talk, was undertaken as part of Level Three of our study of classroom practice, described in full in our eleventh report. The other was a longitudinal analysis of all the Authority's 7+ and 9+ reading test scores between 1983 and 1989. The first part of the latter, dealing with the period 1983–8, is described in Report 9 (Alexander *et al.* 1989: Ch. 3). The second part, extending the coverage to include 1988–91, and reworking the entire 1983–9 analysis in the light of new data, is presented here for the first time. While the studies do not claim to cover English comprehensively as an area of the curriculum, they do shed important additional light on two major aspects which, as National Curriculum Attainment Targets En1 and En2 (DES 1990a), are now of considerable public, as well as pro-fessional, concern.

Speaking and listening

Our combination of quantitative and qualitative analysis of classroom interac-tions (dealt with more fully in the next chapter) indicates practice which sometimes fell some way short of the requirements of the twenty-one National Curriculum Statements of Attainment for Speaking and Listening which are now applicable to the primary phase (DES 1990a). In saying this, we must emphasize that since the study predated the imposition of the Orders for English there was no reason to expect otherwise: the point is made to indicate the extent of change which was needed in order to meet the letter and spirit of the statutory requirements.

Our analysis of the curriculum as both *generic activities* and *subjects* shows that English, as observed during our project, tended to be dominated by writing and reading with relatively little opportunity for structured teacher–pupil or pupil–pupil talk, especially among older children. Even accepting the argument that talk is cross-curricular rather than confined to an area labelled 'English' or 'Language', such opportunities were still surprisingly rare.

Teacher–pupil talk was often dominated by the teacher's questions, frequently of a rhetorical, closed or token kind. Questions inviting or encouraging the child to think were much rarer. Questions were sometimes pitched low: while accessible to all, they then ceased to challenge more than a few. Answers to such questions might be accepted by the teacher, however incorrect or irrelevant.

Too often, the exaggerated or undiscriminating use of praise denied children access to the kind of focused feedback they most needed. Conversely, pupils' unusual and thought-provoking statements and questions were sometimes blocked or ignored if they risked diverting the teacher from his or her agenda.

Much pupil–teacher discourse which had the appearance of being open-ended and exploratory was in fact closed and directive, providing little scope for children to extend their understanding beyond the sometimes very restricted goals set.

Much pupil- and teacher-time could be wasted by what might be called 'pseudo-exploratory discourse'. There is a clear place in teaching for questions, statements and instructions, and for questions, statements and instructions of different kinds. Each should be used appropriately and discriminatingly.

Class size and the complexities of the job of whole-curriculum teaching in primary schools make one-to-one teacher–pupil talk a rare and precious commodity. Schools need to devote much more attention to ways of extending and refining professional skills in this area, and to upgrading pupil–pupil talk within small groups from random exchanges to a structured and genuinely collaborative programme of discourse designed to promote learning. (We further consider the unrealized potential of group work in the next chapter.)

Reading

Our study of reading standards was of a very different kind. Reading scores on the Authority's 7+ and 9+ tests had been used as one of the measures of schools' needs in respect of the PNP. In addition, the scores constituted a rare piece of consistent and objective data covering both the PNP period and that preceding it and thus provided a pertinent indicator of PNP's impact, though not, it must be emphasized, the only or even necessarily the best one. We collected and computer-analysed all available 7+ and 9+ test scores for the six years 1983–9 – some 85,000 in all – in order to gain a picture of trends in each PNP phase, across all 230 or so of the Authority's primary schools, and – for comparative purposes – across all middle schools. No sample was drawn: every child's score was included. The first part of our analysis was presented in Report 9 (Alexander *et al*. 1989: Ch. 3). What follows is taken from the as yet unpublished reanalysis, which added the 1989 scores and some additional data from previous years to give a more comprehensive picture of trends during the six-year period.

We were also able to study four additional reports: the National Foundation for Education Research in England and Wales (NFER) survey of LEA evidence on reading standards (Cato and Whetton 1990) undertaken on behalf of the School Examinations and Assessment Council (SEAC) (Leeds LEA was one of the twenty-six LEAs on which the NFER was able to report in some detail and it did so by drawing mainly on our own data); the HMI survey of the teaching of reading in 120 primary schools (DES 1990c) which, along with the SEAC/NFER study, was undertaken at the request of the Secretary cf State following the controversy generated by Turner's analysis of reading test results in nine LEAs (Turner 1990); the Turner study itself; and Leeds LEA's own analysis of the figures for the two years following our own study, 1989–90 and 1990–1.

Tables 3.2 and 3.3 show means and standard deviations (SD) for each year and PNP phase. Figure 3.1 shows fluctuations in the mean reading ages, again by year and phase.

We now summarize our findings. Reading standards, in as far as they can be defined by test scores (which of course attend to only some of the outcomes of the reading process), both rose and fell very slightly during the period 1983–9. Combining the project and LEA data so as to encompass the period 1983–91 – though with due caution – we find a slight but definite downward trend in recent years, notably in Phase 2 schools at 7+ and Phase 1 and 3 and middle schools at 9+.

However, this does not necessarily denote the beginning of a longer-term decline in reading standards (though the LEA's additional figures – see below – do seem to tip the balance slightly in support of such an interpretation). If the graph had stopped in 1987 the picture would have looked very different.

More significant is the variation within and between the three groups of primary schools and the middle schools. The fact that pre-1985 Phase 1 scores are lowest and Phase 3 scores are highest is inevitable, since that is why the schools were allocated to those phases. The fact that middle school scores are lowest at 9+ might seem at first sight disturbing. However, it must be remembered that in Leeds the middle schools were mainly fed by inner area primary schools and thus their scores should be examined in relation to those for Phase 1 and perhaps Phase 2. In any event, children took the 9+ test so soon after entering their middle schools that it would have been impossible for those schools to have affected the outcomes of the 9+ tests.

Having entered these caveats, it is important to point out that although there is no firm evidence of an overall decline in reading standards at 7+ and 9+ in Leeds during the period 1983–9, neither is there evidence for an overall improvement, either differentially between phases, or across the board. There are thus no grounds for complacency.

A disturbing trend, shown in our ninth report, but not in the tables below, is the slight rise in the proportion of children scoring low (with reading quotients of

Table 3.2 Mean raw scores on the 7+ reading test (reanalysis incorporating additional data)

		1983–4	1984–5	1985–6	1986–7	1987–8	1988–9
Phase 1:	Mean	25.6	24.8	25.8	25.7	25.0	23.5
	SD	10.2	10.4	10.1	10.2	10.2	10.2
Phase 2:	Mean	29.0	29.1	29.0	29.1	28.6	27.3
	SD	9.4	9.5	9.5	9.6	9.6	9.5
Phase 3:	Mean	31.6	32.1	32.7	32.2	32.1	31.7
	SD	8.9	8.7	8.5	8.7	8.8	8.8

Table 3.3 Mean raw scores on the 9+ reading test (reanalysis incorporating additional data)

		1983–4	1984–5	1985–6	1986–7	1987–8	1988–9
Phase 1:	Mean	22.4	21.6	21.9	22.4	22.5	21.5
	SD	7.1	7.9	7.5	7.1	7.6	7.4
Phase 2:	Mean	22.2	23.0	22.4	22.2	23.4	23.0
	SD	7.4	7.0	7.2	7.4	7.1	7.2
Phase 3:	Mean	25.2	25.1	25.0	25.5	25.4	25.0
	SD	6.4	6.1	6.4	6.2	6.1	6.4
Middle	Mean	21.8	21.6	21.0	21.5	21.7	21.2
	SD	7.8	7.9	8.1	8.2	8.1	8.5

80 or below) on the 7+ test. In contrast the proportion of children in the highest-scoring group has remained more or less stable.

The LEA's own analysis was undertaken on a different basis from ours, and we have not had access to their raw data or calculations. However, the analysis is useful because it brings us up to date in two important respects. First the apparent decline noted towards the end of our own data period of 1983–9 is continued into 1990 and 1991. Second, the increase in the proportion of 7+ low scorers is confirmed as a much longer-term trend, going back to 1983 and being particularly marked in PNP Phase 1. The figures for 9+ remain less conclusive.

The figures in Table 3.2 show standard deviations to be largest in Phase 1 schools at 7+. Taken together with figures showing an increase in the proportion of Phase 1 children of 7+ with reading quotients of 80 or below, this means, first, that teachers of young children in the inner-city schools were facing wider gaps between their least and most able readers than were their colleagues elsewhere,

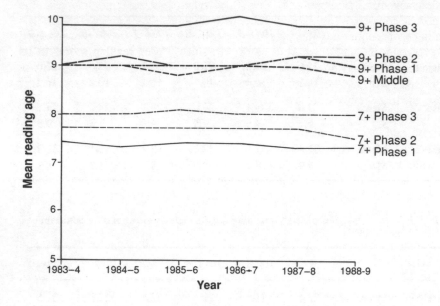

Figure 3.1 Reading standards: primary and middle schools, 1983–9

and second that they had a particular and increasing challenge in respect of the least able readers. Staff in these schools were thus manifestly in greatest need of Authority support in the teaching of reading, and the inner-city weightings in the Leeds PNP and LMS policies would seem to have been vindicated.

However, it would seem that the substantial injection of extra staff and material resources under the Primary Needs Programme had no perceivable impact on reading test scores overall, though the school-by-school figures do show considerable improvements in some cases (and deterioration, PNP notwithstanding, in others). However, it is also possible that without PNP any downward trends would have been even more marked.

The lack of apparent impact of PNP on reading scores raises important questions about the focusing of the programme. If instead of the vagaries of the 'broadly-based curriculum' the Authority had systematically targeted PNP resources on very specific curriculum and school needs, and if reading had been one of them, the picture would almost certainly have been different. Thus, although our figures confirm the PNP policy of greatest support for inner-city schools, they also question the kind of support which was provided, with its emphasis on increasing staff and capitation rather than enhancing those professional skills which teachers need most if they are to cope successfully with the central challenges of inner-city teaching.

In our earlier comparison of five areas of the curriculum, we pointed to the inadequacy of LEA support for English in relation to its importance. In this respect it compared very unfavourably with mathematics. Our analysis of the reading scores underlines this point dramatically. Here was a need acknowledged by everyone (including the Authority itself, since it used reading scores in its allocation of PNP resources), yet having been identified, the need was simply not addressed by the Authority, and the resources were directed elsewhere. In this sense, the neglect might seem almost perverse. In any event it seems to underline two major criticisms we have made of PNP: its confusion and ambivalence of purpose, and its neglect of curriculum specifics.

The question of reading standards cannot be separated from consideration of the wider language environment of primary schools and classrooms. Our cumulative evidence – on reading test scores, on classroom practice, on curriculum development, on INSET, and on LEA policy – indicates that language as a curriculum area was given surprisingly low priority during the PNP period. In any event, the evidence raises important questions about the overall language environment of primary classrooms which must be addressed as part of any serious attempt to improve reading standards.

The SEAC/NFER study (Cato and Whetton 1990) confirms that the position in Leeds during this period was comparable to that elsewhere in the country. In as far as a decline in measured reading standards was detectable in the late 1980s from the NFER data, it occurred mainly among lowest-scoring groups of children. However, while in Leeds deterioration in these scores was most marked in inner-city schools, NFER asserted that 'there is no evidence [nationally]. . . that decline is an inner-city phenomenon'.

Yet it is important to understand that the national evidence on this matter is far from conclusive. The SEAC/NFER study is extremely cautious in its conclusions, since it acquired usable data from a mere 26 of the 117 LEAs, and could report a decline in scores in only three-quarters (19) of them. A more recent study from Buckinghamshire, reported as we went to press, seems to contradict the NFER evidence and concur with our own, suggesting that the sharpest decline in test scores occurred in the most disadvantaged areas (Lake 1991). However, what is not in doubt is the need – voiced frequently in all our reports – for a much more focused approach to curriculum in inner-city schools than that offered under PNP, with literacy given very high priority.

At the same time, as we commented in Chapter 2, some of the root causes of the problem may well be beyond the reach of the educational system, and certainly of individual teachers. The impact of poverty on a child's life and educational prospects is far greater than the rather clinical phrase 'social and material disadvantage' can ever convey. The teaching of reading has been in the public arena for some time now, and the brunt of the political and media attack has been borne by primary teachers and teacher-trainers. While our evidence underlines the need for a considerable sharpening of the educational response, it also suggests that without a change in the political, social and economic circumstances which lead to poverty and social dislocation, teachers will continue to fight a losing battle.

There remains the question of what to do about the LEA's 7+ and 9+ reading testing programmes. Their prime function has been to identify children with learning difficulties. This screening function is now superseded, to some extent, by the introduction, from 1991, of National Curriculum Assessment at 7+, within which a formal assessment of reading is a compulsory part. Dealing with reading assessment in this context is much more satisfactory: the teacher is more involved in the assessment process and reading assessment is contextualized within the wider curriculum. But we have also seen that the testing of reading across the Authority can also yield valuable information about overall trends. The particular tests used in Leeds are by now somewhat dated, and if this kind of blanket testing is to continue, more up-to-date, comprehensive and sensitive tests need to be used.

Accordingly, we recommended the following to the LEA in advance of our report's publication: that the 7+ and 9+ tests should cease to have a screening function, and that this should henceforth be undertaken as part of each school's statutory assessment obligations; that the existing 7+ and 9+ tests should be phased out, and better tests should be phased in with the monitoring of standards firmly in mind; that to maximize the value of the data already gathered, the existing tests should be used for a further two years so that the Authority would gain, through the combination of PRINDEP and LEA data, an analysis for the decade 1983–93 – a period over which claims about longer-term trends may have a reasonable validity; and that the LEA should begin to make systematic monitoring of reading test scores, along the lines initiated by ourselves during the evaluation, part of its response to its statutory obligation to undertake curriculum monitoring and quality assurance.

Finally, it is important to note that the prioritization of reading in the National Curriculum, and in the statutory assessment requirements for Key Stages One and Two, cannot of themselves guarantee higher standards. Reading needs closer attention in initial teacher-training and INSET – that much is evident – and in the summer of 1991 the Secretary of State instructed the Council for the Accreditation of Teacher Education (CATE) to undertake an enquiry into the initial training of teachers to teach reading; but there is an equally important need to look searchingly at the classroom context within which the teaching of reading is located. The emerging evidence is not encouraging. HMI (DES 1990c) reported a link between poor teaching of reading and the complex patterns of classroom organization we consider in our next chapter. The Warwick study of teacher-time at Key Stage One (Campbell and Neill 1990) and the NCC (1991) study of National Curriculum implementation in 1989–90 showed how reading was one of the first casualties of the sheer volume of National Curriculum requirements, particularly those in mathematics and science, which the primary teacher is now obliged by law to accommodate.

The National Curriculum was introduced subject by subject, with maximum pressure from the favoured subject lobbies and no serious acknowledgement of the fact that a curriculum cannot be indefinitely expandable. Primary teachers inevitably responded by concentrating on those subjects which were new or particularly demanding, putting other more familiar subjects on hold. This process had already begun during the PNP period 1985-90 and the problems we have reported – not just in reading but also in respect of wider issues of curriculum balance and consistency – may therefore be exacerbated rather than remedied by the National Curriculum, since curriculum overcrowding and professional overload are now statutory.

CONCLUSION

Notwithstanding its central place in the child's education, its conceptual and operational complexity, and the considerable demands it places on the expertise of primary teachers, and despite being highlighted in the initial aims of PNP, curriculum remained a kind of void in the Authority's policy until the arrival of the National Curriculum. The 'broadly-based curriculum' was elusive because it was never defined or argued through. The questions it invited about purposes, about scope, content and balance, about delivery and differentiation, about planning, management and assessment, were never addressed. Instead, teachers had to be content with recommendations about the physical and organizational context of curriculum, rather than its substance; about the 'learning environment' rather than learning itself.

Meanwhile, curriculum policies emerged *ad hoc*, in response more to the persuasiveness of this or that subject lobby and to community pressure and central government requirements than to any systematic local analysis of educational and professional need. Thus, mathematics, and increasingly science, fared well because they were powerful lobbies with central government policy on their side. In contrast, English, though arguably the most fundamental as well as the most extensive curriculum area at the primary stage, was left to its own devices, with consequences which are now only too apparent. Other curriculum areas – the arts, history, geography – having neither resources nor more than minority support, fared even worse. Although Leeds did far more in the fields of ethnicity and gender than some other LEAs, the *curriculum* applications of its policies were not always followed through, either – as in the case of gender and disadvantage – because of insufficient resources for teacher support and development, or as a consequence of the more general neglect of hard thinking about curriculum planning, content, differentiation and delivery.

The result was an array of confused and confusing messages, very uneven provision within both the LEA and its schools, a failure to provide support where it was most needed, and the general perpetuation or reinforcement of the very curriculum problems most in need of resolution. This, surely, was the worst possible way to construct a curriculum. The Authority needed people with educational vision, with detailed understanding of curriculum matters and with freedom from particular subject prejudices, to map out a primary curriculum which was genuinely comprehensive, balanced, and relevant to the needs of both children and society. These problems remain. The National Curriculum has exacerbated rather than removed them. They require urgent attention.

4 Teaching strategies

In moving now to consider the fate of the third PNP aim – that concerned with the promotion of 'flexible teaching strategies' – we stress the close connection with our discussion of curriculum in the previous chapter. It is not so much that curriculum is the 'what' of education and teaching the 'how', as that the teacher's classroom strategies are what transform curriculum from a mere bundle of inert ideas to experiences through which children learn. In this sense, therefore, the 'how' and 'what' of education are one.

This being so, there is some degree of arbitrariness in the division of issues between this and the previous chapter, and there will also necessarily be some overlap.

The chapter has two main focuses: the character and impact of teachers' classroom strategies; and the wider professional context within which such strategies are developed, supported and improved.

POLICY

As we have seen, the Primary Needs Programme was based on a list of aims rather than a comprehensive statement of policy. The list referred only briefly and somewhat obliquely to classroom practice, recommending (but not defining): a stimulating and challenging learning environment; flexible teaching strategies to meet the identified needs of individual pupils; and specific practical help for individuals and small groups.

Subsequently the Authority issued more detailed and comprehensive statements of its policy in relation to primary education, notably in *Primary Education: A Policy Statement* (Leeds City Council 1988), and *The Curriculum 5–16: A Statement of Policy* (Leeds City Council 1990a). However, neither of these documents was available during the early years of PNP, and neither gives detailed guidance on classroom practice, being more concerned with underlying principles, aims and objectives.

Before the appearance of these two documents, teachers learned of the preferred modes of classroom practice in other, more informal ways: from attendance at in-service courses or from discussions with advisers and advisory teachers, and conversations with their head teachers, PNP coordinators, and other colleagues. However, the main channel during the critical period when schools were being brought into the Primary Needs Programme phase by phase (1985–8) was the Authority's substantial programme of in-service courses mounted at the Primary Schools Centre, and discussed in Chapter 7.

There was an unfortunate lack of clarity about the status of the ideas which were introduced at the courses dealing with classroom practice. Some teachers saw them simply as points for discussion and considered themselves free to accept or reject them without prejudice to their professional future in the LEA. Others believed that practices described and demonstrated at length by persons of high status in the Authority must at the very least be strongly recommended and might even be – or become – mandatory.

In fact the central message of these courses, though diffuse, was consistent. Recommendations about classroom management, group work, the planning of projects, the fostering of pupils' self-reliance, the use of resources, classroom display and a number of other topics, reinforced by the powerful visual device of a model classroom, identified the various items on the advisory team's agenda for reforming classroom practice. Taken together, they conveyed a view of primary teaching which had a distinctive character. The physical and organizational settings in which children's learning took place were to be all-important, and the combination of PNP resourcing, advisory effort and enhanced school staffing were all to be directed to their improvement, or to establishing what advisory staff termed 'the quality learning environment'. The emphasis, then, was on the *context* rather than the *processes* or *content* of learning. Whatever the strengths of this approach as a way of giving teachers a practical basis for beginning to change their practice, it carried the risk that some might presume that changing the physical arrangements of a classroom would of itself produce improved learning.

Interviews and observations carried out during a long-term follow-up study in fifty classrooms revealed that the classroom practice of nearly 50 per cent of the respondents had not changed in any perceptible way as a result of their attendance at such courses. Of these, half had already been working along the lines advocated, and although some of them enjoyed the reassurance of seeing classroom practice like their own being commended to others, several expressed the view that such an experience did not merit time away from their classes. The other half of this group (about a quarter of the entire sample) either rejected the Authority's recommendations entirely or claimed that although they agreed with them in principle they were prevented from implementing them by unsuitable classroom conditions or other school circumstances.

On the other hand, for a little under a third of respondents the courses were highly successful, capturing their interest and provoking major changes in their thinking and classroom practice. A smaller group, comprising just under a quarter of the sample, spoke highly of such courses but had made only very superficial moves or token gestures in the direction of their recommendations. In this group there were some wide discrepancies between what teachers were doing in their classrooms and what they said – and seemed to believe – they were doing.

It is clear that this kind of INSET provision could have been much more effective if the membership of each course had been carefully targeted and hence more homogeneous; many of the teachers who attended would have been better served by a simpler, more sharply focused presentation of recommendations specifically relevant to their own current practice.

The complexity and diffuseness of the Authority's messages had a further effect. There was so much on offer that highly selective and incomplete incorporation of course recommendations was common. This sometimes led to productive and satisfactory change; but in some classrooms it resulted in confusion as procedures became separated from their underlying objectives, and as teachers strove to balance the conflicting demands of a mixture of well-tried and untried practices, of a wide variety of grouping strategies, and of many different activities going on simultaneously in their classrooms. As a consequence, the complexity of some teachers' classroom organization appeared to greatly increase the proportion of the time during which children were distracted, awaiting attention or working only sporadically.

There are, however, three overriding reservations about the approaches commended in Leeds during this period.

First, although their ambience was ostensibly child-centred, they concentrated considerably more attention on teachers and classrooms than on children. Teachers had to take as self-evident what in fact needed to be closely questioned – namely, assumptions about how children learn and claims about the causal connection between such learning and particular strategies for teaching and classroom organization.

Second, although much was made of the principle of 'flexibility' in both the PNP aims and its various courses and documents, there was an inherent contradiction in the notion of flexibility being mandated from above, especially given the didactic power of the model classroom. The message to teachers seemed to be that they could be flexible in the prescribed way but not in their own.

Third, the package of suggestions, recommendations and prescriptions was justified in terms of a notion of 'good primary practice' which was frequently provided as a validating label but never openly defined or explored. Consensus was assumed; the possibility that 'good practice' might be problematic was not.

We shall return to these points later.

PRACTICE

The classroom context: display and layout

Leaving aside for the moment the matter of the educational validity of the principles under discussion, their most immediately apparent influence – as might be expected – was on the physical appearance of PNP classrooms. The extent and quality of classroom display improved dramatically during the period of PRINDEP's evaluation, though we became increasingly aware of a tendency

Figure 4.1 Type One classroom layout

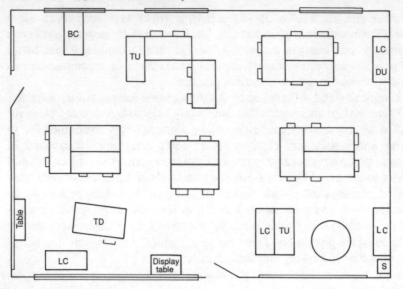

Figure 4.2 Type Two classroom layout

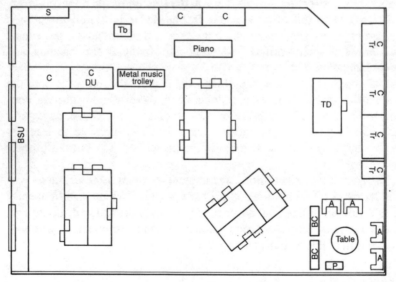

Figure 4.3 Type Three classroom layout

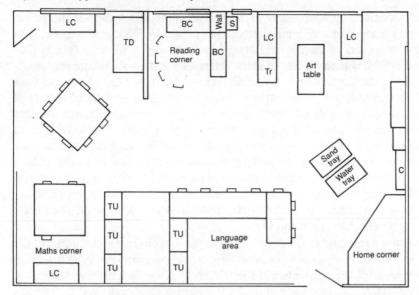

Figure 4.4 Type Four classroom layout

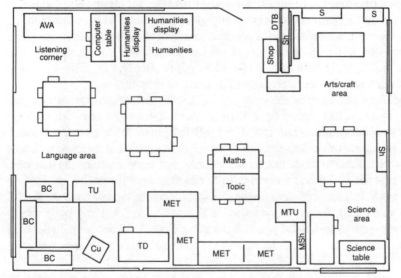

Key

A	Armchair	Msh	Maths shelves
AVA	Audiovisual aids	MTU	Maths tray unit
BC	Bookcase	P	Plant stand
BSU	Built-in shelf unit	S	Sink
C	Cupboard	Sh	Shelves
Cu	Cushion	Tb	Tub-like container on castors
DTB	Daily task board	TD	Teacher's desk
DU	Display unit	Tr	Trays
LC	Low cupboard	TU	Tray units
MET	Maths equipment table	⊓	Built-in tray units

towards a certain repetitiveness in colour schemes and styles of mounting, conveying a sense of conformity rather than creativity. That teachers felt constrained in matters of display and layout by Authority guidelines (Leeds City Council 1989d) was confirmed in many interviews and questionnaire responses.

Of the teachers we spoke to, two-fifths reported that they had rearranged their furniture, and well over nine-tenths of them had made some kind of change to their classrooms as a direct consequence of suggestions or recommendations made to them as part of the Primary Needs Programme. We were able to corroborate such claims observationally. A few of the suggestions about the deployment of furniture were fairly generally rejected. For example, only a minority of respondents were willing to abolish the teacher's desk, and very few felt able to dispense with the convention that each pupil should have his or her own place, or to accept the idea of a classroom in which there were, as a matter of policy, fewer chairs than children.

A common response to the PNP messages was to convert at least a part of the room into workbays which were generally, though not invariably, dedicated to specific areas of the curriculum. Most classrooms had at least one such area, usually a reading or library corner, and a few teachers had organized their rooms entirely in this way, forming as many as six or seven work areas. A popular arrangement involved four areas, devoted to reading, art, maths and language. The area of the curriculum most commonly given a corner of its own was reading. Art came second, with more space devoted to it than either maths or language; it accounted for just over a quarter of all curriculum-specific work areas for younger pupils, and a fifth of those for older pupils. In contrast, only 4 per cent of curriculum-specific work areas were devoted to science.

In seeking to understand the extent of the LEA's influence on primary classrooms it is instructive, as we have already noted, to compare our own findings with those of Mortimore et al. (1988) from ILEA junior schools. In the London sample, one-tenth of classrooms had tables or desks arranged in rows: in Leeds we observed none (though that is not to say that none existed). In London, curriculum-specific layouts were rare: in Leeds they were the norm.

Our analysis produced four main classroom layout types (compared with Mortimore's three), and these are shown in Figures 4.1 to 4.4. The proportions in our sample were as follows: Type 1, 8 per cent; Type 2, 50 per cent; Type 3, 39 per cent; Type 4, 3 per cent. A more detailed analysis appears in Alexander et al. (1989: 247–54).

The strong emphasis on visual appeal and curriculum-specific classroom layout has a distinct local genealogy in the approaches inherited from the West Riding. However, not all teachers found curriculum-specific organization easy to implement or operate, and it provides a good example of a practice commended in the name of 'flexibility' which makes the work of some teachers less, rather than more, flexible (a tension which emerges in research elsewhere – Alexander 1988). Moreover, the practice has been shown by other studies, notably those of Mortimore et al. (1988) and HMI (DES 1990c), to reduce rather than enhance children's learning, in some situations and in the hands of some teachers, at least.

If the practice is introduced from a sense of obligation rather than conviction, the adverse effects on children are likely to be even greater.

In view of the high incidence of these arrangements in Leeds, and their adoption and dissemination during a period when the massive resourcing of PNP appeared to have little impact on reading test scores, it might be worth carefully pondering HMI's finding, referred to towards the end of the previous chapter, that

> some of the poorest work in reading occurred where the organization and management of the class were weak. Examples included too many groups of activities running at the same time and an emphasis on individual work which could not be sustained in sufficient depth for all the children in the class.
>
> (DES 1990c: 15)

The classroom context: grouping

The most obvious influence of PNP on teachers' approach to the management of learning was the encouragement of group work. This was consistently commended by advisory staff throughout the period under review and still remains a central component of expected practice (for example, Leeds City Council 1989a, 1989e, 1990a, 1990c). The norm, as we have noted, was for different groups to be working in different curriculum areas simultaneously.

The most common way of grouping was to sort the children by ability (as informally rated by the teacher) and to make the groups as homogeneous as possible. Groups formed in this way tended to remain relatively stable, moving as a whole from one activity to another, although in a few classes they were formed only for specific activities (generally mathematics) and disbanded for the rest of the day. An alternative form of ability grouping was to aim for as wide a range of ability as possible in each group. A minority of teachers used other grouping criteria. An eighth of them opted for friendship groups for at least part of the time, and a few grouped their pupils by age.

We found that the larger the group, the less time its members tended to spend on task. However, against the obvious conclusion that small groups are more effective one must set the increased managerial challenges of having a larger number of groups.

It was by no means uncommon for teachers to switch from one type of grouping to another as the activities of individuals and groups of children changed. This fluidity of grouping practice, in classrooms dominated by curriculum-specific work areas in which a wide range of totally dissimilar tasks were simultaneously undertaken, occasionally led to extremely complex organizational problems and a good deal of confusion.

Though grouping of some kind was the norm in the classrooms we visited, our interview and observation data revealed it to be a somewhat problematic strategy for many teachers. Grouping children was an organizational device as much as a teaching approach, a way of maximizing the opportunities for productive teacher–child interaction as well as a means of encouraging cooperation among the children and flexibility in curriculum.

However, as we show below, there could sometimes be a significant gap between intention and outcome. One-to-one teacher–child interactions were brief and (for most children) infrequent; and collaborative group work was rare (cf. Galton *et al*. 1980; Galton and Simon 1980).

As for the goal of flexibility, grouping can be distinctly double-edged, permitting teachers to concentrate as much *or as little* of their time on particular children or particular curriculum areas as they wish. The danger, witnessed sometimes in practice, is that certain children (notably the most able, the oldest, the best-behaved, and girls) are tacitly deemed 'undemanding' and may be left to their own devices for long periods, denied the kinds of challenging interaction which they, like all children, need. In turn these children may give no signals to a busy teacher 'scanning' the class while working with another group that they are other than fully and productively engaged in their learning tasks. Indeed, some will actively adopt strategies to convey this impression and secure a quiet life (Galton 1989; Bennett *et al*. 1984).

By the same token, certain curriculum areas (notably topic work and art) might be seen as of low priority and requiring little more than occasional and cursory monitoring by the teacher, with the result that unless the tasks set have an exceptionally high combination of challenge, motivating power and self-monitoring potential, children may spend excessive amounts of time either off-task or only partially engaged, or undertaking low-level learning.

In combination, this double neglect must mean that certain children, when working in certain areas of the curriculum, are getting a distinctly raw deal. Yet many of the teachers we interviewed, far from being unaware of this risk, perceived only too clearly that it was inherent to the LEA's preferred combination of group work and multiple curriculum focus teaching.

The dilemma can be expressed as follows: the more accessible teachers seek to make themselves to all their pupils as individuals, the less time they have for direct, extended and challenging interaction with any of them; but the more time they devote to such extended interaction with some children, the less demanding on them as teachers must be the activities they give to the rest; and the less demanding an activity is of their time and attention as teachers, the more the likelihood that the activity in question will demand little of the child.

The strategy of 'unequal investment' – deliberately concentrating attention on specific groups – was a conscious response to the dilemmas of grouping. In some cases a carefully monitored rolling programme ensured that over a given period of time, say a week or a fortnight, the teacher engaged directly with every child in every area of the curriculum; but in other cases the inequality of investment was not adjusted in this way, and the result was the persistent neglect of certain children and certain areas of the curriculum.

One way through, explored by researchers like Galton (1989) and Bennett (1987), is to exploit much more fully the potential of collaborative tasks within groups. In our own studies, the ostensibly collaborative setting of the group tended to be one in which children spent most of their time on essentially individual reading and writing tasks. Much of this time could be wasted while children awaited the teacher's attention or were simply distracted. The early findings from the Leverhulme Project (Wragg and Bennett 1990) show that where learning tasks are genuinely collaborative, children will use the group rather than the teacher as their main reference point, and the ratio of work to routine interactions will improve.

Collaborative group work is not a panacea, but it is certainly a strategy worth exploring. Equally important, as we urge later on, the kinds of dilemmas and compromises associated with all teaching strategies, and perhaps especially with group work, need to be admitted and addressed. Unfortunately, the climate of PNP did not encourage this.

A final point to note on grouping is the mismatch we frequently witnessed between the ostensibly *collective* strategy of grouping and the predominance of *individualized* work tasks. Common sense dictates that task and setting should as far as possible be consistent. Just as collaborative activity is difficult in a traditionally arranged classroom, so the concentration needed for individualized tasks may be difficult within a group. We gained the impression that – like several other practices in primary education – the strategy of grouping has become an end in itself rather than a device adopted for particular educational purposes; moreover, as a strategy grouping may have become so deeply ingrained in primary consciousness and practice that to ask questions about its educational purposes may seem, to some, almost impertinent.

Our data were gathered, as we have emphasized elsewhere, during the period immediately before the introduction of the National Curriculum. Since it was frequently predicted that the pressures of the latter would lead to an increase in whole-class teaching, it is useful to supplement our comments by reference to more recent data, gathered as part of another project based at Leeds University, the SEAC-funded evaluation of the 1991 Key Stage One National Curriculum Assessment directed by Diane Shorrocks and Robin Alexander. In a national sample of primary classrooms, four fifths were divided into groups and the number of groups per class averaged four to five, with a mean group size of 6.1.

Although those who predicted that the National Curriculum would cause a wholesale shift away from group work are apparently proved wrong by these figures, the matter is not that simple. The national sample of teachers spent only a third of their time interacting with groups: the bulk was divided between whole-class and individual interactions. Thus what the emerging national data seem to confirm is the Leeds data's sense of a pervasive incongruence in classroom strategies between pedagogic style and mode of organization. The Leeds local data pointed up a mismatch between predominantly individualized learning tasks and the collaborative setting in which children were expected to undertake them. The national data suggest a further mismatch – between this same collaborative setting and the teacher's predominantly individual or whole-class mode of interaction.

Two interpretations are suggested. The first is that grouping is the ideal organizational arrangement in that it gives the teacher the flexibility to move freely between individual, group and whole-class activities in a way which the traditional arrangement of desks in rows does not. The second, however, is that the physical arrangement of grouping in primary classrooms has acquired such a powerful doctrinal status that no other arrangement is even entertained. Whatever the interpretation, the cumulative research and survey data since 1978 suggests an urgent need to look at the justifications, dynamics and effectiveness of grouping.

The classroom context: planning

Teachers' planning, as we showed in Chapter 3, varied greatly in its time-scale and degree of formality. The time-scale ranged from the very short-term to the comparatively long-term: from daily to yearly, with many intermediate steps. The degree of formality ranged from elaborate and schematic written documents to a simple mental rehearsal of what would happen next.

There was also considerable variation in the structure of teachers' planning. Some teachers showed a *comprehensive* awareness of the balance of different lessons and their place in the curriculum as a whole, as well as a very clear concern with progression, continuity, the acquisition of underlying skills and the achievement of goals. Others adopted a more *incremental* approach, planning as they went along (Clark and Yinger 1987). They were much less concerned with the details or wider context of future activities, and much more interested in trying out ideas in practice before moving on to further planning. There were also teachers in the sample who were grappling with several complex long-term and short-term schedules and forecasts at a time, and others whose only apparent work plan was to set up a succession of *ad hoc* activities with little long-term coherence or progression.

Methods of curriculum planning are inseparable from teachers' thinking about what has to be planned, and the arrival of the National Curriculum is dictating a much more considered and long-term approach than was adopted in at least some of the classrooms we visited (NCC 1989, 1991; Alexander *et al.* 1990).

The classroom context: record keeping

We found very few teachers who kept no records of any kind. The records which were kept varied from the elaborately formal and comprehensive, involving a good deal of detailed and meticulous clerical work, to the admittedly casual and labour-saving. Some teachers were chiefly concerned to chart the acquisition of underlying skills, but many were satisfied with checklists of tasks completed.

Only about one teacher in three had any kind of supervision in the matters of planning or record keeping.

Again, the requirements of the National Curriculum will make minimalist approaches to record keeping difficult to sustain, let alone justify to parents. The agenda of educational objectives to be charted – and perhaps the record-keeping format too – are now very clear.

The working day

On average, children in the classrooms where observation took place spent

- 59 per cent of their time working;
- 11 per cent on associated routine activities (getting out and putting away books and apparatus, sharpening pencils and so on);
- 8 per cent waiting for attention from a teacher or other adult;
- 21 per cent distracted from the task which had been set;
- 1 per cent other (unclassified).

These figures are averages which cover a very wide variation between individual classes. They are broadly consistent with those from earlier studies carried out in other parts of the country except that children in the present study spent more time waiting for attention, in spite of the presence of an unprecedented number of support teachers and other ancillary staff and helpers.

Figures like these usually occasion adverse lay comment, and these particular figures featured prominently in the press coverage of the Leeds report. The journalistic and political inference was that children in primary classrooms are not working nearly hard enough; generally this was based on an aggregation of the percentages for 'routine', 'awaiting attention' and 'distracted' to produce the claim that 40 per cent of time was 'wasted'.

We wish to distance ourselves from such inferences, even though naturally we would expect our findings to generate constructive discussion about the effective use of pupils' and teachers' time in primary schools. Quite apart from questions of sample size and representativeness, this particular aggregation is wholly inappropriate. The more legitimate aggregation is of the 'working' and 'routine' categories, since both are necessary aspects of the learning task. Moreover, it is impossible to define what constitutes the 'appropriate' proportion of time which a 5-year-old, or a 7- or 11-year-old, should spend on task in a school day of some five and a half hours.

To set the issue in its proper perspective, we might care to consider the way time is used in *adult* work settings. Adults, too, spend much time distracted and on routine activities – indeed, such time may even be dignified as 'incubation' or 'thinking time' – and few work for anything remotely approaching 100 per cent of the time they are employed. We suspect that in many work settings 70 per cent of time spent on task or on associated activities would be a remarkable achievement. Yet we are talking here not of adults but of children.

Nevertheless, the figures give pause for thought. Clearly it is important to find strategies to reduce the proportion of time children spend awaiting attention and distracted. Whole-class teaching, usually seen as the device most likely to keep children on task, may well reduce distraction (or at least distraction of an undisguised kind) but it may also increase the time children spend awaiting attention, and indeed our own figures on group sizes tend to confirm this.

In any event, the global figures above are less significant than variations which can be shown to relate to specific categories of children, kinds of learning and classroom contexts.

Thus, girls generally spent more of their time than boys on work and associated routine activities. Boys were more often distracted, and also spent more time waiting for attention from their teachers.

Older children were less inclined to wait for attention than younger children. In maths and language they were less distracted and spent more time on work and routine activities, although in art the pattern was reversed: older children were more often distracted and did less work.

Children whose teachers rated their ability as average tended to spend less time on work and routine activities and more time distracted or awaiting attention than either those who were thought to be above average in ability or those who were rated as below average. In the absence of any objective index of the children's true ability we cannot know the extent to which the teachers' ratings were themselves unduly influenced by the observed behaviour.

In classrooms where there were two adults, children were generally less distracted and spent more time working than in classrooms where there was only one. Beyond that point, however, there was no tendency for the presence of additional adults to bring about more work and less distraction, partly because extra adults tended to introduce extra challenges and more complex organizational structures. Moreover, as we shall see when we discuss collaborative teaching later in this chapter, it is much easier for two teachers than three or more to undertake the shared planning on which the success of classroom collaboration depends.

Children generally spent less time working and more time distracted as the size of their work groups increased from one to twenty. In even larger groups, however, this pattern was reversed, partly because of the nature of the tasks that were undertaken in large groups, but mainly because of the whole-class style of supervision to which they were subjected.

We noted in Chapter 3 that the large amounts of time allocated to language and mathematics were sometimes the least efficiently used. The overall percentages are shown in Table 4.1.

Such figures appear to challenge the conventional assumption that the way to improve standards is to give the subjects deemed most important more and more time. Perhaps familiarity breeds contempt – among teachers as well as children. Perhaps, too, there is a Parkinsonian effect at work here: the standard allocation for mathematics in primary schools, often regardless of the ground to be covered, has for decades been the equivalent of an hour a day.

A clearer understanding of such anomalies, however, comes from probing beneath the curriculum labels. In Chapter 3 we identified ten 'generic activities' which we found to underpin primary classroom practice regardless of the subject labels used by the teacher, and argued that these activities therefore constitute at least as important a curriculum reality – certainly for children – as terms like 'topic' or even 'language'. Table 4.2 shows how each of these generic activities generates different patterns of task-related behaviour.

Table 4.1 Percentage of time spent by pupils on task-related behaviour in different areas of the curriculum

	Working	Routine	Awaiting attention	Distracted	Not observed
Language	55	11	7	26	<1
Maths	59	10	9	23	<1
Science	64	8	5	20	2
Admin.	64	5	11	18	1
Art	65	16	3	16	0
PE	51	21	18	10	0
Topic	55	21	6	16	3
Play	70	10	2	18	0
CDT	69	5	4	22	0
Choosing	63	16	7	14	0
Music	67	8	9	13	2
Environmental studies	63	6	6	26	0
Sewing	57	20	14	8	0
Table games	69	13	6	13	0
Computer	51	19	26	5	0
Cooking	55	15	0	30	0
Television	58	0	32	11	0
All curriculum areas	59	11	8	21	1

Table 4.2 Task-related behaviour in different generic activities (percentage of pupil time)

	Working	Routine	Awaiting attention	Distracted	Not observed
Writing	52	13	8	28	<1
Apparatus	65	12	6	17	<1
Reading	57	12	6	24	<1
Listening/looking	68	6	10	15	1
Drawing/painting	55	14	5	25	1
Collaboration	67	11	6	15	<1
Movement	54	15	14	17	<1
Talking to teacher	71	11	6	10	2
Construction	70	7	3	20	0
Talking to class	100	0	0	0	0
All activities	59	11	8	21	1

Thus, children in our classroom practice sample spent a high proportion of their time working when they were engaged in tasks which involved talking to the class, talking to the teacher, construction, listening or collaboration. Their work levels were lowest in writing, drawing/painting, or tasks which involved movement from one part of the room to another, and all three of these activities generated very high levels of routine behaviour. For the most part, high levels of distraction were found where work levels were low, and the highest distraction levels of all were in tasks involving writing, drawing/painting, and reading.

In general, the most work and the least distraction occurred in the rarest activities. The striking feature of the activities at which children worked for a high proportion of the time was involvement with other people; conversely, most of the activities at which children worked for the lowest proportion of time – writing, reading, drawing/painting – involved no other people and could have been carried out most effectively in isolation. Thus, there could be a significant mismatch between the tasks which children were given, and the setting in which they were required to undertake them.

The importance of these variations in children's use of classroom time lies less in the precise quantifications than the questions they provoke. Why do such variations occur? To what extent are they inevitable? Does the situation warrant improvement? If so, what?

There was a common sequence to nearly every teaching session observed: the teacher settled the children down; explained the tasks; allocated children to groups; interacted with one or more groups while they worked; initiated finishing off or tidying up. Whole-class sessions were very rare, though many sessions had a whole-class element, usually at the beginning and/or end. Within this basic framework the amount of time allocated to each stage varied considerably. Thus the time spent on the settling-down and clearing-up stages varied from 7 to 45 per cent of the total session, and the introductory stage varied similarly, largely because some teachers treated it as a purely administrative matter to be dealt with as succinctly as possible, while others incorporated it into the session as the whole-class teaching in an arrangement otherwise dominated by group work. Three examples, taken from our eleventh report, show something of the variation.

A class of thirty-eight 5- and 6-year-olds:

2 minutes	teacher settles class down after playtime;
2 minutes	allocates tasks;
2 minutes	works with language group;
1 minute	gives a task to an unsupervised number group and asks the nursery nurse who should be with them how long she will be;
16 minutes	returns to work with language group;
2 minutes	monitors jigsaw group;
1 minute	gives new task to computer group whose supervising nursery nurse has given them a task which is too difficult;
5 minutes	works with writing group whose teacher has been called away;

5 *minutes*	supervises change over of free-choice activities and then monitors maths group and two language groups;
3 *minutes*	supervises tidying up;
3 *minutes*	children sit and sing in the book corner;
9 *minutes*	teacher tells a story;
5 *minutes*	informal activities (e.g. clapping a rhythm).

A class of twenty-nine 8- and 9-year-olds:

3 *minutes*	teacher talks with class about a Victorian penny brought in by a child, and about penny-farthing bicycles;
7 *minutes*	sorts out group choices for the afternoon session;
11 *minutes*	allocates tasks for current session;
11 *minutes*	works with maths group;
16 *minutes*	monitors the work of all groups and responds to individuals seeking help;
7 *minutes*	supervises tidying up.

A class of thirty-six 7- to 8-year-olds

8 *minutes*	teacher takes register and then describes and allocates tasks;
14 *minutes*	monitors the work of all groups and deals with individuals who seek help;
7 *minutes*	works with language group;
8 *minutes*	works with science group;
2 *minutes*	monitors work of language and maths groups;
7 *minutes*	gives new task to maths group;
11 *minutes*	works with science group and deals with individuals seeking help.

As Bennett (1978, 1987) points out, one of the most important determinants of pupils' learning is simply the amount of time they spend in it. In a class where almost half the time is spent on administrative matters, the time left over for active engagement in learning tasks is severely curtailed.

Though some of the foregoing indicates diversity, the questions they raise are common to all teachers:

• How can the time children spend in classrooms most effectively be used?
• How far is the fairly low proportion of time spent on task in some classrooms attributable to factors unique to those classrooms – the teacher's mode of organization, the quality and appropriateness of the learning tasks he/she devises, the personalities of the children and adults present, and so on? How far is it attributable to more generally prevailing patterns of teaching and classroom organization in primary schools, including those commended by Leeds LEA? We believe that our evidence suggests that the latter is indeed a critical factor.
• What can be learned from the differential figures for particular groups of children – boys and girls; older and younger children; those rated by their teachers as of average, above average and below average ability or attainment?

How far are such differences inevitable? How far are they a consequence of the teacher's assumptions about and expectations of the children in question?
- Do the figures on the impact of increasing the number of adults in classrooms challenge the conventional assumption that the more adults there are, the better?
- Do the figures suggest that there is an optimum size for groups?

More generally we might ask the following:

- What is the best way to introduce and allocate learning tasks?
- How can the time and opportunities for children to engage in these tasks be maximized?
- What kinds of classroom environment will most support children's learning?
- What kinds of task is it most appropriate for groups to undertake?
- How can we achieve the best possible match not only between learner and task but also between task and classroom setting?

The curriculum

In Chapter 3 we outlined the findings on curriculum in practice as they emerged from the quantitative data. We do not propose to repeat this material here. However, the questions and issues this material raises about the way primary classrooms are organized are worth presenting as an extension of those above.

- Is the balance of time between the various parts of the curriculum appropriate?
- Where teachers have sought to accommodate the subject requirements of the National Curriculum, have they achieved a better balance than that shown by our figures, or has the result been an imbalance even more marked than that which obtained previously?
- If it is indeed the case that time is used least economically in those subjects to which most time is allocated (see Table 4.1), should not schools, LEAs (and indeed the NCC and DES) look afresh at their assumptions about how much time these subjects (that is, the National Curriculum core subjects) really need?

We found that regardless of the subject labels adopted, the curriculum in practice consisted of a further and perhaps more influential 'core' of ten *generic activities* (writing, using apparatus, reading, listening, drawing or painting, collaboration, movement, talking to the teacher, construction, talking to the class – see Table 3.1). While there is some inconsistency within and between classrooms where subject labels and subject relationships are concerned, there is rather less inconsistency in this 'alternative curriculum', and for children it has a much more profound impact than the labels teachers use. In raising questions about curriculum content and balance, therefore, the balance and disposition of these generic activities must be looked at as searchingly as the balance of subject time. Indeed, it is very clear from our studies that to define curriculum balance solely in terms of subject time allocations is both superficial and misplaced. Yet this is precisely how the problem tends to be approached by official bodies.

Balance, in our alternative sense, needs to be tackled in two ways. One is to appraise the overall mix of generic activities undertaken by children during, say, a typical day or week. The other is to examine the mix within each curriculum area or subject. Our figures suggest that many of the subjects were neither what their proponents claimed, nor what their nature demanded that they should be. Particular concern is merited over the dominance of writing, especially where this is a low-level, time-filling activity; over the general failure to exploit the potential of collaborative activity – especially since every one of the sixty classrooms we visited in the classroom practice study used a grouping system of some kind; and over the limited opportunities given to children for work-related talk of a challenging kind.

This point is all the more necessary in view of our finding that collaborative, interactive tasks kept children's attention more effectively than solitary tasks – yet solitary tasks predominated. This does not mean that there is no place for the latter. Rather, we might infer first that the potential of collaborative tasks needs to be more fully exploited; second, that the conditions in which children are expected to undertake solitary tasks may frequently be inappropriate. Indeed, common sense must tell us that there is something paradoxical about setting up primary classrooms in which 'busyness', diversity, movement and activity are counted as virtues if within these classrooms children are mainly engaged in solitary activities requiring concentration. But then, common sense is usually one of ideology's earliest casualities, in education as in politics.

Teacher–pupil interaction

Teachers spent a very high proportion of their time in class interacting with pupils. The type and frequency of their interactions are summarized in Table 4.3. Work and associated routine interactions accounted for nearly two-thirds of the total. Disciplinary interactions were comparatively rare because experienced primary teachers, particularly of younger children, have a repertoire of 'oblique' disciplinary strategies which avoid direct confrontation except in extreme cases (King 1978). Control tends to be exercised by means of work and monitoring interactions.

Table 4.3 Type and frequency of teacher–pupil interaction (based on systematic observation of teachers)

Type of interaction	Frequency	%
Work	4,564	37
Monitoring	2,452	20
Routine	3,322	27
Disciplinary	1,260	10
Other	729	6
Total	12,327	100

Although there were large differences between classes, in general individual children (as in other studies, notably Galton *et al.* 1980) were involved in very few interactions with their teachers. Table 4.4 clearly shows that in spite of all the additional resources of PNP, and in spite of the fact that, on average, their teachers were involved in more than three teacher–pupil interactions every minute, individual children took part in only eleven teacher–pupil interactions per hour, of which fewer than half were task-related: indeed in some classes the mean hourly rate of individual pupils' task-related interactions with their teachers was as low as two, and in no class was it higher than eleven.

Tabel 4.4 Rate of each type of teacher–pupil interaction (based on systematic observation of teachers and pupils separately)

Type of interaction	Teachers	Pupils
Work	58	5
Monitoring	43	2
Routine	58	2
Disciplinary	22	1
Other	10	1
Total	191	11

Note: Rate = mean number of interactions per hour.

These overall figures conceal considerable variation between classes, as the comparison of ten sample schools in Table 4.5 shows. The figures raise important issues. For instance, the considerable differences in the number of interactions (compare, for example, the pseudonymous Claybourn and Greystock) is partly a function of their length: a relatively low number of interactions does not indicate prolonged periods of silence, and most teachers were interacting with children most of the time. Fewer interactions, therefore, indicate more sustained conversations between teachers and their pupils. A very high interaction rate indicates a succession of extremely short interactions, characteristically in the context of brief and necessarily somewhat superficial monitorings of individuals and groups. The two styles are – or should be – a conscious response to the question of whether the brief monitoring of many or even all the children in a class is more effective in promoting learning than more sustained interactions with a smaller proportion.

The question, however, may be about control as much as learning. Engaging in sustained interactions with a relatively small proportion of the class presupposes that the remainder are willing and able to work with little attention. Conversely, a very high rate of short interactions may sometimes reflect a poor level of control or a lack of structure in the tasks set. Having said that, it is important to add that interaction rate is also related to children's age: older children are usually expected to sustain concentration for longer periods than younger children.

Table 4.5 Rate of each type of teacher–pupil interaction in ten schools (based on systematic observation of teachers)

	Work	Monitoring	Routine	Disciplinary	Other	Total
Applegarth	67	56	88	26	8	245
Blakemore	44	31	40	19	11	145
Claybourn	54	35	131	22	15	257
Deacondale	52	26	52	47	14	191
Easterbrook	68	87	34	4	17	210
Freshwater	47	62	55	17	14	195
Greystock	48	15	41	23	4	131
Hartfield	59	40	28	19	4	150
Illingworth	61	31	45	7	4	148
Jeffcote	79	43	62	31	13	228
Mean rate	58	43	58	22	10	190

Note: Rate = mean number of interactions per hour.

Another matter raised by these figures is that of the proportion of different kinds of interaction. Again, these vary considerably from one classroom to another. The challenge, clearly, is to reduce the proportion of 'routine' and 'disciplinary' interactions and increase the proportion concerned with work. A high proportion of disciplinary interactions may reflect (as in the case of Deacondale) a lack of 'oblique' disciplinary strategies and a tendency to adopt a more confrontational style; and a high proportion of routine interactions may stem from an excessively complex organization or an inability to engage in depth with the content of the tasks given to one's pupils. Teachers, therefore, need to look both at the *frequency* and the *proportion* of their interactions in considering how to make the best use of the strictly limited time available for interacting with each of their pupils. This brings us to the more important underlying issue, that of the *quality* of teacher–pupil interaction, as revealed by the transcript data.

Though questioning was a prominent mode of teacher discourse, the full potential of questioning as a teaching strategy was not always exploited. Thus, questions might feature as little more than conversational or rhetorical devices; they might be more token than genuine; they might be predominantly closed; and they might lack cognitive challenge. Moreover, in some classrooms where teachers asked many questions, their pupils were able to ask relatively few, and having done so they might risk having their questions blocked or marginalized. Teachers were clearly conscious of the pressure of time and the need to cover the ground intended. Yet the urge to press on, paradoxically, could lead to questioning becoming not more but less effective and therefore a somewhat inefficient use of the time available.

Report 11 (Alexander and Willcocks 1992) contains a large number of annotated examples from our considerable body of transcript material: they repay close analysis.

A common tendency, reflecting perhaps a consciousness of the taboo on didacticism which has been such a strong feature of recent primary education, was for some teachers to ask questions rather than make statements or give instructions. In some circumstances this remained true even in straightforward administrative interactions where strings of questions about what was going to happen next sometimes led to complicated and unproductive guessing games, and where a simple clear statement would have saved a great deal of time.

Teachers tried to strike a reasonable balance between the challenges they were setting and the skills of their pupils. Their ability to motivate children was heavily dependent upon the precision of this balance since tasks which are too difficult invariably generate frustration or anxiety while those which are too easy soon lead to boredom and a general sense of purposelessness. It is not always easy to balance challenges and skills even when working with a single child on a relatively straightforward task; for these class teachers working with mixed ability groups in settings where the normal practice was for several different tasks in different curriculum areas to be undertaken simultaneously, an adequate balance between challenges and skills throughout the group had to remain an aspiration rather than an achievement. Some children experienced the balance for some of the time; others inevitably did not.

Frequently, strategies were adopted which camouflaged the intractability of this particular problem. A common device was to ask large numbers of token questions (or pseudo-questions) which gave the illusion of educational dialogue without making any demands at all on the children's skills.

The imposition of a small amount of easy work was another popular strategy, particularly in situations where children were offered some degree of choice of activity. This reduction of demand to a low level maximized the number of children who could proceed without assistance, and offered at least the illusion of motivation through enjoyment.

There was a reluctance among some teachers to say openly that a particular answer to a question was wrong. Incorrect answers were sometimes ignored; more often they were praised as if they were right, and then ignored. Conversely, correct answers were sometimes treated as if they were incorrect. The problem here was that genuine open dialogue is unpredictable and can lead anywhere; it is not consistent with the pursuit of a detailed prearranged plan of work, yet it is widely accepted as an appropriate medium for teaching. Consequently, the fate of children's contributions sometimes had less to do with their quality than with their ability to sustain the teacher's pre-existing intentions for the session as a whole.

Teachers showed a great deal of skill in dealing with the many interruptions of the classroom day, generally managing to neutralize them either by simply refusing to be distracted by them, or by transmuting them into a part of the teaching session.

More damaging to the continuity of sessions were the frequent occasions when teachers interrupted themselves, either because they did not have a very clear idea of what they were trying to say, or because their organizational structure was so complicated that they were trying to do too many things at once. The problem of time in primary classrooms does not arise solely from external pressures. It may in part be a function of the teacher's own practices, and when this is so an analysis of his or her use of time, from the broad organizational strategies right down to the minutiae of moment-to-moment interactions with the children, could help both in creating more time and in making for a more effective and efficient context for learning.

The patterns of interaction explored and illustrated in detail in our eleventh report and briefly summarized here raise important issues for teachers, heads and advisory staff:

- Is the balance of questions and other kinds of utterance in primary classrooms right? Should we not be more discriminating in our use of questions, statements and instructions, being prepared to tell or instruct if the occasion warrants?
- What can be done to shift from pseudo-questions to those which genuinely invite an answer?
- What can be done to shift from closed questions to those which encourage children to reflect and solve problems rather than recall low-level information?
- Should children themselves be asking more of the questions?
- What are the contexts in which it is most appropriate to adopt a questioning stance?
- When is it appropriate to tell rather than ask?
- How can we strike the right balance between steering discussion down a prescribed path and recognizing that apparently divergent responses may contain considerable learning potential?
- How can we learn to listen to children as well as get them to listen to us?
- How can we encourage them to talk and listen to each other?
- How can we make our use of praise discriminating and therefore meaningful, rather than profligate or ritualized?
- How can we balance praise and encouragement with clear and useful feedback?
- How can we use classroom dialogue to promote genuine learning and understanding?

In the context of these questions the rarity of genuinely collaborative group work is unfortunate. It is educational in itself, encouraging the kinds of interaction in which effective learning is grounded. It promotes self-monitoring by encouraging children to use the group as well as the teacher as their point of reference. It shifts interaction between pupils away from casual social conversation in the direction of discussion about the task in hand, and in doing so it reduces the amount of time spent by the teacher on matters of routine.

Although most teachers would recognize the desirability of appraising their classroom practice in terms of questions like those listed above, the difficulty of applying such a process to one's own discourse should not be underestimated. In the 1984 study by Bennett *et al.*, teachers thought that their learning tasks were considerably more challenging than they were. In the hitherto unpublished Leeds University evaluation of the 1991 Key Stage One National Curriculum Assessment, teachers rated the tasks they gave to children as rather more challenging than did observers, and were rather more generous than the observers in their estimates both of the frequency of open questions and of the opportunities they gave pupils to volunteer opinions. On the other hand, observers felt that teachers were needlessly pessimistic about the clarity of their explanations.

Self-monitoring in a busy classroom is not easy, yet the need for training in the skills of classroom discourse is evident; as part of that training the trainee or serving teacher needs to be able to objectify his or her modes of discourse in order to begin to improve them. Video and audio recording are helpful in this matter, and the particular use of radio microphones in the Leeds study – less obtrusive and yet more effective than conventional microphones – deserves to be developed.

However, issues like those listed above can only begin to be seriously addressed if more fundamental assumptions about primary practice are challenged at the same time. We have indicated that the unthinking and undiscriminating use of questions – often closed or low-level – may reflect what we term a 'taboo on didacticism', a sense that children at all costs must not be told. The result, as the transcripts and analysis in Report 11 show, can be a charade of pseudo-enquiry which fools nobody, least of all the children, but which wastes a great deal of time. Similarly, the indiscriminate and thus unhelpful use of praise – rather than more judicious and exact feedback – may stem from a laudable concern that children should be encouraged and supported in their learning. Yet in the end this too can be counterproductive, with children becoming confused or cynical in the face of what they may begin to see as so much mere noise. Teachers' interactions with individual children – as is clear from figures in Report 11 and from other research (notably Galton *et al.* 1980; Bennett *et al.* 1984; Mortimore *et al.* 1988; Galton 1989) – are rarer than they may realize. Such interactions must never be other than supportive; yet they must also carry as much potency as possible for moving children's learning forward.

However, behind the tendencies we have charted lurks a more intractable problem, that of curriculum expertise. There may on occasions be sound educational reasons for adopting a style of interaction in which unfocused questions predominate. Equally, the strategy may serve as another of the various 'camouflaging' devices we have identified; in this case what remains disguised is the extent to which a class teacher's limited grasp of specialist subject matter may make unavailable the options of adopting a more focused and challenging mode of questioning, or making judicious use of a didactic mode.

The same difficulty may discourage a teacher from permitting the children to ask too many questions themselves. To confine the interaction to what is known is the safest course, and there are limits to the number of times a teacher can reply – as primary teachers are encouraged to – 'I don't know, but let's find out, shall we?' without straining their credibility and frustrating their pupils.

This particular problem emerged most tellingly in the context of our studies of

TTT. Here, some teachers found themselves, often for the first time in their careers, with the opportunity to engage in depth with a small number of individuals, yet were not always able fully to exploit the possibilities because sustained questioning and discussion at that level required them to have a clear framework of the kinds of question they wished to promote and a grasp of the ways a sequence of such questions related to the wider map of the curriculum area in which a particular learning task was located. One of the preconditions for productive teacher–pupil interaction, therefore, must be curriculum mastery on the part of the teacher: keeping one step (or one SOA) ahead of the children is not enough.

The matter bears as much on *assessment* as on learning, and indeed the two are intimately connected. Accurate diagnosis and assessment require two kinds of professional knowledge: knowledge of the child, and knowledge of the aspect of the curriculum in which evidence about the child's capacities and progress is sought. To form judgements about a child we need evidence. Asking questions is one of the most powerful tools at the teacher's disposal for establishing the nature and extent of a child's understanding; providing feedback is a necessary way of registering whether the understanding is correct or complete. Both questions and feedback have a *prospective* as well as a *retrospective* function: they enable the child to build on present understanding and to move forward into new areas of learning.

The urge to question and praise are but two of many possible examples of commitments which are deeply embedded in the conventional wisdom about what constitutes 'good practice' in primary education. Despite the growing weight of conceptual and empirical evidence (Dearden 1968, 1976; Bennett 1976; Bennett *et al.* 1984; Galton *et al.* 1980; Galton and Simon 1980; Galton 1989; Alexander 1984; DES 1978b, 1982, 1983, 1985; Mortimore *et al.* 1988; Tizard *et al.* 1988, etc.), there was a tendency to acquiesce in this conventional wisdom and all that went with it: the reduction of what ought to be a complex and multi-faceted debate to the simple adversarialism of 'formal' versus 'informal', 'didactic' versus 'exploratory', teacher as 'instructor' versus teacher as 'facilitator', rote learning versus 'discovery', 'subjects' versus 'integration', class teaching versus group work, 'traditional' versus 'progressive', 'bad practice' versus 'good'. This primitive style of discourse, in which complex issues are reduced to simple polarities, was a powerful and persistent feature of English primary education at the start of PNP. Even now, the National Curriculum notwithstanding, it still provides the basic framework for much professional discussion, and the culture of some schools makes the entertaining of alternatives difficult.

The need for a review of teaching strategies in the light of the National Curriculum requirements is evident. However, the vocabulary for such a review will need to be more subtle and precise, and much less polarized, than that which has dominated discussion of such matters in primary education for the last two decades or so (Alexander 1984, 1989, 1991).

At the same time, we may have to accept that the National Curriculum finally forces us to address the question of how far the polarization of the discourse, and the adopting of classroom strategies which celebrate something called 'process' at the expense of content, may both stem in part from a posture of defensiveness in the face of the problem of the primary class teacher's curriculum knowledge. (This hypothesis is explored more fully in Alexander 1984: 74–5.) In turn, to open up these issues to honest and realistic scrutiny must entail our preparedness to challenge the ultimate article of faith in primary education: the inviolability of the class-teacher system.

TEACHERS TEACHING TOGETHER

Before PNP, Leeds primary schools were staffed on the conventional basis of a head plus a teacher for each registration group, and in the national league table many Leeds primary classes were very large. Enhanced staffing under PNP gave schools two broad possibilities: to continue the traditional arrangement of one teacher per class, but with smaller classes; or to maintain class sizes but have more than one teacher working in some of them.

Advisory staff encouraged the latter, using labels like 'support teacher', 'collaborative teaching' and 'working alongside' and arguing in courses and documentation that enhanced staffing used in this way would enable the central goal of PNP – to meet the needs of each and every child – to be met. Schools responded variously, some taking up the opportunity, or challenge, of collaborative teaching while others seized the chance to reduce class sizes, for decades a source of frustration and complaint in the primary profession. In this section we summarize our findings on what we termed 'Teachers Teaching Together' or TTT – a label we introduced as being as neutral as possible and free of the particular value-orientations of 'team' or 'collaborative' teaching. This label allowed us to start from the simple proposition that in some classrooms more than one teacher was present and to explore without preconception what they were doing. Others adopted the term, sometimes using it more prescriptively than we had intended.

Our original analysis, outlined in the fourth report, showed that TTT involved four main dimensions or areas of decision-making:

- Participants (who the collaborating teachers are);
- Purposes of the collaboration;
- Collaborative style of the teachers concerned;
- Pupil organization (the ways pupils worked with each teacher).

Our fieldwork revealed a number of emerging possibilities, practices and issues in respect of each of these.

Participants

Most collaborations involved the class teacher and one other: a PNP appointee (coordinator or Scale I/MPG teacher) or an existing colleague released from his/her own class duties by PNP staffing.

A great deal hung on the relationship participants were able to establish, and in this any status differential could prove problematic. Traditionally, primary class teachers attach much importance to having 'their' class, and notions of territory, ownership and autonomy are deeply embedded in professional consciousness. TTT could threaten these, especially if the visiting teacher had higher status than the class teacher. The issue called for a great deal of understanding on both sides, which inevitably in many cases could not be guaranteed. Yet at the same time the question of who was in charge had to be addressed, in the interests of effective planning and action, and to avoid any later confusion. Both partners could find the situation difficult, for different reasons. For the class teacher the problem was one of territory and ownership. For the visiting teacher it was one of access.

Purposes.

Three main purposes for TTT emerged:

* special educational needs;
* curriculum enhancement;
* professional development.

Given the strong emphasis on children with special educational needs during the early days of PNP it was not surprising that many collaborations concentrated their attention on these children. However, there was a clear distinction between those schools which used TTT to achieve greater *integration* of SEN children into a class, and those in which there was *segregation*, with one or other of the participating teachers adopting the traditional 'remedial group' model of SEN provision.

By 'curriculum enhancement' we initially meant the use of TTT to spread the specialist curriculum expertise of individual members of staff, along the lines commended by HMI since 1978 (DES 1978b, House of Commons 1986). Our later fieldwork showed three variants of curriculum enhancement (discussed in more detail in Chapter 3): *shared delivery of the whole curriculum* (the use of specialist expertise across the school in pursuit of whole-school curriculum policies), *curriculum intensification* (support for specific groups of children in particular areas of the curriculum) and *curriculum invigoration* (meeting the subject needs of particular teachers on an *ad hoc* basis).

The boundary between curriculum enhancement and the third TTT purpose, professional development, is not clear-cut: curriculum enhancement necessarily involves professional development but TTT of this kind acquires the latter label when its purposes are quite explicitly directed at improving teacher competence. Moreover, the focus for the professional development purpose of TTT can be aspects of teaching other than curriculum expertise and delivery.

However, making the intention explicit meant that the dynamics of collaboration had to be handled very carefully. With the goal of *curriculum enhancement* it was possible for a junior member of staff with specific subject expertise to support a senior colleague without such expertise; but when the goal was *profes-*

sional development it required a clear status differential between senior partner as trainer or consultant and junior partner as trainee or client. Yet even in these cases the situation could be an awkward one: senior partners needed both credibility and backing from the head; they also needed tact and skill in the development enterprise, and such attributes are not an automatic concomitant of experience; and client teachers needed to be able to accept that their practice needed such attention.

Collaborative style

There were two main forms that TTT collaborations could take in the classroom: *working alongside* and *withdrawal*. The first was the advisory team's preference when the Authority introduced enhanced staffing as a strategy, while the second, being the traditional way of using extra pairs of hands in most contexts other than nursery, was the initial preference of many schools.

Clearly, it is far less problematic for the teachers involved if they each take full responsibility for separate groups of children and work independently – especially when their independence is underlined by physical separateness. Moreover, there is no doubt that in large classes this practice can ease the burden on the class teacher. But the strategy of working alongside is more likely to bring about significant change in professional thinking and classroom practice, because the partners have no alternative but to confront questions of planning and organization, and hence to explore each other's ideas.

However, we came across many examples of teachers who had failed to tackle the imperative of genuinely shared planning ostensibly working alongside each other in pursuit of shared goals. As a result the climate of collaboration could be full of unresolved questions and tensions, children could be confused about what was going on and the potential of the collaboration could be subverted. In some of these cases the collaborative style was really withdrawal, and such was the tension and confusion generated by the participants claiming to be working together but not really doing so, that it would have been better to drop the pretence and designate the practice withdrawal.

The prerequisite for successful collaboration, therefore, was *shared planning*; the precondition for such planning to be coherent was *shared values*. In turn, both of these required that the participants were open and honest in presenting and discussing their individual value-positions on matters of curriculum and classroom organization.

Pupil organization

There were three patterns of pupil organization:

• equal division;
• no division;
• small group/rest of class.

Where the class was equally divided, two mini-classes were in effect created, each teacher taking responsibility for one of them. Where there was no division, one or both teachers started the session off, then both moved freely round the whole class. In the third case, one teacher took responsibility for the majority, while the other looked after a small group, or even an individual. The latter was particularly favoured as a strategy for dealing with children with special needs.

It is our contention that each of these dimensions – participants, purposes, collaborative style and pupil organization – is intrinsic to TTT, wherever it takes place. Moreover, the dimensions can be variously combined, producing a wide range of ways of exploiting the potential of TTT. We also believe that the dimensions constitute an essential discussion agenda for the teachers concerned. Both parties need to be absolutely clear about the purposes of the collaboration; they need to resolve matters of leadership, status and responsibility; they need to plan together in order to sort out these matters and practical questions to do with who is responsible for what activities and which children. Only then will the potential of TTT be fully realized.

As PNP progressed, we came across many examples of collaborations which were clearly working well and which had liberated staff to work in new ways, to increase their understanding and skill, and to attend more closely to the needs of particular groups and individuals. We were also aware that 'TTT' began to be in danger of becoming yet another over-used and under-defined primary slogan and all kinds of claims were being made for its educational efficacy for *children* simply because of the novelty, stimulus and enjoyment which it could give to their *teachers*. Such self-indulgence needs to be guarded against: what is pleasurable for teachers is not necessarily beneficial to children. TTT at best is a complex and sophisticated way of working. When the participants fail to address the agenda referred to above, it may do more harm than good. Flooding schools with teachers in itself solves nothing, and may merely disrupt effective solo teaching. Indeed, as our data on adult–pupil ratios showed, increasing the number of adults in a classroom can sometimes detrimentally affect children's task-related behaviour. TTT has considerable potential, but it is not a panacea.

CONCLUSION: THE PROFESSIONAL CONTEXT OF CLASSROOM PRACTICE

The Authority recognized that classroom practice would not improve without a considerable investment in INSET and in professional support at both LEA and school level. In this chapter and others, we describe and comment on the strategies for professional development adopted and/or commended, ranging from day-to-day collaboration in the classroom, as discussed above, to whole-school strategies such as those explored in Chapters 3 and 6, and LEA courses and the work of advisers which we consider in Chapter 7. In this final section of the present chapter we pull together some important issues relating to the context within which the LEA sought to improve the classroom practice of its primary teachers.

Versions of 'good practice'

As we have shown, the prevailing model of 'good practice' was in certain important respects incomplete. In focusing on the physical and organizational features of the 'quality learning environment' it neglected the necessary questions about the purposes and content of primary education on which decisions about layout, organization, grouping and so on should be contingent. Equally serious was its neglect of the issue of children's learning.

It should go without saying that questions about the purposes and character of children's learning are of fundamental importance not just to teachers but also to those who undertake the task of constructing the policies and strategies through which teachers' ideas and practices are shaped. To neglect these questions and concentrate instead on the 'environment' of learning, however important that might be, is to risk encouraging the belief that teachers are judged and advanced on the basis of how their classrooms look rather than how and what their pupils learn; consequently, some may feel that it is strategically sensible to concentrate on surface at the expense of substance. The implied agenda is in any event back-to-front. Questions about purposes, content and learning are logically prior to questions about layout and organization: the latter should be set up to implement goals set out on the basis of attention to the former. Learning is the end, organization the means. Teaching strategies and classroom organization should never be viewed as ends in themselves.

There was an even more profound sense in which the prevailing version of good practice was deficient. Nowhere in our considerable quantity of data is there any sense that the notion of 'good practice' was presented to teachers as problematic. Nowhere were teachers invited to note that 'good' implies questions and judgements of *value*, and that the whole issue of good practice might raise controversial yet essential questions about the claims made for particular approaches, the arguments and evidence for and against them, the educational values they represented, or the practical problems of implementing them. Instead, despite the ostensible commitment to 'flexibility' there was apparently just one version of good practice, presented as a package of recommendations and principles and exemplified in the model classroom. This was viewed by teachers as having the force of policy and therefore being not open to challenge.

Further, it has to be asked whether in any event layout, display, grouping and organization are proper subjects for central policy or prescription. Clearly, an LEA has an obligation in the words of a recent Audit Commission report (Audit Commission 1989a) to 'articulate a vision of what the education service is trying to achieve' and to 'support schools and help them to fulfil this vision', but it could be argued that the most appropriate focus for such a vision, necessarily generalized because of the range of institutional contexts and pupil needs involved, should be on identifying broad goals and the kinds of learning which schools might seek to promote. It might also be suggested that for officers of an LEA to concentrate time and resources on prescribing how the physical arrangements of classrooms should be attended to represents a rather demeaning view of teachers and heads, whose proper concern such matters undoubtedly are.

Responding to officially commended versions of 'good practice'

Many teachers had difficulty accommodating what they thought others expected to see in their classrooms, partly because they were frequently unclear about what was expected, and partly because of practical and personal difficulties. Some ignored the recommendations; others implemented them wholeheartedly; others changed – as they were implicitly invited to do – the surface of their practice without engaging with deeper issues about what purposes such practice might serve.

For many, the sense of having to adopt a preferred version of practice accentuated the dilemmas which are always part of everyday teaching. Our reports provide many examples; for the present we note three which were both prominent and recurrent. In these cases the pressures and dilemmas could not only prove intractable but might also have adverse consequences for the children.

The first example is the view that it is good primary practice to have children working in groups. For some teachers, problems arose when they sought to reconcile this expectation with their simultaneous sense of obligation to monitor, diagnose, assess and interact at the level of the individual child. In this case a solution was at hand, although it helped the teacher rather more than the children: it was to neglect those children working in curriculum areas perceived to be relatively unimportant (such as art and topic work), to devise for them low-level activities which could be tackled with minimal teacher intervention, and to focus attention on those children who demanded it. The strategy was deliberate, and indeed was often referred to as focused, or unequal, investment. Yet as we noted in our tenth report: 'The price that some children may pay for demanding little of the teacher may be that they are given work which demands little of them' (Alexander *et al.* 1989: 284).

The second example, a frequent concomitant of the first, is the notion that it is good primary practice to have the different groups pursuing different areas of the curriculum at any one time, because only thus can the goals of 'seamlessness' and 'flexibility' in curriculum and learning be achieved. For some teachers not only was this difficult to plan and implement as an organizational strategy *per se*, but the increased demands imposed on them by the strategy meant that their opportunities for systematic and sustained monitoring of children's progress were further reduced, while at the same time the increased levels of movement and disturbance in the classroom might adversely affect children's concentration and time on task.

The third example is the view that it is good primary practice to adopt a predominantly 'enquiry' or 'exploratory' mode of teacher–pupil interaction and to couple this with plenty of encouragement and support for children's responses. We discussed in Report 11 the way this can be taken to excess by those teachers who couch the majority of their utterances in the form of questions, even when statements or instructions are more appropriate, and how such questioning can then become further debased by being low-level or closed. We also showed how the indiscriminate use of praise is a poor substitute for positive and specific feedback. We believe that many teachers who adopt such modes of interaction, though they do so partly as a matter of habit, are also responding to what they feel is expected of them. Though they might thereby earn their spurs as 'good practitioners', their children may gain rather less than if they had experienced a more varied and exact mode of discourse.

These are just three examples. Our reports contain many others. The general principle they all provoke is this: all teaching involves dilemmas which arise when teachers seek to reconcile the various circumstances, contingencies and expectations of which the job, by its nature, is constituted (Berlak and Berlak 1981; Nias 1989; Alexander 1988, 1989). No approach to professional support and development, still less an account of 'good practice', can afford not to identify and confront these. Yet many teachers clearly feel that to admit to facing dilemmas is somehow an admission of weakness, and that at all costs a front of professional equanimity and consensus must be maintained in respect of the validity and practical viability of mainstream primary orthodoxies. In suppressing their dilemmas and in failing to challenge the orthodoxies they help neither themselves nor the children they teach.

Lest we be misinterpreted on this matter, we are not advocating the abolition of grouping or the withdrawal of encouragement. Far from it: encouragement is essential and grouping, appropriately used, is a highly effective classroom strategy. We are arguing, on the basis of what actually happens in classrooms, that a purist adherence to any methodological orthodoxy can generate considerable problems, that these need to be addressed openly, and that in any event the notion that the act of teaching can be made the subject of procedural mandates is suspect and unrealistic.

Strategies for improving practice

Leeds LEA sought to improve classroom practice by a combination of two main strategies:

- enhanced staffing, and the exploitation of its potential to encourage classroom-based professional development;
- the work of the advisory service in general, and of adviser-led INSET in particular.

Schools recognized the potential of these strategies, and our discussions elsewhere of PNP coordinators and TTT explore some of the possibilities and problems of having staff work together with the improvement of classroom practice in view.

However, in this chapter we have identified certain reservations about the models of teaching commended during the period under discussion, and to the extent that teachers felt obliged to implement these the effectiveness of enhanced staffing must have been blunted. A strategy for improving teaching has not one but two components: not only must there be an effective means for helping teachers to change their practice along the lines required, but the preferred approaches to teaching must be coherent, defensible and demonstrably capable of securing a quality of learning superior to that available previously. On this latter aspect, regardless of the successes claimed for enhanced staffing, we are less sanguine.

Three fundamental changes are called for in this regard. First, it is clear that the way classroom practice is defined and talked about must change. The quasi-consensus of 'good primary practice' must be replaced by a mode of professional discourse in which the difficulties of determining what practice is good must be addressed. The focus of discussion must be greatly extended to take in more issues to do with learning and with educational purposes and content. The day-to-day challenges and dilemmas of practitioners must be explored much more openly and honestly.

Moreover, and this concerns policy-makers at least as much as teachers themselves, where certain dilemmas remain unresolvable because they are rooted not so much in particular classroom strategies as the inbuilt limitations of the generalist class teacher system, the professional, political and resource implications must be squarely faced.

Second, there needs to be a substantial shift in primary education from judgements of quality based on visual cues to one based on engagement with what and how children learn. What we called in our tenth report 'the inviolability of practice', or the tendency to skirt round the issues at the heart of education, needs to be breached. Such a shift needs to take place in two contexts – one, as we have said, is professional discourse; the other is the strategies adopted by those responsible for promoting and encouraging teachers' development.

Finally, the idea that an LEA – let alone a national government – can be the sole definer, arbiter and guardian of good practice must be abandoned. The assumption is offensive to teachers; it encourages professional dependency; it discourages professional autonomy and self-motivated development; and it is in any case empirically unsustainable.

These have far-reaching implications, especially for the strategies and styles adopted by advisory staff and heads, and for the ways class teachers view themselves as professionals. They are particularly important – and problematic – at a time when government policy seems to be introducing a serious tension into the local administration of the education service. On the one hand, advisory roles are shifting more towards inspection and quality control, and the accountability of advisers and inspectors to their employing LEAs is being more firmly underscored (Audit Commission 1989b). On the other hand, schools are being encouraged in a much greater degree of financial and professional self-determination. At the same time, the rhetoric of 'partnership' has never been stronger: used by policy-makers it seeks to soften the blow of centralization; used by the professionals it smacks of a desperate clinging to more liberal values. These matters will not be easily resolved.

5 Links with parents and the community

At the time of our third report, in May 1987, the LEA had no written policy on home–school links, and no officer carried overall responsibility in this area. It is fair to add that Leeds does not seem to have been unique in this respect: reporting on an inspection carried out in 'ethnically diverse areas within three LEAs' (including five Leeds Phase 1 PNP schools) in March 1988, HMI remarked that 'none of the three LEAs had specific policies for parent school liaison' (DES 1988a). However, the HMI report sampled only three LEAs, and we are aware of others which have been considerably more proactive and inventive in the area of home–school links. Frequently, such LEAs operate at two levels simultaneously: at the school level fostering and encouraging changes in attitude and practice, while at LEA level opening up direct two-way communication with parents through a variety of channels.

By the end of the project we could report that there had been some changes and developments in practice. Many of them were initiated independently by the schools, and some were a direct consequence of national legislation, but the Authority's own profile in this area continued to be remarkably restrained. There was still no official home–school links policy document to which interested parties might turn for clear and authoritative guidance.

However, in April 1989 an advisory teacher attached to the Primary Division was given responsibility for 'parents and community' along with her existing workload. At an in-service course which she led three months later it was proposed and agreed that a working party should be set up to produce a draft policy for links with parents and the community. Nine more months passed before the group convened. It consisted of the advisory teacher, an educational psychologist and sixteen of the teachers who had been at the course. At the time of going to press the working party's document is still awaited.

In view of the level at which responsibility for parents and the community was allocated, the pace at which action was taken, the apparently arbitrary way in which membership of the working party was decided and the omission from its membership of key figures in the area of home–school links, it must be assumed that the formulation of an LEA policy in this area was a matter to which the Authority attached a rather low priority during this period. The situation contrasted sharply with the high profile initiatives taken in relation to the other three PNP aims.

PRACTICE

Our third report outlined a number of schemes and initiatives which were intended to further the general aim of closer links with parents and the community: the appointment of a team of home–school liaison assistants (later redesignated home–school liaison officers); the Portage scheme, described in more detail below; in-service support courses; and a wide range of everyday practice, including a great diversity of activities (forty-seven in all) which are listed in Table 5.1.

Table 5.1 Strategies for home–school links in thirty Leeds primary schools

	Phase 1 (n = 10)	Phase 2 (n = 10)	Phase 3 (n = 10)
Transmitting information			
Booklets about the school	6	9	6
Letters and notes	10	10	10
Regular newsletters	5	6	9
School magazines	0	2	1
Articles in parish magazine	1	1	0
Formal meetings	7	9	9
Informal meetings	9	9	9
Talks on curriculum/education	4	6	4
Notices pinned up in school	6	9	10
Admission of new pupils			
Letters	10	8	10
Meeting pupils before admission	9	10	10
Home visits before admission	3	3	2
Pre-admission play sessions	7	7	5
Parents' and toddlers' groups	4	3	3
Activity packs	3	2	3
Parents involved in settling in	6	8	5
Involving parents in school life			
Home-school liaison assistant(s)	2	0	0
Secondary/junior/infant liaison teacher	0	1	0
Home visits	6	3	2
Parents' assemblies	6	7	6
Parents' room	1	1	1
Parents' self-run support groups	1	1	2
Coffee mornings	2	4	6
Crèches	3	1	0
Open days	10	8	9
PTAs	3	8	4
Invitations to concerts/sports/plays	10	10	10
Shared church activities	1	0	1
Book sales	4	9	7

Table 5.1 Continued

	Phase 1 (n = 10)	Phase 2 (n = 10)	Phase 3 (n = 10)
Parents helping			
Teaching their children at home	6	6	8
Parents' workshops	2	1	3
Portage	2	0	2
Helping in class with reading/numbers	5	2	5
Helping in class with cooking/sewing	9	6	8
Helping in class with art/craft	4	5	5
Helping in class with music	2	0	2
Helping in class with the computer	4	2	4
Helping with structured play sessions	4	1	1
Helping with stories/library sessions	4	4	5
Helping with games/swimming	3	3	6
Helping run school library	0	3	2
Making costumes/scenery for plays	7	7	7
Helping with general repairs	2	3	7
Fund-raising	8	9	8
Parents' dances	3	2	5
Family discos	4	5	6
Christmas parties/trips, etc.	10	9	9

The report also examined the very real difficulties which sometimes beset home–school links, suggesting that a clash of basic objectives between teachers and parents may sometimes lead to a confrontation between widely differing models of home–school links. We identified four pairs of complementary roles commonly adopted by teachers and parents in their encounters with each other:

- consultant and client;
- bureaucrat and claimant;
- equal partners;
- casual acquaintances.

Problems arise when there is a mismatch between the models adopted by the teacher and the parent – when, for example, one wants to make a complaint while the other wants to give advice. With only four models in operation (and of course in reality there are many more) this kind of mismatch can take no fewer than twelve possible forms. When any one of them occurs, the teacher and the parent are likely to experience each other's behaviour as inappropriate and hence strange and uncooperative, and both may leave the encounter bewildered and disappointed.

Through comparison with an earlier survey undertaken by Leeds LEA itself, it was possible to report:

that most of the present range of home–school links was already to be found in local primary schools well before PNP, and that activity in this field since 1985 has involved the further development and dissemination of existing practice rather than the devising of innovative techniques.

Even so, PNP has clearly brought along with it a few entirely new initiatives. The 1985 study reports no examples of parents teaching their children at home under the guidance of a teacher; no activity packs for use at the time of the children's first admission to school; no parents helping in the classroom with music, and no home–school liaison assistants or secondary/junior/infant liaison teachers.

(PRINDEP 1987a: 9–11)

The questionnaire sent to all primary heads in July 1989 revealed that the combined resources of PNP were thought to have had far less impact on home–school links than on any of the programme's other objectives. Few heads had allocated any of their extra capitation to the development of productive links with parents and the community, while nearly all of them considered that such PNP resources as the Authority's advisory and support staff, the INSET programme and even the refurbishment of their own schools had made little or no impact on home–school links, however effective they may have been in furthering the programme's other objectives.

Only enhanced staffing and, in particular, the PNP coordinators were thought to have made a slight to moderate impact. By far the most widespread activity of PNP staff in the general area of home–school links involved reading or other language work with parents and their children. Number work was also common, as were programmes of home visiting and initiatives involving the parents of children with special educational needs. In all, well over sixty different specific activities were listed by heads in this context, including cooking for special occasions, a paired play project with a neighbouring special school, and the development of links with local elderly people.

The Education Acts of the 1980s greatly increased the responsibilities and powers of school governors, including parent governors. In response to the introduction of the local management of schools the LEA organized a series of measures to train and inform governors on such topics as the appointment of staff, provision for children with special educational needs, and the formulation of school policy on discipline, equal opportunities, child protection and a number of other matters.

The Governors' Unit serviced by the Education Department also produced a news-sheet which contained updates on government and LEA reports and initiatives, and offered lists of issues for consideration.

The 1980s legislation also gave parents the legal right to be informed about, and be involved in, certain aspects of school life. In the Summer Term of 1989 the LEA published and distributed a short booklet (Leeds City Council 1989e) which was 'intended to help parents to appreciate what constitutes the best primary school practice and also to highlight aspects of education that the

Authority wishes to promote'. Home–school links did not feature prominently in this booklet although its content clearly implied that the Authority wished to:

• provide parents with basic information about its schools;
• suggest the kinds of questions they should be asking about their children's education;
• encourage them to participate in their children's early reading experiences;
• urge them to seek regular discussions about their children's progress;
• help them to find their way around school buildings.

At the time of going press, primary and middle schools are being reorganized. As part of this procedure the Authority has been involved in meetings with parents and governors of the schools concerned.

Home–school liaison officers

The setting up, training and work practices of the home–school liaison team were described at length in our third report. There we noted that:

> as a matter of policy, all ten of the home–school liaison assistants are them-selves members of ethnic minority groups. The reasoning behind this is clear. Any minority group is likely to include a substantial number of people who feel the need of . . . help and reassurance, . . . and many members of ethnic minorities suffer an additional persistent burden of racial discrimination which may well cause them to wonder what hope they could ever have of a fair hearing from a representative of the culture which treats them in this way . . . . Yet of course each of the schools in which the assistants work has pupils of many different ethnic origins, and in practice no single head has expressed any other intention than that assistants should work with families from all parts of the local community.

> (PRINDEP 1987a: 17)

After HMI's inspection in March 1988, a set of guidelines about the use and deployment of home–school liaison officers was produced by the LEA and distributed to the heads of primary schools concerned.

In May 1988, the team of home–school liaison officers was augmented by two additional members and the LEA applied to the Home Office for funding for three more posts under Section 11 of the Local Government Act of 1966.

March 1989 saw the formal appointment of a coordinator for home–school liaison officers and bilingual support assistants, who was to be responsible to 'the appropriate adviser in the Primary Division' and whose job description listed eight major duties including close liaison with the schools involved in the two projects, cooperation with heads to provide a positive and coherent service, and attendance at appropriate working parties and committees 'as agreed with the Primary Adviser'. Contact with the advisory teacher who was subsequently (April 1989) given responsibility for parents and the community was not written into the job description.

In keeping with the exclusive emphasis on racial and multicultural matters in the job descriptions, the entire team of officers and their coordinator were all members of ethnic minority communities.

Portage

Portage is a method of working with pre-school children whose development is delayed: parents teach their children at home under the guidance of a Portage worker who visits the family once a week. The worker also attends weekly meetings with a supervisor who provides help and support, records details of the teaching programmes, writes reports, and helps the family with problems involving contact with other agencies.

The Leeds Portage Scheme serviced twenty families across the city. It was set up under Educational Support Grant funding in 1986, but was financed by the City Council when the grant expired in April 1989. It was not part of the Primary Needs Programme but the method was advocated through PNP INSET.

Early Education Support Agency

A broadly similar philosophy underlay the work of the Early Education Support Agency (EESA). Again, this was not a PNP initiative but is reported here because it concerned parents, children and schools and gives an example of the practice from which the LEA's unwritten policy on home–school links has to be inferred. It was set up in September 1987 under the Department of Education Special Services Division, and its brief was threefold:

> to find out the needs of parents of children under five and work with them to help facilitate those needs, . . . to help parents help their children acquire useful skills and act as a bridge between home and school, . . . and to increase a shared community spirit and foster an attitude of sharing and support between parents and other parents in the local neighbourhood, alongside the paid professionals and voluntary agencies.
>
> (Leeds City Council 1987b)

The EESA team consisted of the educational psychologist who originally proposed that the agency should be set up, a supervisor, and eight workers who were selected for such qualities as their apparent ability to empathize with their clients without seeming patronizing, and to deal with difficult situations.

After the initial training of staff, and discussion with other agencies, EESA's work began with a pilot project in two inner-city areas. The success of the pilot project led to a decision in principle that EESA should extend its activities throughout the city. In September 1989, with the existing funding and personnel, five school groups were set up, one in each inner area of the city, while the original groups still met and were run by parents with minimal support from the EESA workers.

By this time the formally stated aims of EESA were:

To support children, parents and teachers to enable children to start at the same starting line.
To help children to happily acquire useful skills in order that they might take full advantage of nursery provision and formal schooling when that time begins.
To help raise parental esteem so that they become equal partners in this process; and so that young children are able to see their parents as problem solving, confident role models.

(Leeds City Council 1989b: 4)

Primary Needs Programme INSET

Our analysis in Chapter 7 will show that the LEA's programme of in-service training was much more concerned with the other objectives of PNP than with home–school links. We know also that according to the Authority's primary heads, PNP INSET made no impact on their practice in this area.

Nevertheless, there were some INSET initiatives in this area, and in particular the Special Services Division organized and ran a small number of very ambitious courses. Firmly based in the educational and psychological literature and on research findings on home–school links, these courses involved detailed planning, comprehensive support material, built-in evaluation techniques and follow-up meetings.

It must be emphasized, however, that whether the criterion be the number of courses or the number of teacher-days devoted to this topic, the development of productive links with parents and the community did not account for more than a one-hundredth part of the Authority's in-service programme during the evaluation period.

CONCLUSION

This brief chapter has included details of the major LEA and school initiatives in the home–school field between the start of PNP in 1985 and the end of our fieldwork in 1990. At that point (and indeed at the time of writing, in 1991) the Home–School Working Group was still in existence, and still apparently moving towards the eventual drafting of a policy document. Although individual schools reported some degree of increased activity in this area, facilitated by extra staff, it was clear that except in certain well-known cases, home–school links was not a PNP priority. Those schools who changed their outlook and practice in respect of relationships with parents and the community did so for their own reasons and in response to their own sense of priorities and needs.

Home–school links was the forgotten PNP aim. The fact that by 1991 the situation had begun to change more generally was due less to Authority initiatives – which remained on a relatively small scale – than to a combination of growing commitment at school level and the legislative requirements in respect of school governing bodies and the provision of information to parents about curriculum and assessment.

It could be argued that home–school links is precisely the kind of issue where a generalized LEA policy is least appropriate, since the chemistry of relationships between each school's staff and its parents is a unique and subtle matter, hardly conducive to centrally determined procedures. Equally, it could be argued that the promotion of a sense of community, of which the primary school is a vital part, can only be achieved by local commitment and action.

In a fundamental sense this is true. Each of the schools we visited pursued the matter differently, and in some the quality of relationships established with parents and the community was impressive, the more so for being the result of long and painstaking work by heads and teachers, often encountering frustrations and setbacks on the way to success. Yet questions remain about those many schools still locked in the traditional relationship of 'casual acquaintances' or 'bureaucrat and claimant' discussed earlier. In these schools, while national legislation will nudge staff to introduce procedures for involving and informing parents where this is required by law, it will not encourage them to go beyond such procedures to establish the kinds of voluntary open dialogue and day-to-day collaboration which can do so much to enhance the quality of a child's education.

We believe that an LEA has an important role to play here. Indeed, there is something distinctly paradoxical about the Leeds stance on this particular aspect of PNP in comparison with the others. For while it was happy for the advisory team to devise policies which went into considerable detail about aspects of classroom practice which are surely for schools and teachers to determine, it remained relatively aloof from one area of school life – home–school links – where policy might usefully and helpfully have stipulated not just goals and commitments but also a range of procedures from which schools could choose.

The LEA, then, appears to have been interventive on matters which schools themselves ought to have dealt with, and *laissez-faire* on other matters in which it had a wholly legitimate interest.

6   Managing reform within the school

Our discussion in the previous four chapters has focused in turn on the substance and implementation of each of the aims of the Primary Needs Programme as set out by Leeds LEA in 1985 and as reinforced in numerous contexts subsequently. Although management as such did not feature in these aims, the Authority perceived from the outset that their successful implementation would depend as much on schools' internal management styles and strategies as on external guidance, advice and support.

Accordingly, the PNP resource package included not merely extra staff of varying levels of experience and seniority, but also a *particular category* of extra staff – the PNP coordinator – appointed to a specific managerial role. Within each school, PNP coordinators were to be the LEA's main agent for interpreting, explaining and implementing the goals of the programme. They therefore featured prominently in our evaluation of PNP.

However, PNP coordinators could achieve little in isolation. They were introduced into established professional cultures, dominated – as are all primary schools – by the personality and outlook of the head. They had to work alongside deputy heads and postholders who also had managerial responsibilities, some of which overlapped considerably with their own. Each school had its own unique circumstances, its particular history, strengths and weaknesses. Managing PNP in the school, therefore, could never be a one-person affair.

This presented us with a problem. Our task was to evaluate PNP. We recognized PNP's central managerial dimension – the coordinator role – and included that in our programme. Yet we also recognized that the success of PNP in general, and the coordinator in particular, depended vitally on aspects of the professional workings of schools which PNP addressed neither explicitly nor implicitly, and which were therefore not really within our evaluation brief. Moreover, we had neither the resources nor the time to undertake a comprehensive anatomy of primary school management and professional relationships along the lines pursued, for example, by Nias *et al.* (1989).

Consequently, we took a middle course. We made PNP coordinators the object of a detailed study, but in addition we gathered data on the managerial and professional contexts within which coordinators and other PNP appointees worked, so that we could identify those contextual factors which bore most heavily on how, and with what success, schools implemented the programme's goals.

ENHANCED STAFFING AND THE MANAGEMENT OF CHANGE

Table 1.1 (see Chapter 1) lists in full the various categories of PNP appointment and the numbers in each category, year by year. The staggered introduction of Phases 2 and 3 means that years and phases do not correspond, but it is evident that there were considerable differences in the overall numbers of extra teaching staff allocated to each phase. The 71 Phase 1 schools shared 178 extra staff – some gaining a substantial complement – with the allocation averaging 2.5 per school. In the larger proportion of Phase 1 schools there were two appointees, one coordinator and one Scale 1 teacher, although many schools had considerably larger PNP enhancements – up to 7.5 in two schools, or a staff increase of 38 per cent. In contrast, the PNP enhancements for Phases 2 and 3 were 96.5 and 92 (full-time equivalents), producing an average enhancement per school of 1.7 in Phase 2 and 0.9 in Phase 3.

The disparity between PNP phases was accentuated by two factors. One was that in many Phase 3 schools with fewer than 150 pupils on roll the allocation was only 0.5, giving them a much smaller range of support and development possibilities than was open to those schools with a full-time enhancement. The second was the level of seniority at which appointments were made. The 1985–6 Phase 1 initial staffing profile shows a balance of senior and junior appointees – 53 coordinators and 60 Scale 1 teachers. This represents a senior/junior staffing enhancement ratio, in percentage terms, of 47:53. By Phase 3, the balance had shifted to a preponderance of main professional grade teachers (11:89), and while in Phases 1 and 2 PNP coordinators were created from the PNP staffing enhancement, most Phase 3 schools had to appoint coordinators from their existing staff.

All these discrepancies, of course, were deliberate. PNP was a programme explicitly grounded in a philosophy of positive discrimination in favour of the schools with the greatest social and educational needs, as represented by free school meals and low reading scores. Assuming these measures to be fairly reliable indicators of the needs in question, the differential allocation of staffing was appropriate and just. However, while the LEA maintained, as was its obligation, a global view of primary schools' needs, heads and teachers in individual schools were less likely to do so. For them it was a matter of how many extra staff they received in comparison with a school down the road, and judged in these terms the disparities aroused great resentment, especially among Phase 3 heads.

The issue which these allocations does raise, however, is whether the level of Phase 3 resourcing was too low to have any significant impact. Primary schools are very tightly staffed, to the extent – as the 1986 Parliamentary Select Committee Report recognized – that an enhancement of less than one teacher above establishment can generally achieve relatively little (House of Commons 1986). Once the enhancement is one full-time teacher or more, then a whole range of managerial roles and strategies becomes available because it is possible to combine full-time class responsiblity – which many heads see as vital to the integrity and continuity of children's education – with substantial cross-school management, development and support. When the appointment is of someone who is experienced and well-qualified in both teaching and professional leadership, as all coordinators were required to be, the potential of enhancement is even greater.

All PNP appointees had job specifications – a welcome and important innovation. Scale 1/MPG appointees were recruited to a fairly open brief, which set out a number of options for negotiation between appointee and head: taking a class, releasing a teaching head, releasing other staff, working alongside colleagues in a 'support' role, facilitating and/or organizing school visits, covering for colleagues, and so on. Probationers were expected to teach a class full-time, in order to meet DES requirements. Among the many statements about the character of PNP which were issued, orally and in writing, by officers and advisers in the early days of the Programme, two points were particularly forcibly expressed. One was that PNP appointees were 'real' teachers, not supplies or ancillaries, and were to be treated as such, even though their roles might be more diverse than the traditional anchor of class-teaching. The other was that in defining individual teachers' roles, schools were asked to recognize the importance of job-satisfaction. Clearly, the Authority perceived a risk that junior PNP appointees might be exploited or marginalized, and took steps to prevent this.

What, then, did the very large number of Scale 1/MPG teachers (some 267 overall, or 68 per cent of the teachers appointed under PNP) actually do? Our annual surveys yielded a range of roles and activities. Table 6.1 shows the distribution of PNP Scale 1/MPG roles revealed by the survey of all schools over the period 1986–9. It should be noted that the percentage column in the table sums to considerably more than one hundred because most staff in this category combined more than one role. Typically, those (the majority) who did not have a full-time class teaching responsibility, might 'float' and cover for an absent colleague one day, act in a support TTT capacity the next, and so on. The average number of such combined roles, across all three phases and over the four years in question, was just over three.

There were, however, significant differences between PNP phases in how such staff were used. Generally, there was more diversity of role in Phase 1 than later phases – not least, presumably, because the higher staffing complement allowed this. Perhaps more significant is the fact that SEN-related roles were more prominent in Phase 1 schools than in Phase 3, and using extra staff to cover for others was a more common use in Phase 3 than in Phase 1. This tends to bear out the point raised above about the level of Phase 3 staffing. With an average staffing enhancement in Phase 3 schools of 0.9, and with the majority of appointments made at MPG level, many such teachers found the developmental aspects of their job specifications constantly subverted by the need to cover for colleagues.

Disentangling Phase 3 heads' analysis of their use of PNP staff from their collective sense of outrage at the phasing policy is difficult. Again and again in

Table 6.1 PNP Scale 1/MPG roles, 1986–9

	Frequency	%
Releasing class teachers	170	88.1
TTT	141	73.1
Special educational needs	93	48.2
Class teaching	87	45.1
Curriculum responsiblity	63	32.7
Work with parents	37	19.2
Miscellaneous administrative	14	7.3
Unclassified	6	3.1
Work with outside agencies	5	2.6
Other special needs (not SEN)	1	0.5
Total responses	617	

Note: Number of respondents was 193; mean number of roles was 3.2.

the responses to our 1989 survey of all heads, those in Phase 3 schools commented negatively on their PNP staffing: that it had little impact; that it even exacerbated their previous staffing problems; that it was too little too late; that the LEA did not understand the problems which their schools were trying to tackle. Positive responses, very much in the minority in Phase 3, therefore, focused mainly on the way PNP appointees freed heads and senior staff for managerial tasks and facilitated classroom collaborative activities, especially TTT.

In contrast, Phase 1 heads, and to a considerable extent Phase 2 heads also, listed gains such as enhanced management, TTT, curriculum review and development, staff development, and others to do with the quality of professional life in the school: improved morale; increased enthusiasm and vitality; the sharing of ideas and expertise; and the collective appraisal of alternative practices. (It should be noted that the Phase 3 heads' comments came from a group whose schools had only recently been brought into PNP and that expressions of dissatisfaction were also voiced at equivalent points in Phases 1 and 2. However, these were rarely as vehement or focused as those of their Phase 3 colleagues.)

In the period leading up to and immediately following the introduction of the National Curriculum, such qualitative gains were in themselves an essential resource. Where schools, aided by PNP resourcing, had lifted their professional climate and decision-making processes out of the slough of low morale, crisis management and paternalism, they were able to confront the next wave of change constructively and with confidence, having the will, expertise and procedures to tackle the very difficult questions about curriculum and assessment which the 1988 Act provoked. This transformation of professional climate may prove to be one of the most important legacies of the Primary Needs Programme.

Although the perception that Phase 3 schools were under-resourced was widespread, the effectiveness of the PNP staffing enhancement was certainly not a consequence of numbers alone, any more than it is when schools are staffed at the conventional establishment figure. We came across many cases of schools using minimal resourcing to maximum effect; and of schools with a substantial PNP staff enhancement manifestly failing to take advantage of what that enhancement could offer. Many of these problems centred on the way schools deployed their PNP coordinators (see pp. 102–8), but Scale 1/MPG staff could also find themselves marginalized or used as supply teachers or even ancillaries in the very way the Authority had warned against. Moreover, given the fact that classes have always been much larger in primary schools than elsewhere, and that primary teachers have persistently urged the need to improve pupil–teacher ratios, it is not surprising that many heads saw the opportunities afforded by PNP only in terms of smaller classes.

For schools to exploit fully the potential of enhanced staffing after a century of working on the basis of n class teachers plus the head, they needed the imagination to conceive of alternatives; a shift in attitudes away from the entrenched belief in the inviolability and supremacy of the traditional twin roles of head and class teacher; and the will to enact such alternatives and live with the discomfort which the changing of professional roles inevitably generates. In some schools these attributes were in short supply, and the PNP staffing enhancement was largely wasted. This problem, too, is still with us: radical changes in professional culture and structure cannot be achieved overnight.

Although advisory staff delivered warnings on this matter, they were not always followed through into the PNP INSET programme. PNP staff attending these courses complained of being told what to do but not how to do it, and of receiving dismissive or baffled responses to their anxieties about coping with colleagues who were reluctant or unable to accommodate to new ways of working. There was also a critical gap in the INSET programme where heads were concerned. Heads' support was cited as the most important factor in the assimilation and success of PNP staff, yet the need to explore with heads, thoroughly and openly, the implications and potential of enhanced staffing, was not addressed at all in the early days of PNP. The Authority responded to our interim statements on this matter and increased its INSET commitment to management issues and leadership roles (including that of the head) as PNP progressed. However, as our reference above to the power of historical habit and precedent indicates, this is a long-term challenge, demanding radical change in the way schools conceive of management and the deployment of staff.

MANAGING CHANGE: THE PNP COORDINATOR

PNP coordinators were perceived and presented as the managerial linchpin of the Primary Needs Programme. The role was an innovative one, and its initial scope was set out in the 1985 job specification (Leeds City Council 1985c). It included working with colleagues and support agencies to further the four PNP aims, a particular brief for special needs provision, and a further injunction to work alongside other teachers to fulfil this brief.

The 1985 specification's emphasis on special needs was consonant with the mixed origins of PNP, and it reinforced initial – and persisting – confusion about whether PNP was a special needs programme or something else. The specification was also very comprehensive, and the 1987 version added the significant message that heads and coordinators should select from and adapt the list rather than seek to implement it in its entirety. In the same year, and in response to these and other difficulties – several of them identified by our project's fifth interim report – the Authority circulated *Guidelines for Headteachers in the Use of PNP Staff* (Leeds City Council 1987c). This document made it clear that the responsibility for determining coordinators' roles rested with the heads, who were encouraged to choose from the 1985 specification provided by the Authority. However, the document also emphasized that heads' room for manoeuvre was not unlimited, and that coordinators should be part of a senior management team which would determine and implement school policy. Further, it identified three main ways in which coordinators could expect to contribute to the school's teaching programme:

- taking responsibility for a class;
- working alongside other teachers;
- helping provide non-contact time by covering for colleagues.

In the event, a considerable diversity of roles emerged. On the basis of our initial fieldwork, we were able in our fifth report to group these under five main headings:

- special educational needs;
- curriculum development;
- staff development;
- home–school links;
- whole-class responsibility.

Further, the curriculum development role had four main versions:

- curriculum manager;
- curriculum consultant;
- curriculum enhancer;
- curriculum facilitator.

These latter four roles are defined and discussed in some detail in Chapter 3, and are therefore not elaborated here.

The annual questionnaire returns from PNP coordinators confirmed the validity of our initial framework, provided that 'staff development' now subsumes TTT and the release of colleagues, and that 'home-school links' includes working with outside agencies as well as parents. With this proviso, the framework represented, in 1990 as in 1987, the main areas of school life in which PNP coordinators were deployed. In addition, we can now indicate, in Table 6.2, the frequency of each role over the whole evaluation period. Of course, these are not necessarily discrete categories: for example, curriculum development and staff development are intertwined. But the categories and frequencies provide a useful commentary on the ways schools chose to implement the main managerial aspect of PNP policy, as contained in the various documents and courses relating to the coordinator role.

Within these overall figures there were significant phase differences. Special educational needs was always a much more prominent aspect of the work of Phase 1 coordinators than of those in Phases 2 or 3, and for the first three years of PNP SEN was the dominant coordinator task in Phase 1. In contrast, the Phase 2 list was consistently headed by staff development and support, particularly TTT.

There were also important changes over time. Coordinators' involvement in special needs declined while their full-time class teaching commitments increased, as did their participation in school management, especially curriculum development. TTT, carefully nurtured in the early days of PNP – especially after our fourth report had provided both a label and a framework for its development – became less prominent as coordinators returned from a collaborative to a solo teaching role. Thus, where the first coordinators fulfilled a brief dominated by special needs, with curriculum development and TTT level-pegging a little way behind, they and their successors in 1989 were as likely to be concerned with curriculum management and teaching, in collaboration or alone.

Our 1985–6 pilot study suggested that coordinators were having to take on more roles than they could cope with. This was confirmed in the 1987 study and was acknowledged by the Authority, as we have seen. Thereafter, the average number of roles (regrouped from the full list of ten above) was between three and four per coordinator, diminishing slightly towards the end of the evaluation period. The growth in curriculum-related roles is particularly significant. It predated the arrival of the National Curriculum, but was without doubt given a considerable boost by the publication of the government's initial National Cur-

Table 6.2 Coordinators' roles, 1986–9

	Frequency	*%*
Curriculum development	109	68.1
TTT	100	62.5
Special educational needs	97	60.6
Miscellaneous administrative	56	35.0
Class teaching	55	34.4
Releasing class teachers	37	23.1
Work with parents	33	20.6
Unclassified	21	13.1
Work with outside agencies	17	10.6
Other special needs (not SEN)	8	5.0
Total responses	533	

Note: Number of respondents was 160; mean number of roles was 3.3

riculum proposals in 1987, and the Education Reform Bill and Act, both in 1988. Our data show the generalized and somewhat ambivalent role of PNP coordinator being translated, by 1988–9, into that of *curriculum* coordinator. (For an extended discussion of curriculum coordination and management, see Chapter 3.)

Judging the impact of PNP coordinators in absolute terms is as problematic as judging the impact of the Programme as a whole. Coordinators themselves, in the annual surveys, had no such doubts about the main gains at least. Their league table is headed by *improved attitudes*, *increased staffing* and *staff development*; but there was little consensus about the rest.

- *Widespread agreement* (in order of frequency):
  improved attitudes;
  increased staffing;
  staff development.
- *No clear agreement* (in order of frequency):
  curriculum change;
  collaborative teaching;
  better management;
  release of staff;
  more individual and group work;
  improved SEN provision;
  more parental involvement.

Heads were asked to rate coordinators' impact on their schools' pursuit of the four PNP aims. Their response was broadly in line with the frequency of the various roles listed above. It should be noted, however, that heads were on the whole reluctant to ascribe much more than moderate success to their coordinators in respect of any of these aims. On the other hand, coordinators were seen as more effective than most other PNP resources.

Coordinators' unanimity about attitude change in their schools is significant for two reasons. First, because it is evident that many of the problems which the Authority identified in 1985 when it established PNP were centred as much on professional attitudes as professional expertise – attitudes to children, to curriculum, to teaching methods, to parents, to ethnic minority groups, to gender issues – and indeed we have picked up and reported the resilience of many of the attitudes which the Authority sought to change. Second, coordinators as a group were acutely conscious of the way their own success depended in large part upon how they and the practices they were promoting were regarded by existing staff in the schools where they were placed. However, 'improved attitudes' is both elusive as a claim and difficult in practice to demonstrate. It is also possible that in some cases 'improved attitudes' is another way of saying that nothing of substance was achieved.

In our fifth report we identified three main areas within which attitude and related attributes like personal manner and professional style were critically important for coordinators' success:

- the influence of the head;
- the attitude of other staff;
- the persona and style of the coordinator.

As far as heads were concerned, coordinators needed from them a properly negotiated version of the Authority's job specification, support for the difficult tasks they were required to undertake, and a preparedness to include them within the team of senior staff involved in the development of policy. All too often these prerequisites were withheld, especially but not exclusively in the early stages of the Programme.

Equally influential for most coordinators were the attitudes of other staff. There was an initial suspicion among teachers at all levels, including some heads, that coordinators were agents of the LEA, charged with identifying and reporting on inappropriate practice. As the Programme became established, and as co-ordinators became a part of the staff team, they were increasingly judged on the practice they delivered rather than the power they seemed to represent.

Coordinators themselves were to a greater or lesser extent sensitive to these anxieties: some fuelled them while others quickly or painstakingly dispelled them. But the job was rarely easy, especially where support from the head was withheld or accorded only grudgingly. Coordinators had to acquire skills in leadership and in handling people and ideas which the majority of them had not developed in their previous jobs. They felt that the Authority provided too little support here at first, although curriculum leadership courses introduced in the later stages of the Programme provided some help subsequently.

As coordinators' roles shifted towards curriculum responsibility, so *curriculum expertise* itself became a further factor in their success, to be added to the three other factors discussed above.

Coordinators operated, as we have seen, in five broad areas – special needs, curriculum development, staff development, home–school links and whole-class teaching. The first four of these were generally school-wide roles, and three broad styles of implementing these emerged:

- *Whole-school manager* involved at a senior level in school policy- and decision-making.
- *Enactor* of policy developed by others.
- *Facilitator* to other staff to enable them to undertake intiatives.

These styles represent different levels of power, authority and influence within a school, and therefore different possibilities for action. All coordinators, as we have seen, worked to the same basic job specification, adapted to meet the circumstances of their school. Whatever version of this specification was negoti-ated, they needed appropriate authority and resources, and access to the decision-making process, to carry it out. Their chances of success were far less where they were relegated to the position of *enactor* or mere *facilitator*, as some were. The tasks identified for coordinators by the Authority could not be carried out with anything less than *enactor* status. The discrepancy between job-specification and status became acute for some coordinators, and remained a problem in some schools, not just for coordinators but also for many other staff with significant cross-school managerial responsibilities. Again, the remedy is largely in the hands of the head.

In our fifth report we compared the Leeds conception of PNP coordinator with other versions: the role of SEN coordinator which emerged after the 1981 Education Act, and that of curriculum coordinator, first tentatively identified by Plowden (CACE 1967), then developed in the 1970s and 1980s by HMI and others (DES 1978b, House of Commons 1986, Campbell 1985, Taylor 1986). The Leeds role was initially, and to some extent remained, broader than either of these, though it tended to become less and less distinguishable from that of curriculum leader. In addition, it lost its uniqueness and force as a result of two developments. One was the extension of school-based curriculum leadership roles across a much wider range of curriculum areas than was covered in the mid-1980s (see Chapter 3): in this sense, nearly every teacher is a curriculum leader (or even a coordinator) now. The other development was budgetary delegation to schools (LMS) under the 1988 Education Reform Act (DES 1988b, 1991d), which appeared to reduce the scope for enhanced staffing, despite the Secretary of State's approval of PNP-style weightings for social disadvantage, ethnic minority groups, special needs, and small schools in the Leeds LMS formula (Leeds City Council 1989c).

However, the idea of a free-wheeling change-agent and catalyst in each school remains a powerful one. It is dependent not so much on the generous staffing levels of PNP Phase 1 (though that obviously helped a great deal) as on a combination of a degree of staffing flexibility and a basic preparedness to accept that this kind of role is important and needs to be built into a school's staffing arrangements under whatever label is deemed appropriate. There is no reason why schools should not include within their plans for the 1990s the full range of managerial and support roles which emerged from PNP during the 1980s. If it is now less likely, because of LMS, that one member of staff can combine several of these roles, it is certainly practicable for them to be spread across the staff as a whole, or at least its more experienced and talented members. The most unsatisfactory outcome of LMS in this context would be if schools felt obliged to return to the traditional concept, so inimical to professional and curricular development, of there being just two professional roles in primary schools, those of class teacher and head, each confined to and jealously defending his or her territory.

The residual force of this traditional view was one of the main reasons why PNP coordinators so often encountered anxiety and resistance. As we noted in our fifth report:

> The idea of a coordinator . . . signals the limits to the generalist class teacher's whole curriculum/whole child capacities. It denotes different levels in the staff hierarchy. It overlaps (and perhaps threatens) the head's role as traditionally defined. And it raises questions about what, once the division of labour

between head and coordinator is determined, there is left for the deputy head to do .... Beyond innocent labels like 'coordinator' and the comfortable language of 'working alongside' are some tough realities.

(Alexander *et al.* 1989: 188–9)

The PNP coordinator idea, whatever its problems and imperfections in practice, represents a vision of professional collaboration, development and decision-making which schools can ill afford to abandon, least of all in the era of the National Curriculum.

MANAGEMENT STRUCTURES

Notwithstanding the above, some schools persisted with, or only cosmetically adapted, their existing management structures. Overall, however, our studies showed schools tending to cluster towards the following main types:

- *Type 1: 'My School/My Class'*. The classic division of labour between a head and class teachers, each with clearly defined roles and 'zones of influence'. In this situation, the role of the deputy head might be undefined or non-existent, except in a symbolic sense. Type 1 structures were commoner, for obvious reasons, in small schools than large, though there were examples of large schools persisting with this model despite the arrival of coordinators. In such cases the tensions were greater than in the smaller schools.
- *Type 2: Head, Deputy and Class Teacher*. Still a two-tier structure, but with three rather than two basic roles. Here that of the deputy was clearly defined, and entailed engagement with policy, management and development rather than merely covering in the event of the head's absence.
- *Type 3: Senior Management Team*. With the arrival or designation of the PNP coordinator, some heads constituted the three senior posts as a senior management team, meeting regularly to review and agree policy.
- *Type 4: Embryonic Departmentalism*. As the focus of concern shifted towards curriculum matters, and as HMI, DES and others argued with increasing insistence that each area of the curriculum should be led by a staff member with appropriate expertise, so designated curriculum leaders assumed greater importance in the overall management structure. However, the structure remained essentially two-tier, with curriculum leaders not involved in major policy matters.
- *Type 5: Three-Tier*. Whereas Types 1–4 are all variants of the basic two-tier model of primary school management, in this type the coordinator and curriculum leaders represent a significant and formally recognized additional layer in the management structure, running their own meetings and development programmes, reporting back to the head and the staff as a whole, and contributing in a distinctive way to overall school policy.
- *Type 6: Management Matrix*. In larger primary schools, the roles of head, deputy, coordinator and curriculum leader might be complemented by those of year leader, head of infants/juniors, and indeed by other posts of responsibility.

Where the year-group was large, year leadership became a post of some importance, counterbalancing the cross-school role of curriculum leader, and
introducing potential tensions over who was responsible for what. These were
resolved by the formal recognition that the structure was no longer one of
layers or levels, but a curriculum/year-group *matrix*, requiring close
collaboration between the parties and the involvement of all of them in policy
discussions.

A number of points should be made about this typology. First, like all others, it
represents general tendencies rather than exact categories. Second, although
there is a clear relationship between school size and management structure –
there is limited scope for extended curriculum leadership roles, let alone year-
group responsibilities, in smaller schools – the relationship is not inevitable.
Some medium-sized schools had shifted to a three-tier model, while some large
schools were still operating a rather unsatisfactory and somewhat stressed
version of Type 2 or even Type 1. Generally, however, by the end of the period
in question, larger schools tended towards Types 4, 5 and 6. Third, as we
monitored our representative sample of schools over a three year period, we
could perceive some of them undergoing a process of structural transition,
shifting away from the simple two-tier model towards departmentalism and/or a
matrix structure. Finally, although we have represented the senior management
team as a particular type or stage, the emergence of a senior team within schools
was a more general characteristic of the PNP period. The arrival and ambivalent
status of the coordinator forced many heads to look afresh at structures and
decision-making, to delegate more extensively than hitherto, and to establish
more regular consultation procedures than the traditional combination of informal encounters and unstructured or semi-structured staff meetings.

DEPUTY HEADS

The role of deputy head did not always feature in this process of management
review. When we surveyed deputy heads towards the end of the evaluation
period, we found a somewhat surprising proportion – over half of those surveyed
– without job specifications. Since they were working with coordinators whose
jobs were – at LEA insistence – properly specified, their anomalous position in
the school could be severely aggravated by PNP. It seems not unreasonable to
argue that in a modern primary school all staff, and especially those with formal
responsibilities of any kind over and above the class-teacher role, should have
clear and properly negotiated job specifications.

Deputy heads undertook very diverse responsibilities. Every one of those
surveyed had a class, though some were released from part of their teaching
duties to undertake other activities. In order of frequency, deputy heads' responsibilities were as follows:

• class teaching;
• curriculum leadership;

- general managerial responsibilities, delegated by the head;
- staff development and staff pastoral support.

These four were particularly prominent. Some way behind was a more random and idiosyncratic collection of responsibilities, again listed here in order of frequency:

- taking assemblies;
- staff–head liaison;
- pastoral care;
- discipline;
- buildings;
- home–school;
- library;
- odd jobs – tuck shop, festivals, etc.

It should be noted that just as all deputies combined a school-wide responsibility with teaching a class, so most combined a major school-wide responsibility from the first list above with one or more of those from the second list. However, there were some whose role appeared to involve, apart from class teaching and standing in when the head was absent, no more than relatively low-level jobs like reporting on leaking gutters or running a tuck shop.

Although the latter cases are probably a diminishing minority, especially now that budgetary delegation under LMS has made it essential that heads in their turn delegate a greater proportion of their managerial functions to senior staff, our studies indicate a more general need for primary schools to continue to review the role of deputy headship, to define more exactly the range of tasks it is appropriate for someone at that level of seniority to undertake, and to ensure that all deputy heads have appropriate job specifications.

DECISION-MAKING

To some extent, management structure and decision-making are directly related. A head develops a particular structure in the light of the decisions which have to be made and the people he/she believes should be involved in making them. The traditional 'My School/My Class' model (Alexander 1984: 161–8) is based on the assumption that there are two sorts of decision: about the school as a whole – its goals and ethos, its children, its staff and its curriculum – and about the translation of these whole-school decisions into day-to-day teaching. The head deals with the first, class teachers with the second, and there is little blurring at the edges. In the Three Tier model, the head acknowledges that there is a substantial field of decision-making to do with the content and development of specific aspects of the curriculum which requires the expertise and time of others. In the Management Matrix model there is an even broader conception of the range of decisions calling for specialization and delegation.

There are three inevitable consequences of these very different approaches.

One is that the further from a Type 1 structure a school is, the greater the need for communication and coordination in decision-making. The second is that while all primary school decision-making is dependent upon both formal and informal relations and contacts, the more complex structures require a much greater expenditure of time on formal decision-making processes; at the same time, there is greater risk of divisiveness if groups and individuals feel that they are being excluded from the formal processes or that the latter are less important than informal, behind-closed-doors negotiations. The third consequence is that while in Type 1 structures leadership is synonymous with headship, in the more complex structures leadership is shared among several people.

The development of PNP is in part a story of growing sophistication over such matters in Leeds primary schools. As schools shifted generally from a dependence on informal contacts to role specialization, delegation, and a greater investment in formal procedures, so they were forced to acquire the vocabulary and skills which formal decision-making dictates.

The formalization of decision-making could have adverse side effects. Coherence in policy could become less easy to achieve where its components were fragmented among different groups and individuals. Sub-groups could become oppositional rather than cooperative. Consensus could not be guaranteed where particular groups had had little or nothing to do with a particular policy.

The more effectively managed schools understood these problems and sought to ensure that sub-groups and delegated roles and responsibilities remained part of a wider collegial culture in which all participated, and within which divergences of opinion were openly explored.

However, these processes – central though they were to the success of PNP – were at first given little attention in the LEA's in-service support programme. Coordinators had their own courses and conferences from the outset but courses for curriculum leaders started rather later in the programme, as did management courses for heads. Such courses were initially based on the notion of management as something one person does to others; but the management of a school, it is now generally acknowledged, is a process in which all members of the school's staff are, in different ways, engaged: it is a multi-directional process. All staff, not just the 'managers', need skills if they are to participate successfully in delegated or collegial management and decision-making, since every person in such contexts has a managerial role of some kind. Even the newly arrived probationer needs managerial skills – for working with colleagues and participating constructively in meetings, for example.

Management, then, has become a whole-school process, and it should be approached as such in any INSET and support programmes organized by the Authority or its schools. This view was endorsed in the School Management Task Force report (DES 1990f), and by 1991 Leeds LEA had a policy and programme for management training (Leeds City Council 1991a) which sought to address the management needs of all staff – heads, deputies, staff tutors, INSET coordinators, curriculum coordinators and probationers. Some of this activity focused on what were termed 'generic' management issues and skills.

However, the need for whole-school approaches to management is only part of the problem. It is also essential, as Alexander (1984) emphasizes, to avoid the historic tendency for management training to concentrate on how schools should be run while neglecting the purposes they serve. Shipman puts the point uncompromisingly:

> Learning is the business of schools. It should be the priority for school management. Yet it is usually ignored in school management training. Means have got confused with ends.
>
> (Shipman 1990: v)

More generally, bearing in mind some of this book's observations about the thinking behind the Primary Needs Programme:

> Specialisation, consultancy and the streamlining of headship may produce greater efficiency, but in respect of what? Ideas imposed more effectively on children and teachers than in the 1960s, but which remain, as ideas, as ill-conceived as ever? Primary education certainly needs to review its professional procedures, but far more pressing is the need to review the ideas which such procedures seek to implement.
>
> (Alexander 1984: 209)

As governors, heads and teachers become increasingly enmeshed in the complexities of managing *resources* under LMS (Audit Commission 1991) it is important that they are able to keep the management of *learning* as their central objective. LEAs can offer schools significant support in maintaining the balance, and can provide appropriate frameworks to encourage this. One such might be the school development plan, now a statutory requirement. In Leeds, the LEA's current framework (Leeds City Council 1991b) might usefully be monitored – and modified where appropriate – with this issue of *balance* firmly in mind.

THE HEAD

Notwithstanding the current shift to collegial and whole-school management, the head remains pivotal to the successful management of a primary school. Yet though Leeds LEA understood this from the outset, its approach to heads seems to have been curiously negative. As we saw in Chapter 1, it was believed in the early 1980s that much primary classroom practice in Leeds was outdated, uninspiring or downright bad; that heads bore much of the responsibility for this state of affairs; and, therefore, that the same heads could not be expected to put matters right. In evolving PNP policy, therefore, officers consulted no more than a few carefully chosen heads, leaving the rest ignorant and deeply suspicious of what was going on. A new role was then established, that of coordinator, which bypassed the head and was intended to carry the new vision of good practice directly from Merrion House (the Education Department's offices) to the classroom. Such an approach was bound to backfire. Not only were many primary heads suspicious of and unclear about PNP, but the PNP experience provided further fuel for those who felt that Leeds was an authority which treated its heads badly, neither consulting nor supporting them. Relations between schools and the Authority deteriorated seriously as a result.

All this is now history, and the Authority, to its credit, has done much to try to repair the damage done during this period. However, in the present context it is important to make two points of continuing concern. First, though heads are indeed crucial to the character of a school and the quality of the education it provides, they can never be held entirely to blame if these prove unsatisfactory. The policies pursued by Leeds LEA before 1985 – lower than average per capita spending on primary education, higher than average pupil–teacher ratios, a stagnant staffing profile exacerbated by the ring-fence policy on new appointments, little investment in advisory support – played their own part in producing the conditions of which the LEA itself suddenly became so critical. Second, the way heads responded to PNP, and with varying degrees of success exploited its opportunities and resources for the children's benefit, must be set firmly against this background.

A number of factors emerged from our studies as bearing particularly significantly on how heads managed PNP, and these we now outline.

It is a basic tenet of primary headship that each school should have a distinct 'ethos', 'philosophy' or set of beliefs and aims to guide and inform its policies and practices. Traditionally, determining this philosophy has been the head's prerogative, and few have contested this. While the 1988 Act requires a greater involvement of governors in such matters, the head's role in shaping the professional and educational culture remains critical, and certainly this was the expectation during the period of PNP.

We gained ready access to heads' thinking on such matters, especially in the sample schools. The recurrent theme was 'informality' or 'progressivism': the same value-orientation which they saw the Authority itself espousing as the touchstone for good practice. However, despite the apparent consensus, there were notable differences in style, presentation and treatment where these values were concerned.

- *Purists and sceptics*. While some heads subscribed wholeheartedly to progressive orthodoxies, others were more doubtful or circumspect. Where the former used the full vocabulary of informality, and seemed unprepared or unable to accommodate the possibility that alternative viewpoints might exist, the latter were more aware of the limitations of progressivism, both as an idea and as a basis for practice.
- *The influence of context*. While some heads saw progressivism as providing a basic recipe for primary practice in any context, others admitted to having their 'philosophy' shaped more by the particular social and cultural circumstances within which they worked, especially the backgrounds of the children and the attitudes and expectations of their parents. Such realities, as pressing for some heads in the suburbs as in the inner city, presented an agenda which primary orthodoxies addressed only partly, if at all.

- *The influence of other ideas.* Similarly, some heads sought to accommodate to their 'core' philosophy ideas and concerns from other sources – their reading, their membership of award-bearing courses, their out-of-school reference and membership groups, their professional and social networks. Such sources were, to them, more significant than those within the Authority, and often provided a more neutral and open context for sharing and debating ideas.
- *Rhetoric and reality.* The mismatch between a head's espoused values and what was actually going on in the classroom could be startling – and indeed is a recurrent theme in several of our interim reports, notably 10 and 11. As a general rule, the more purist and dogmatic the value-orientation of the head, the bigger the discrepancy with observed practice. In these cases, a school's philosophy acquired a life of its own: paraded for governors, advisers, parents and visitors, reflected superficially in those aspects of practice like display and decor that such outsiders tended immediately to note, but seldom followed through.

These differences were only partly about value-orientations as such. Some heads were temperamentally and intellectually less inclined than others to perceive education in terms of grand statements and ringing slogans. On the other hand, a gap or mismatch between rhetoric and reality might reflect a gulf between head and staff, and indeed the discrepancies were most marked in schools where heads were relatively isolated, where communication was poor, and where class teachers were not involved in policy matters.

Thus there was an intimate connection between heads' philosophies and their views of their role, and between these and school management.

Heads perceived their roles in different ways. Of the many perceptions apparent in our data, four seemed particularly prominent.

- *Head as 'boss'*, controlling – benignly or otherwise, but at any rate firmly – the character and direction of the school and its staff. Decision-making tended to centre on the issuing of directives and instructions.
- *Head as chief teacher*, believing, and demonstrating, that the teaching function of a school is pre-eminent and that the head must play the leading part, by action and example, in advancing it.
- *Head as managing director.* Where the 'boss' tended to be autocratic or paternalistic/maternalistic, the 'managing director' was more likely to be bureaucratic, delegating specialist roles and responsibilities and instituting formal procedures for decision-making.
- *Head as team leader.* Here there was less social distance between head and staff, though the head accepted the main responsibility for initiating and leading. At the same time, the leadership roles and potential of other staff were valued and developed, and decision-making tended to be collective.

Heads adopting a 'chief teacher' or 'team leader' role tended to be more visible and accessible to staff, especially in respect of their need for support and advice on everyday teaching problems: their physical base was the classroom as much as, or more than, the office. Heads adopting a 'managing director' or 'boss' role were more likely to be office-based and thus to run the risk of appearing remote from everyday classroom concerns, especially in larger schools. However, 'bosses' were less prone to such detachment than 'managing directors', since they tended to place a high value on knowing, and hence controlling, all aspects of school life. To achieve this they needed to keep in touch with the classroom directly rather than through intermediaries. They might spend much time, therefore, patrolling their school and its classrooms, talking with children and offering comment to teachers. However, it should also be pointed out that the 'boss' view of headship manifested itself in a continuum of behaviour ranging from the clubbable to the autocratic or even tyrannical, with various shades of paternalism/maternalism in between.

This issue bears importantly on that of the degree of fit between a school's stated philosophy and its observable classroom practice, as discussed above. The closer a head is to the classroom and the challenges confronting class teachers, the greater his or her opportunities for evolving policies which reconcile ideals with practical circumstances. The more extreme flights of rhetoric we encountered were almost always associated with managerial detachment from the classroom.

The shift towards greater delegation, role specialization and collective decision-making in primary schools, and the emergence of what we have termed departmental, three-tier and matrix management structures, appears to be an inevitable and necessary consequence of the growing complexity of the work of primary schools and the diminishing currency of the 'jack of all trades' view of the class teacher's and head's roles. However, if staff are to remain in touch with each other, and the head is to remain in touch with all staff, close attention needs to be paid to communication, and to ensuring that managerial procedures like school philosophies and policy statements remain rooted in day-to-day needs and realities rather than take on a life of their own. Thus, formal procedures are not so much an alternative as an adjunct to the informal collaboration which is such an important feature of the best primary schools; and the part played by the head in securing the most productive mix of formal procedure and informal consultation/collaboration remains central.

We noted earlier the need for investment in support for heads and in management training, while acknowledging the Authority's recent (that is, post-PNP) initiatives in respect of the latter (Leeds City Council 1991a). We also argued that training should focus on management as a collective, whole school enterprise rather than on the role of the manager alone. Our fieldwork pointed up two further areas of concern, both of which need close and urgent attention in programmes of professional development for heads.

The first is staff relationships. Our survey and interview data revealed a small number of heads who appeared to have difficulty in dealing with their colleagues as people. Some treated their staff in a high-handed and tyrannical way. Some were less overtly overbearing, but no less effective in undermining their colleagues' confidence. Rather different were those heads who avoided not only confrontation but also contact, taking refuge in their office and resorting to memoranda rather than face-to-face encounters. In between were those heads who dealt much more effectively and constructively with some staff than with others. In such cases, as in all human relationships, the presence or absence of personal rapport was a critical element. Equally, some heads were struggling to deal with colleagues who were challenging by any standards – individuals who were combative, touchy, recalcitrant, bitter, lazy or in any of a variety of other ways uncooperative. The roots of such personal antipathies are notoriously difficult to disentangle, but their effect on a school's professional climate can be deeply damaging.

The second area of concern is professional knowledge. A few heads with whom we came into contact seemed alarmingly out of touch with recent developments in primary education. They showed little awareness of, or interest in, HMI surveys and official reports, let alone other published research and writing on primary education. Their grasp of LEA and national policies bearing directly on the task of headship was at best tenuous. Frequently they took refuge in platitudes and rhetoric, delivering as unassailable truths ideas which are elsewhere accepted as very much open to debate. About ideas and practices other than their own they tended to be contemptuous, dismissive or hostile; usually such attitudes were grounded in ignorance of, rather than engagement with, the ideas in question. Their lack of commitment to extending their own professional knowledge and understanding, and their rampant anti-intellectualism, tended to infect the whole professional climate of their schools, depriving them of the spark of lively discussion about issues which is essential to educational progress, and dampening the enthusiasms of those staff who were otherwise inclined. Such a stance, it has also to be said, was sharply at odds with the educational aims to which their schools were purportedly committed, with their emphasis on engendering open, questioning minds, a love of reading and so on, a contradiction of which such heads seemed unaware.

These two concerns – staff relationships and heads' professional knowledge – are vital ingredients in effective school management and in the head's professional credibility. That being so, they should feature prominently both in the selection process for headship and in subsequent management support and training. However, since management courses tend to concentrate on basic tasks and procedures, there is a risk that the much larger matters signalled here will be treated rudimentarily at best. The LEA will need to look at other routes as well. It will also need to be aware that concerns such as these expose a major limitation of the school-controlled model of INSET which Leeds, in common with other LEAs, has adopted, and which is reinforced by current government funding arrangements and LMS. In a school having the professional climate characterized above, the capacity – let alone the will – to identify INSET needs with accuracy and honesty will simply not exist, and a self-generated INSET programme may well merely reinforce a school in its inadequacies. For this reason, LEAs must always maintain a major stake in INSET and professional development, above all where heads are concerned.

CONCLUSION

We noted at the start of this chapter that our study of school management was not intended to be comprehensive: our concern was the management of PNP rather than that of every aspect of a school's professional work. To this end, we devoted particular attention to the contribution of PNP enhanced staffing, to the work undertaken by support staff and PNP coordinators, and to the contexts within which such staff were working.

However, we showed that the contribution which PNP appointees were able to make was inseparable from the wider management structures within which they were located, and in particular that the head played a key role in facilitating and supporting their endeavours.

It is a truism that every school is unique. However, it is also the case that schools have a lot in common. Our evaluation identified some of these shared features, and showed how primary schools tended to cluster towards a number of broad types in respect of certain issues bearing on the management of PNP: for example, the roles undertaken by support staff and coordinators, and by deputy heads; the managerial styles of senior staff; the management structures which framed the defining and implementing of school policy; the policies themselves; heads' stance, on the ideas and practices which have constituted mainstream primary thinking since Plowden; and heads' leadership styles.

Like other studies (for example DES 1977, 1987; Rutter *et al.* 1979, Mortimore *et al.* 1988; Nias *et al.* 1989), ours identified or underlined some of the main factors in effective school management: the style and quality of the head's leadership; the intellectual and professional climate of the school; the explication of the management roles of staff with posts of responsibility – curriculum leaders, year leaders, coordinators and deputy heads; the importance of formal structures and mechanisms for decision-making; the need to strike an appropriate balance between such formal structures and informal processes; and the importance of involving all staff in decision-making.

Such issues are likely to be important in any primary school, anywhere. However, there were others, more distinctively local in their orientation: the gradual demise of the traditional two-tier model of primary school management and its replacement by three-tier and matrix models; the desirability of building on the diversification of staff management roles which PNP has produced, avoiding any contraction of such roles as a consequence of LMS; the need to acknowledge the pivotal role, for good or ill, played by primary heads, and to work with and through rather than round or against them; the need to expand the focus of management training courses to encompass the roles and needs of all staff (not just those of the 'managers' as conventionally defined), to locate management strategies in whole-school analysis, and generally to broaden the concept of 'management' which currently informs such courses; the importance of training, support and INSET for heads, and of ensuring that these give close attention to the broader aspects of the expertise needed for headship, such as professional knowledge and personal relationships as well as the more obvious tasks, roles and strategies.

The recurrent factor in this analysis has been the inseparability of primary school and classroom practice from the policy, resourcing, support and guidance provided by the LEA. These are the concern of our next chapter.

Our evaluation of PNP caught schools during a period of transition, from *laissez-faire* to the much greater LEA intervention that PNP signalled, and from a largely local orientation to one framed by national policies and directives. For all concerned, the agenda is now substantially different from 1985, or even 1989. For primary class teachers, the National Curriculum and assessment provide the overwhelming preoccupation. Alongside these, heads contend with school development plans, changing relationships with parents and governors, and the pressures and constraints of budgetary delegation under LMS. They find their thinking and decision-making dominated by market and resource considerations which in their scale and complexity are a long way indeed from the traditional concept of primary headship (Audit Commission 1991). By 1991, Leeds LEA had set up services and procedures to guide and support schools in these novel areas of activity, and there was no shortage of advice from other sources. However, even when the agenda is clarified and the tasks are clear, choices still remain at school level as to how the agenda and tasks should be managed. In this matter the PNP experience is of considerable relevance. The items on the agenda may change, but the questions about strategies, roles and procedures remain the same.

7 Supporting reform: the role of the LEA

During the 1980s, Leeds LEA set itself the task of reforming an entire local system of primary education. It diagnosed the main weaknesses in the schools it had inherited from earlier decades and set out its alternative vision, a Primary Needs Programme intended to meet children's needs by transforming schools into exemplars of 'good primary practice'.

The LEA then identified the resource needs of the system as a whole and voted the additional resources to meet them, determining precisely which schools would receive what level and kind of additional resources, and when. It set up mechanisms for coordinating, controlling and servicing the new programme, and expanded its advisory and support staff to ensure that such mechanisms would be effective. It determined the job specifications of the 530 teachers and other staff appointed to the programme, and officers themselves were involved in many of these appointments. It also devised a substantial programme of centralized in-service support for such appointees in order to ensure the successful dissemination of the various strands of the LEA's version of good practice.

Finally, the LEA agreed procedures for monitoring and reviewing the entire programme, and this included an invitation to the University of Leeds to undertake an independent evaluation.

This gives some measure of the boldness and scale of the programme. It also indicates how interventionist it was, especially by comparison with the practices of some other LEAs. In the present chapter we consider some of the main issues of policy and strategy which the Leeds approach raises: the way PNP policy was formulated and communicated; the substance and interpretation of the policy; and the LEA's own strategies for implementing the policy – as opposed to those adopted in the schools which have been considered in previous chapters – with particular reference to the INSET programme.

PNP POLICY: FORMULATION AND COMMUNICATION

All LEAs have a statutory duty to have policies on the various aspects of the education service for which they are responsible. Leeds LEA took this duty very seriously, especially in respect of primary education. However, on matters of substance and strategy LEAs retain discretion. From the various strategies available, Leeds LEA opted for the one which was simplest to enact quickly but was also most likely to provoke adverse reaction – namely, a centralized approach involving minimal consultation with those most affected.

As a result, while the Authority can justifiably take much of the credit for the transformation of certain aspects of primary education in Leeds which PNP began to yield, it may also need to accept responsibility for some of PNP's manifest weaknesses.

The advantages of a centralized policy are the speed and scale of reform it allows; the disadvantages, particularly in a complex arena like education, are the resistance and disaffection it may generate, and the inevitability that the practice which emerges will be rather different from that intended because those at the receiving end may have insufficient understanding or commitment to secure its implementation. The experience of PNP, as recorded in our eleven interim reports and the previous six chapters, suggests that the extent of LEA centralization over PNP was excessive, and that in certain crucial respects it was counter-productive. There are important lessons here both for future policy formulation and for the way an LEA's officers work. The lessons apply as much to the policies and strategies of central government as they do to LEAs.

The resentment and resistance generated in the schools by the way PNP was developed and implemented was a prominent theme in our early data, and in some schools it persisted until our last major data-gathering exercises: the 1989 questionnaires sent to primary heads, coordinators and advisory staff, and the 1990 home–school links follow-up study. Our subsequent contacts with school staff in the city indicated that the legacy was a powerful and often negative one, and that it continued to be reinforced because despite a general loosening of LEA control and a government-sponsored shift to a greater measure of school self-determination, the Authority was perceived by schools as continuing to present itself as the main definer and arbiter of good practice.

What made this situation peculiarly problematic for primary teachers was their sense that the firm stance on good practice taken by the Authority's advisory staff was inseparable from the part they played both in the formal processes of promotion and appointment and in the many informal and subtle ways whereby individual teachers were encouraged and advanced – or discouraged and held back.

In any field of employment a successful application depends to some degree on the applicant's being seen to say and do what is expected during the selection process, and to this extent conventional selection methods can always be faulted for the way they may presume that words uttered on a form or in an interview are reliable indicators of future performance. This much is commonplace. However, the situation in Leeds was felt to reach deeper than this, and there were few other issues on which our questionnaires, interviews and observation between 1986 and 1990 yielded such widespread agreement or such strong expressions of anxiety, cynicism or disaffection. Many teachers and heads felt that getting on in the primary sector required verbal and practical allegiance to certain quite specific canons of 'good primary practice', and that anything less, let alone any open challenging of the orthodoxies in question, could damage their professional prospects. Moreover, this normative process was felt to operate at several levels, from appointments, promotions and other career aspirations to the much more subtle everyday processes whereby individuals come to acquire a sense of their professional worth from the comments and valuations of 'significant others' – advisers, advisory teachers and heads in particular.

The fact that heads and teachers of very differing professional styles and values were working in Leeds throughout this period demonstrates, of course, that other factors were at work and that the wilder accusations of patronage which came our way needed to be treated with considerable caution. Clearly, the service was by no means monolithic. On the other hand, there are different levels and degrees of both conformity and dissent, and in a context where prevailing versions of good practice tended to emphasize the visual and organizational, a strategic surface conformity allowed the more subtle and perhaps significant aspects of practice to be retained and underlying attitudes and assumptions to persist.

It is likely that these findings will be strongly disputed in some quarters: understandably, because no individual or organization wishes to be depicted in terms other than those of the most scrupulous integrity and open-mindedness where such matters are concerned. However, as with some other issues we have explored, the problem here is centrally one of *perception*. If people believe something to be true, then its consequences are the same, whether or not it is *actually* true. In the present case, the perception seems to have adversely affected both the quality and climate of professional discourse and the credibility of structures, procedures and people at LEA and school level. In any event, we have stressed that the perceptions relate as much or more to the *informal* context within which teachers and advisory staff work as to formal procedures. It is a relatively straightforward matter to sort out guidelines for the conduct of the latter; much more difficult to control the character of the former. Moreover, agents of the process may be genuinely unaware of what they are doing for as long as they see good professional practice as unitary, consensual and unproblematic. For if there really is only one version of good primary practice then it becomes obvious that everyone should subscribe to it. However, since it is to be hoped that the essentially problematic and contestable nature of good primary practice has by now been adequately demonstrated, the state of affairs described here must give rise to some concern.

We recognize that the shift in the balance of power in appointment matters from LEAs to governing bodies may seem of itself to resolve this issue. It does not: proposals currently under discussion make it clear that advisory influence on individual careers will remain highly significant (Leeds City Council 1991c). However, the issues here will now need to be considered by governing bodies as well as advisory staff. It is vital that the teaching profession has full confidence in the processes of career development and advancement. The statutory responsibilities of LEAs and governing bodies in respect of quality control should be exercised with due acknowledgement of teachers' special knowledge and skills and their freedom and right as professionals to adopt those strategies which build on their personal strengths and reflect the unique circumstances of each school and classroom.

PNP POLICY: SUBSTANCE

The four key focuses of PNP, each discussed in detail in Chapters 2–5, were:

- children's needs;
- the curriculum;
- teaching strategies and classroom organization;
- links between home, school and community.

There is little doubt that these are proper, necessary and central focuses for educational policy and practice. Each of them, however, raises certain basic requirements of a conceptual and empirical kind. The *conceptual* requirements are to be clear and exact in our use of these and subsidiary terms, and to confront and seek to resolve the many and often contentious value issues which each of them raises. The *empirical* requirement is to seek, evaluate and make explicit the evidence upon which claims for particular ideas and practices advocated as policy are based. (We develop this argument, and an analysis of the 'good primary practice' problem, in Chapter 11.)

In formulating and presenting the various PNP policies, neither of these basic requirements appears to have been even entertained. Schools were expected to make sense of ideas which had not always been thought through fully, and to implement practices whose justification frequently consisted of little more than unsubstantiated assertion. The force of such ideas and practices lay partly in their 'progressive' origins, which few teachers would be prepared to gainsay; and partly in the authority of those who devised and presented them, whom few would dare to contradict.

It should be added that the absence of proper justification of the ideas and practices underpinning major aspects of the education experienced by primary school pupils is not unique to Leeds. On the contrary, it is an extremely common condition in post-war English primary education, and the agents of PNP policy in Leeds were merely conforming to the general tendency.

There is, however, no good reason why Leeds or any LEA should follow this particular trend. The only proper way to arrive at sustainable definitions of good educational practice is by sharing and analysing ideas and values, marshalling and examining evidence, and applying both processes to the task of formulating principles. Arguments and evidence for and against particular propositions are now abundantly available, both from the growing body of research and analytic study in primary education and from the cumulative experience of teachers. Published analysis and research are already in the public domain and are liberally referred to in this report. Teachers' experience, which is at least as valuable a source of insight, is also readily accessible, but only if those responsible for policy are prepared to acknowledge its validity and are willing to make efforts to bring teachers into the debate. The shift is necessary, but it requires a fundamental readjustment in the relationship between the Authority and its schools, and between officers, advisers, heads and teachers. The adjustment needed is towards a partnership of fellow professionals rather than a hierarchy of expert superordinates and inexpert subordinates.

Questions about the *characteristics* of LEA thinking on aspects of primary practice are inseparable from questions about its *focus*. In one sense, the concentration on needs, curriculum, teaching strategies and home–school links is suitably comprehensive: it appears to encompass all the main elements of educational practice. However, our interim reports and previous chapters have shown major omissions and distortions *within* each of these elements. Here are some examples.

The needs policy was generally more concerned with children's problems than with their potential, and it totally omitted certain kinds of needs and therefore certain kinds of children, despite its claim to be comprehensive. With the exception of children with special educational needs, the approach to needs was uneven and sometimes weak in the vital areas of diagnosis, assessment and provision. (See Chapter 2.)

The approach to curriculum was strong on rhetoric about the whole, but weak on detail about specifics. Such specifics appeared to receive attention in a fairly random way, and there were notable omissions from the specifics attended to. Among these, the omission of aspects of language was particularly serious. (See Chapter 3.)

The proper concern with curriculum breadth and balance could be subverted at three levels: the Authority, the school, and the classroom. At Authority level, the INSET programme, as later sections of this chapter will show, attended to some areas at the expense of others. At school level, the programmes and strategies for curriculum review, management and development, and the staffing of curriculum leadership posts, could sometimes reinforce such discrepancies. At classroom level, the attention on some areas of the curriculum could sometimes be achieved only by the deliberate neglect of others, the reasons having to do partly with teachers' attempts to conform to other advisory expectations: those relating to classroom organization. Moreover, at this level, PRINDEP's analysis of the *generic activities* of which all curriculum practice is constituted showed the considerable imbalance discussed in detail in Chapters 3 and 4.

The commended approach to teaching strategies was highly partisan in respect of the particular kinds of practice which were endorsed. Moreover, it tended to present a view of practice as constituted largely of issues to do with the visual appearance of classrooms and matters of organization relating to children's grouping. There was a general neglect of the teacher–pupil and pupil–pupil interactions on which learning depends, and indeed of learning as such; the message appeared to be that if the 'environment of learning' was correctly established, learning, and appropriate learning at that, would follow. Coupled with the neglect of diagnosis and assessment in the 'needs' part of the programme, this constituted an approach to children's learning which was too generalized and unfocused to have any significant impact. (See Chapter 4.)

The policy on home–school links was never properly defined, despite its prominence in the programme's initial aims. (See Chapter 5.)

The lessons for the future are clear. First, the Authority's approach to each of the elements of practice central to PNP – needs, curriculum, teaching strategies and home–school – can now be strengthened and extended in the light of the material presented in our twelve reports; each of these elements, though specific to PNP, is also a perennial concern in education and the issues therefore remain important. Second, the formulation of the Authority's educational policies and programmes, especially those which teachers are expected to translate into day-to-day practice, should from now on be grounded in prior consultation with teachers and others, together with analysis of relevant conceptual and empirical research, and those devising such policies and programmes should be able to justify them in terms of the considerations which this process will reveal.

PNP POLICY: IMPLEMENTATION

The main strategies for implementing PNP policy can be divided into two groups, LEA-based and school-based:

LEA-based strategies:
• the day-to-day work of advisory and PNP support staff;
• the administrative service of the Education Department;
• the Authority's centrally mounted in-service courses;
• the work of the Primary Schools Centre.

School-based strategies:
• enhanced staffing under PNP;
• the PNP coordinator;
• extra capitation;
• refurbishment.

The various school-based strategies have been considered in Chapters 2–6. In the present chapter we consider aspects of the LEA-based strategies in greater detail.

Advisory staff

The LEA judged the role of the advisory staff to be pivotal to its attempts to improve the quality of primary education in Leeds. Though not part of the Primary Needs Programme, the parallel expansion of the advisory service needs to be noted in this context, since members of the service became the Authority's chief agents in PNP's interpretation and implementation. Before 1985, there were four specialist primary advisers; the LEA then started to rapidly expand the service, the exercise coinciding with restructuring of the administration as a whole. The result, by 1988, was a separate Department of Primary Education with seven advisers, eight advisory teachers, various support staff based in Merrion House, at the Primary Schools Centre or elsewhere, and an administrative officer and clerks, all headed by a Director of Primary Education. This was another powerful signal that primary education had ceased to be the Cinderella of the education service in Leeds. After the 1988 Education Reform Act, the primary team expanded further to accommodate the additional responsibilities placed on LEAs by the Act.

Because the advisory service was so deeply enmeshed in PNP, it is difficult to divorce its contribution from the many aspects and contexts of the programme which are discussed elsewhere in this report. However, certain general observations are merited.

Advisory staff were tireless in their advocacy of PNP and in their efforts to secure its effective implementation. A careful division of labour within the team sought to ensure that most aspects of the programme (with notable omissions referred to in previous chapters) would be effectively managed.

Though subject to shared procedures, each member of the advisory team worked in a different way, modifying formal responsibility in the light of individual personality and experience. Thus, though our surveys document a generalized view of the service as being at best only moderately effective, heads and teachers viewed individual members of the advisory team very differently, being unstinting in their praise of some, rather less so of others.

The advisory attributes to which teachers responded most positively were: ready availability, especially in a crisis; visibility, especially in the classroom; credibility at both classroom and managerial levels; preparedness to give a clear lead coupled with a willingness to listen and acknowledge that the schools, too, had expertise; a combination of authoritativeness with humility; an open, friendly and supportive manner. It goes without saying that the attributes which most antagonized teachers were the opposite of these, especially in the context of the perceptions about the need to conform referred to earlier.

One of the main difficulties for the advisory team was the way, particularly following the Education Department's reorganization, they had to combine their advisory role with considerable administrative responsibilities, both for 'their' schools and across the system as a whole. All members of the central team at Merrion House (the Education Department's offices) were severely stretched in terms of both time and the range of roles they were expected to encompass, and it was therefore inevitable that some aspects of their job could be successfully accomplished only at the expense of others. The need to retain the primacy of the professional advisory function is surely paramount, and the Authority might well wish to find ways of reducing the administrative burden on advisory staff. These matters ought to be included in the 1991 advisory restructuring exercise (Leeds City Council 1991c).

The physical conditions in which Merrion House members of the advisory team had to work were, and at the time of going to press remain, grossly inadequate. They shared a cramped open-plan area in which they were disposed rather in the manner of a traditional typing pool. There was no privacy for the interviews and telephone conversations of a sensitive kind which are part and parcel of an adviser's job. When most or all of the team were present, noise levels and constant interruptions effectively frustrated work which needed sustained thinking. Clerical and administrative backup were provided at only a modest level. The fact that the conditions outlined here seem to be all too common in LEAs nationally (Audit Commission 1989b) does not diminish the need to do something about them. The upgrading of the working environment of advisory staff must be treated as a priority.

Administration

As we have noted above, the administrative arm of PNP acquired a poor image. This judgement – as with that of the advisory service – can be accounted for partly in terms of the traditional antagonism of schools to 'the office' which pervades many LEAs. Such antagonism is often almost unthinking, is frequently unmerited, and seems in any event a necessary device whereby the professional culture of a school sustains itself. An LEA, then, fulfils a scapegoat function – as, indeed, do other contingent groups like teacher educators and HMI.

However, in our many interviews with teachers and heads in individual schools, this generalized view was sometimes fleshed out by reference to specific instances and frustrations, of which the most common were the following: the difficulty of obtaining vital information; the persistent unavailability of individuals who possessed such information; the lack of departmental awareness about who was responsible for what; the classic 'doctor's receptionist' tendency among clerical staff to prevent heads from gaining access to advisory staff and other officers; the Byzantine complexity of the departmental arrangements at Merrion House; the lack of reciprocity in information flow: schools felt that Merrion House tended to bombard them with directives and requests, many of them urgent, yet was unwilling to reciprocate by supplying the schools with what they, often equally urgently, required; and the failure of Merrion House officers and staff to answer letters.

Our final questionnaire to all Leeds primary heads asked, *inter alia*, for ratings of the effectiveness of the LEA's various mechanisms for supporting its primary schools: the administration at Merrion House; communication and consultation between the LEA and its schools; the work of the advisory service. In view of the points above, it is hardly surprising that none of these was rated as more than moderately effective, and only the advisory staff were rated as significantly better than ineffective. On this there was general agreement between the three PNP Phases, with a tendency for Phase 2 schools to be most satisfied and Phase 3 least.

The PNP in-service support programme

This section reverts to a finer level of detail because it includes hitherto unpublished material. We discussed the Authority's INSET provision briefly in Report 1, then in Report 6 we explored the style and initial impact of courses and the assumptions about professional development which they reflected. The present section is more concerned with the facts and figures of PNP INSET between

1985 and 1989. Its basis is systematic monitoring of the full complement of courses over this period, and its direct evaluation of some twenty-five of them.

Centrally provided INSET was an essential and substantial part of the Primary Needs Programme. Most courses were mounted at the Primary Schools Centre, also a PNP innovation. In the early days of the programme, these courses all bore the label 'PNP' and many were for PNP staff only. As the programme expanded, the courses lost their specificity of content and audience and became largely indistinguishable from the rest of the Authority's central INSET programme for primary schools. However, it is important to note that PNP provided the resources and framework for the considerable expansion and diversification of such courses between 1985 and 1990: it was not so much that PNP was submerged as that PNP and primary provision became synonymous. The messages of the new courses were clearly rooted in PNP. In the analysis which follows, we have concentrated on courses mounted at the Primary Schools Centre.

The general diversification of INSET in the later stages of PNP came too late for us to include it in our programme, and in any case our resources were already fully stretched. However, it is important to list these alternative modes and thus acknowledge the variety of provision in the Authority. They included, in addition to the extensive programme at the Primary Schools Centre: programmed school-based INSET; INSET supported by the Authority but provided by external agents; INSET related to school reviews; and the expanding school-led INSET initiative. The programme at the Primary Schools Centre remained by far the largest part of the Authority's central INSET commitment during the evaluation period and an important medium for the transmission of advisory views on good practice.

During the first four years of PNP, the Authority appears to have mounted no fewer than 376 primary in-service courses at the Primary Centre. The courses covered a very wide range in both style and content. In style they ranged from formal talks to intensive workshops and such innovative features as the model classroom to which course participants were invited to return with interested colleagues by appointment to discuss its features with an advisory teacher. A detailed discussion of the implications of the different course styles can be found in our sixth report. The variation in content was enormous, although for the purposes of this analysis the course topics have necessarily been grouped into rather broad categories.

In descending order of frequency:

- 31 per cent of the courses dealt with specific individual areas of the curriculum;
- 18 per cent were concerned with social issues, covering such topics as race, gender, drugs and child abuse;
- 16 per cent were dedicated to specific professional roles such as those of PNP coordinators, probationers or permanent supply teachers;
- 12 per cent were concerned with the introduction of the national curriculum;
- 8 per cent dealt with issues of classroom management, including teaching strategies, children's behaviour, and so on;

- 8 per cent covered such whole-school issues as management and curriculum leadership;
- 6 per cent dealt with special educational needs;
- a nominal 0 per cent (in fact a quarter of 1 per cent, or one course out of the total of 376) was concerned with home–school links.

It would be dangerous to assume that this balance of topics necessarily reflects the Authority's PNP priorities very accurately. Courses vary a great deal in both their length and the number of people who attend them, and it would clearly be unjustified to assume that a single course on one topic was outweighed by, say, five courses on another if the single course involved fifty teachers in a full day's attendance each week for a term, while each of the five other courses lasted only a couple of hours and catered for half a dozen teachers. For a closer indication of the Authority's priorities, we have therefore incorporated the length of each course and the number of participating teachers into an index of *teacher-days:* for example, a three-day course for eight teachers would involve twenty-four teacher-days ($3 \times 8 = 24$), while a half-day course for seventeen teachers would involve eight and a half teacher-days ($^{1}/_{2} \times 17 = 8^{1}/_{2}$). We took half a day as the minimum duration for a course, recording that amount of time even for courses which, for example, took place after school hours.

Figure 7.1 shows the allocation of time (measured in teacher-days) to each of the course themes listed earlier. It is immediately clear that some topics received considerably more, or less, attention than would be suggested by the number of courses allocated to them.

Thus, although material tailored to specific professional roles was delivered in only 16 per cent of courses, it accounted for well over a quarter of all the teacher-days devoted to primary INSET, a proportion of time exactly equal to that spent on all individual areas of the curriculum together.

Social issues, which between them were the subject of almost a fifth of the courses, accounted for only 9 per cent of the total number of teacher-days: they tended to be short, workshop-style courses with few participants. At the other extreme, special educational needs – with only a third as many courses as social issues – accounted for slightly more teacher-days, although still only 11 per cent of the total time.

The National Curriculum, as well as specific curriculum areas, received slightly fewer teacher-days than would be suggested by the number of courses allocated to them.

Home–school links, the promotion of which was originally considered important enough to make it one of the four original aims of PNP, accounted for only one teacher-day in every hundred devoted to primary INSET.

The curriculum areas accorded the greatest number of teacher-days were maths, English and science, with English accounting for more than twice as many as science, and these two areas between them taking up about as many teacher-days as maths on its own. A number of other areas of the curriculum – art and craft, PE, music, CDT, computers, dance and so on – were given comparatively

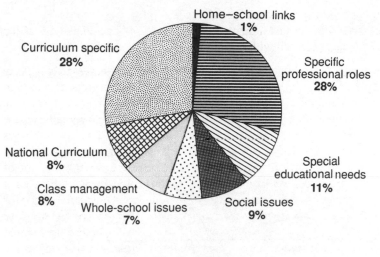

Teacher-days

Figure 7.1 Primary INSET: allocation of time to course themes, 1985–9

little time, amounting to the same number of teacher-days between them as were spent on science alone.

With the passage of time there were changes in both the overall amount of INSET provision at the Primary Centre and in its priority areas. The 9,714 teacher-days spent in this way during the school year 1988–9 (a threefold increase since 1985–6) reflect a very substantial investment of human and material resources, although it should be added that with about 2,400 primary teachers in the Authority the figures represent a rise from an average of only just over one day's provision per teacher in 1985–6 to about four days' provision in 1988–9.

The major areas of increased provision during the four years are illustrated in Figure 7.2.

From the beginning of PNP, the recruitment of new staff, often with new and untested areas of responsibility, demanded intensive in-service provision tailored to specific roles. Even in the first year, when fewer than a third of Leeds primary schools were involved in PNP, this requirement accounted for 760 teacher-days; but from year to year, as more and more schools became involved and as roles proliferated, the investment of time increased until in the fourth year it stood at 2,035 teacher-days.

In-service provision relating to special educational needs, though involving a much more modest investment of time throughout, showed a steady and regular increase from year to year.

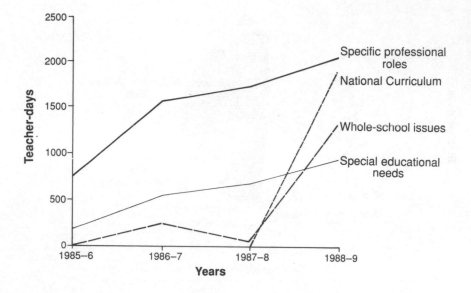

Figure 7.2 Primary INSET: major increases in provision, 1985–9

During the first three years, very little time was spent on such whole-school issues as management and curriculum leadership, but in 1988 an apparent change of priorities led to a dramatic increase in provision in this area from an average of 102 teacher-days a year to a somewhat startling 1,280. If to these one adds other emerging initiatives in management INSET – the management training programme now firmly in place (Leeds City Council 1991a), school-led INSET, and external management courses supported by the LEA – then the massive scale of provision for management training by the 1990s becomes very clear.

The impending introduction of the National Curriculum imposed a new demand towards the end of the four-year period, and during the final year 1,813 teacher-days were spent preparing teachers for their new responsibilities.

Within the area of curriculum-specific courses at the Primary Centre there were some marked changes of priority during the four years, and these are illustrated in Figure 7.3.

The graph shows how mathematics courses followed an alternating on–off pattern in which a year of massive time investment in courses was followed by a comparatively quiet year. During the first three years an average of well under 200 teacher-days a year were spent on English courses, a surprisingly modest allocation of time in view of the status of English as a core curriculum area. As if to make up for this, in the fourth year the number of teacher-days shot up to 1,254, an amount of time exceeded only by courses devoted to specific professional roles. No courses at all were devoted to science during the first two

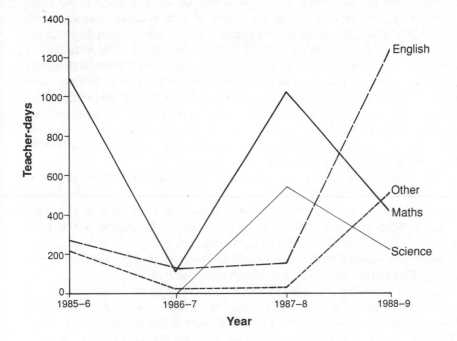

Figure 7.3 Primary INSET: changing curriculum priorities, 1985–9

years. The third year saw a major initiative in this area, involving 545 teacher-days, while in the fourth year there was something of a reversal as the amount of time was cut back by well over a half. Finally, though the rest of the curriculum was allocated well under 100 teacher-days during the first three years, there was a substantial rise during the fourth year.

In view of the fact that INSET was only one integral aspect of a very large and complex package of PNP resources, it is difficult to pinpoint its unique effect on daily practice in the Authority, although this is precisely the task we undertook in relation to one major series of courses for our sixth and tenth reports. We found that in the long term a little under a third of the participating teachers had been significantly influenced by what they had heard and seen and had made major changes in their classroom practice as a result. Others had made more superficial changes.

To augment this kind of study, in the summer of 1989 we asked all Leeds primary heads to rate the overall effectiveness of the PNP INSET provision in relation to each of the four PNP aims. At best the programme was rated no more than moderately effective, being considered completely ineffective in respect of home–school links.

In general our direct evaluation of the sample of courses referred to here showed that a course's effectiveness is closely bound up with the nature and substance of the messages being conveyed. Any tendency to diffuseness or ambiguity led to a wide range of interpretations and allowed teachers and heads to assert in good faith, whatever the nature of their practice, that they were implementing the LEA's policies and principles. They were able to do this partly because some of the messages were generalized enough to allow virtually any interpretation, and partly because messages sometimes combined minute practical detail with broad general principle, allowing teachers to feel they were taking a step in the right direction by changing the surface appearance of their practice without altering its substance. Change at deeper than surface level was maximized as a result of those courses whose messages about practice were clear, unambiguous and precise as to both their substance and their status (as policy, recommendation, suggestion or option).

The effectiveness of courses was also heavily dependent on the degree of consistency and general agreement between the advisers, heads and coordinators who each had a role in the improvement of practice and who each brought their separate influence to bear on the teachers who attended the courses. Where these agents of change were in accord with each other, and where some at least of them were directly engaged in the deeper levels of the everyday classroom practice of the teachers concerned, significant change tended to follow.

During the later stages of the Primary Needs Programme, as we have noted, the Authority started to introduce school-led INSET, first on an experimental basis to some 30 per cent of primary schools, then across the sector as a whole. Since this initiative was financially and administratively separate from PNP, we cannot comment on it here. However, it should be noted that the demands of the National Curriculum, assessment and LMS have been such as to require the Authority to maintain at least as high a centralized INSET profile as previously, and present provision retains, alongside the new agenda of concerns dictated by the 1988 Education Reform Act (ERA), many of the courses and themes established during the PNP period. Moreover, as we argued earlier, the circumstances of particular schools are such as to make it imperative that LEAs maintain a significant stake in centralized INSET. Schools without the quality of leadership or the collective capacity or will to identify and meet their professional development needs are by no means uncommon, and they will always form a problematic minority in any LEA's provision. The current ideology of devolution may favour letting such schools, along with all the others, sort out their own affairs, but that is hardly fair to their teachers, still less to their pupils.

For as long as the Authority retains its commitment to centralized INSET, therefore, the points we raised in our sixth report about the *style* of such courses remain relevant. There we identified and discussed in detail a number of factors critical to the quality and impact of any such course: the clarity and appropriateness of the messages conveyed; the degree of match between messages as intended and as received; the appropriateness of the methods used to convey the messages in question.

We also identified three key questions which need to be addressed as part of the process of devising such courses:

- *General or specific target?* The more precisely a target audience is defined, and the more homogeneous it is, the greater a course's potential for an extended impact.
- *Who defines teachers' professional needs?* Such needs can be defined by others (advisory staff or heads, for example), by teachers themselves, or through a process of discussion and negotiation.
- *Professional training or professional self-development?* An in-service activity can be conceived as something one person does to another, with the assumption that change is most effectively produced from outside; or as a process in which teachers are centrally involved in analysing their own situation and needs and working out the best ways of tackling these.

We showed how although such questions allowed a wide range of possible approaches to INSET, even within the context of a central provision, and despite the market research which preceded the drawing up of each year's programme, the Authority tended towards a particular combination of imprecise targeting, top–down views of teachers' needs, and external agents adopting training or instructing roles.

It could be argued that centralized INSET has this character of necessity, and that the other possibilities can be achieved through school-based INSET. Our knowledge of approaches to INSET offered by a variety of providing bodies – other LEAs, higher education institutions and so on – shows that the style and quality of INSET have less to do with where they take place than with how those involved stand in relation to questions such as those above, not to mention fundamental prerequisites like their professional knowledge and skill. In this sense, therefore, the now fashionable polarization of school-led and agency-provided INSET is misplaced and misleading. There is no guarantee at all that the former, simply by taking place in a teacher's place of work, will somehow be more relevant or valuable than the latter (a point made over a decade ago – Alexander 1980 – in the context of a previous incarnation of current debates).

We argue therefore, now as in our sixth report, that among the critical requirements in an INSET programme are the following: the diversity of teachers' needs must be acknowledged and addressed; teachers themselves must be central to the process of defining their needs; and to meet diverse needs there must be diverse INSET programmes: not just as to their *content* and *level*, but also in their *style* and *venue*. A mixed economy of school-led, LEA provided, and independent agency provided would seem to be the minimum requirement

It is clear that the Authority adjusted its approach to INSET quite considerably after the early days of PNP and in the light of our sixth report and feedback from schools. More courses and activities were targeted on specific groups; more attention was paid to consumer opinion; and there was greater diversity within the system as a whole. Preserving such diversity in the context of diminishing INSET budgets and the trend to school-led INSET is going to become increasingly difficult, but since it is very much in the interests of the professional health of the teaching force it must remain a priority.

CONCLUSION

This chapter has made a number of points about the way in which PNP policy was formulated and communicated; about the means and manner of its interpretation; its substance; and the strategies adopted to secure its implementation. We have acknowledged the vital, substantial and positive role played by the LEA in all these matters. However, we have also drawn attention to some less satisfactory features, several of them fundamental.

Among these was the basic stance adopted by the LEA towards its primary heads and teachers, as demonstrated in numerous aspects of the Primary Needs Programme. The shift we commend – from a stance which teachers view as authoritarian and bureaucratic to one founded on professional partnership – is not only preferable in terms of the quality of relationships within the Authority, but is also far more likely to deliver the very improvements in professional practice for which the Primary Needs Programme was established.

In this and other chapters we have discussed the various LEA-based and school-based strategies devised to secure the implementation of PNP. In our tenth report (Alexander *et al.* 1989: 289–90) we acknowledged that these ought to have been an 'irresistible combination'; yet too often they failed to deliver their potential because of a lack of *linkage* between the key elements, particularly between advisory staff, heads, PNP coordinators and class teachers. It must be clear that improved liaison between these parties will help, but this is only part of the requirement. If the basic relationship between LEA and schools is divisive, liaison will remain frustrated by problems of power, status and value. For effective linkage to be achieved between the various elements in the Authority's policies for educational reform, relationships as well as procedures must change.

Throughout the present chapter, and indeed elsewhere in this report, we have intimated that policies too must come in for scrutiny. We have raised many questions about the particular package of policies, recommendations, messages and specifications through which the Authority sought to implement its vision of primary education.

However, beyond the question of the character, quality and impact of such particular ideas are two more fundamental questions about LEA policy in general: how should it be arrived at, and on what should it focus? Is it really appropriate for policy to deal with such matters as classroom display, layout, grouping and teaching methods, to take four by now familiar examples? Should an LEA be telling teachers how to teach? Or should policy concentrate more on clarifying the goals and outcomes of *learning*, and on providing the kind of support which will enable schools to identify for themselves the best possible ways of achieving such goals and outcomes? It could be argued that Leeds LEA sought and expected consensus on aspects of primary education (such as classroom practice) where consensus is neither possible nor appropriate, while at the same time neglecting those other aspects (such as the curriculum and home–school links) where consensus was both desirable and possible.

Just as there are many ways of organizing and running an effective school, so there are many ways of running an LEA. It was not part of our brief to undertake a comparative study of policy, strategy and professional roles and relationships in different LEAs, but we strongly commend the study as an adjunct to the appraisal of Authority practices to which Leeds committed itself in response to the recommendations in our final report. Those undertaking it will encounter an extent of diversity which they may find surprising, as well as numerous examples of local authority practice in which members, officers and advisers have successfully managed to reconcile their statutory responsibilities with a commitment to genuine partnership with teachers and parents.

We note that at the time of going to press a restructuring of the advisory service is under consideration (Leeds City Council 1991c). The draft proposals tend to emphasize advisory *structures* and *roles*. We believe that the Authority should also consider, in the light of our report, the *focus* and *style* of advisory activity, especially in respect of the day-to-day work of primary teachers and heads.

In the light of the foregoing, it is worth recalling the six tasks commended by the Audit Commission (1989a) for post-ERA LEAs. These include:

- leadership and the articulation of an educational vision;
- partnership and support;
- planning;
- provision of information;
- regulation and quality control;
- channelling funds.

The PNP experience suggests that several of these will need careful thought. LEA leadership is vital, but we have raised questions about the form it might take and the aspects of education with which it should be concerned. Leadership, of course, should be confused neither with autocracy nor omniscience. Partnership should be genuine, rather than paternalism in disguise. As the Audit Commission notes: 'Schools will need support in the new environment. That support should not maintain institutions in a client or subservient role. Rather it should be designed to assist them to achieve autonomy' (Audit Commission 1989a). The provision of information presupposes a two-way exchange both as a concomitant of genuine partnership and in order that LEA decisions and information are grounded in an exact and sympathetic understanding of schools' situations and needs. Finally, quality control: it is a complex, sophisticated and highly responsible enterprise, demanding knowledge and skills which cannot be presumed and therefore require proper training, together with a full and open debate with those whose work is under review about the criteria whereby quality is to be judged. Without such a debate, as the PNP experience has amply demonstrated, an LEA's judgements of quality will certainly not lack power: but they may well lack legitimacy.

8   Summary of main findings

In this chapter we compress into summary form the main findings and issues discussed so far. With a few minor amendments (such as the deletion of paragraph numbers and cross-references to the relevant numbered paragraphs in earlier chapters) they are presented as they appeared in the final report.

AIMS OF PNP

The four aims of the Primary Needs Programme were appropriately focused – on children's needs, teaching strategies, the curriculum and links between school and home – but they were too generalized to provide a secure base-line for a substantial programme of financial investment and structural change.

However, the statement of aims was but one of a large number of written and oral policy statements about primary education which the Authority issued between 1985 and 1990. Some of these, too, suffered from problems of ambiguity and opaqueness. Moreover, heads and teachers were often expected to adopt ideas and practices on the basis of belief and exhortation rather than argument and evidence. This approach does little to help teachers cut through the educational rhetoric and sort out those practices which are most productive in terms of the quality of children's learning.

PHASES OF PNP

There were 71 mainly inner-city schools in PNP Phase 1, 56 schools in Phase 2, with the remaining 103 schools being in Phase 3. Given PNP's commitment to positive discrimination in favour of children and schools with particular needs, the phasing system for introducing schools to the programmme was, by and large, appropriate and equitable. There were of course anomalies, but some would have occurred whatever mechanisms for resource allocation had been adopted.

RESOURCES FOR PNP

The Authority allocated £13.75 million pounds to PNP over the four years 1985–9. Most of this money (£11.25 million) was spent on the main strategy of enhanced staffing, with over 500 additional appointments made during this period. The remainder was divided between increased capitation for all schools, refurbishment of some twenty-five of them, and in-service support. The Phase 1 schools had the largest share of these resources.

CHILDREN'S NEEDS

The main aim of PNP was 'to meet the identified needs of all children, and in particular those experiencing learning difficulties'. The intention was to address the needs of the majority of children through a combination of the 'broadly-based curriculum' and 'flexible teaching strategies', and to use additional programmes and resources to cater for certain specific categories of need. These included special educational needs, ethnic minority and multicultural needs, equal opportunity and gender-related needs, and social and/or material disadvantage.

We identified four features essential to a properly founded needs policy or programme: a clear *definition* of the categories of needs in question; procedures for the *identification* of children within each category; means for the *diagnosis* of the precise needs of each child so identified; and appropriate educational and curricular *provision* to meet these needs. The four categories of need chosen by the Authority varied considerably in the extent to which they met these conditions, at both LEA and school level. Needs policy in general, despite its centrality to PNP, evolved piecemeal with some parts not fully thought through.

In terms of resourcing, comprehensiveness of focus and perceived impact, the most extensive and successful part of the needs programme was that designed for children with special educational needs, with well-thought-out and systematic procedures for identification and diagnosis, highly regarded INSET courses, and initially generous provision through a combination of enhanced staffing and central support. However, the provision was concentrated mainly in Phase 1 schools, and in the later stages of PNP even these schools claimed to be encountering increased difficulty in sustaining their earlier staffing commitments in this area.

Despite the integrative intentions of recent legislation, the Authority continued its administrative separation of special educational needs from primary education. This generated confusion in policy and a certain lack of coherence in practice, which the Authority sought to address in its 1990 advisory restructuring.

The Authority displayed a clear commitment to meeting the needs of children from ethnic minority groups, to combating racism, and to extending multicultural understanding. This commitment was backed by a range of resources, facilities and support staff.

Nevertheless, and notwithstanding the generally good quality of what was provided by the LEA, the actual scale of professional support remained inadequate to the task. Provision was patchy, and professional attitudes ranged from a sensitive understanding of the issues to the blandly ignorant. Some staff failed to distinguish between ethnic minority and multicultural needs, and as a result refused to acknowledge their obligations in respect of the latter.

There is much work to be done here. Professional attitudes and perceptions need to change, and professional knowledge and understanding about societal and cultural matters, as well as about strategies for multicultural education, need to be increased.

Equal opportunities and gender were given a high profile in Authority policy, but again the situation on the ground was uneven and in some cases inadequate. For too many teachers, gender was not taken seriously as an issue. The problem was exacerbated by the way gender inequality was often built into school management structures, and to some extent into the curriculum. Provision was sparse, and often tokenistic. LEA support for developing professional understanding of gender issues was qualitatively good but quantitatively inadequate. However, there were notable exceptions to these trends at the level of individual schools and classrooms.

The larger part of PNP resourcing was concentrated on schools where significant proportions of children were experiencing social and/or material disadvantage. Beyond this, policy offered little. There was no guidance on provision other than the commitments to improving the visual environment and offering a broad curriculum and flexible teaching. While *context* was attended to, therefore, *curriculum content* was largely ignored, and especially those basic areas of the curriculum like reading which are so critical to the improvement of children's educational and career prospects. There was a tendency to acquiesce in low expectations of disadvantaged children and to define their needs in emotional rather than educational terms. Of all aspects of PNP, this one raises the most serious questions about value for money. At the same time, and regardless of the lack of other than financial support from the Authority, certain schools were tirelessly and effectively tackling the needs of these children in the comprehensive way required.

There was no policy for other categories of need. A particularly notable omission was children of high ability, the more serious in view of the widespread evidence nationally that such children underachieve in primary schools, partly because too little is expected of them. The lack of Authority policy was frequently mirrored at school level.

Overall, thinking on children's needs, despite its commendable focus on specific categories, was incomplete. It tended too often to falter on the issue of provision, and it seriously underestimated the extent to which professional attitudes and understanding are vital factors in the improvement of practice. More fundamentally, it was grounded in a *deficit* view of needs. That is to say, it tended to focus on what children *cannot* do rather than what they *can* do, and in (rightly) attending to their *problems* it underplayed or ignored their *potential*. Such an approach can encourage low expectations and a failure to attend properly to the needs of children other than those with 'problems'. In this respect, despite the main PNP goal, the PNP was not really about the needs of *all* children. Policy and provision were less well-developed in the areas of diagnosis, assessment and curriculum – in other words, the precise points where a policy has its greatest potential to affect the individual child. There is a cycle of low expectations and unchallenging curriculum experiences here, which the Authority itself could help to break – not least by retaining a significant stake in centralized INSET. At the same time all concerned should look carefully for ways of meeting the needs of all children, as well as those minorities for which the Authority demonstrated a proper and necessary concern. We add that this agenda is no less important in the context of the National Curriculum and mandatory assessment: although these seek to raise expectations and improve standards, of themselves they will achieve little unless professional attitudes, knowledge and skill are also attended to.

THE CURRICULUM

Authority policy on the curriculum was contained in various documents. Regrettably, like some of its other statements on primary education, many of these were strong on values and assertion but weak on substance and justification. They thus combined, in a frustrating way, a lack of precision and argument with an expectation that they would become the mandatory cornerstones of classroom practice.

More successful in terms of their perceived impact on teachers and children were those programmes associated with certain specific subject initiatives such as PrIME and ESG science.

The Authority's curriculum policies produced various responses from heads and teachers. While some were happy to espouse them without question, others were more critical, the more so because of the Authority's failure to consult any but a small number of heads about their content. But the main problem was that the PNP plank of the 'broadly-based curriculum' turned out to be fairly meaningless. At the same time, PRINDEP data repeatedly showed that the curriculum in action in many schools and classrooms was not, by any of the possible definitions of the phrase, broadly based. The Authority's lead on matters concerning the character, range and balance of the primary curriculum as a whole, therefore, was inadequate.

Schools exploited PNP resources in a variety of ways for reviewing, developing and managing the curriculum. PNP coordinators played a prominent part, whether as *managers, consultants, enhancers* or *facilitators*. Schools made constructive use of the potential of enhanced staffing to secure a collaborative approach to curriculum development in the classroom through teachers teaching together (TTT). The data show a wide range of strategies overall, and we would trust that more of these could enter the management vocabulary of more schools. In some, the potential of TTT was wasted because support teachers were marginalized; in others, highly experienced and qualified coordinators had to be content with a merely facilitating role.

The processes of curriculum review at school level took various forms. Less variable was the tendency to concentrate on reviewing and developing some subjects while neglecting others. The list tended to be dominated by mathematics and language, with science occupying an increasingly important place over the evaluation period. The review process was buttressed by PNP INSET and

Development Fund support for the subjects chosen. The neglect of many other curriculum areas was a persistent problem, the more serious in view of the close correspondence between review and development on the one hand and the quality of curriculum provision in the classroom on the other. Certain subjects now in the National Curriculum – notably art, history and geography – were, and remain, particularly vulnerable. We accept that curriculum review and development, and indeed INSET, may have to be selective. However, care should be taken to construct a cycle of attention which eventually includes all aspects of the curriculum. Without this, as has happened in Leeds, certain subjects are perennial losers, and the principles of curricular balance and entitlement are seriously compromised.

There was a significant relationship between curriculum leadership, staff status and gender, and this reinforced discrepancies in the review process and could convey inappropriate messages to staff and children alike. Schools need to be constantly alert to this problem.

Overall, schools used a wide range of strategies for curriculum review and development. These can usefully be viewed as a repertoire from which schools taking a more restricted approach to review could learn a great deal. In particular, we commend attention to the potential (and challenges) of staff meetings. They are a common ingredient in the review and development process, but were handled with widely varying degrees of competence.

One area in which the advisory team made its views on curriculum clear was the way classrooms should be physically disposed to deliver curriculum breadth and flexibility. Some teachers adopted the recommended practices; some found difficulty in doing so; others rejected them. However, while the advisory team's views had the undoubted consequence of making many Leeds primary class-rooms seem busier and more attractive, the beneficial consequences for children's learning were less clear; and for some teachers, the claim of 'flexibility' had exactly the opposite effect, strait-jacketing them into practices to which they had no real commitment and which they had difficulty in managing.

We commend close attention to the way time is used in the curriculum. At one level we discovered time being spent on different curriculum areas in similar proportions to those recorded by HMI and by other research projects. However, we also found an inverse relationship between time and efficiency: time was sometimes used least effectively in those subjects to which most time was allocated. We also noted a tendency for some teachers to create time to monitor children's learning in prioritized areas like mathematics and language by treating other areas as time fillers. Such findings have serious implications for curriculum planning and provision: children are entitled to a curriculum which is consistent in its quality across all subjects, not just those accorded most time. Moreover, the findings challenge conventional assumptions about the amounts of time the different subjects should be allocated. Given the time constraints to which primary teachers have felt increasingly subjected since the introduction of the National Curriculum, this set of issues deserves very careful attention.

We uncovered four quite distinct ways in which the curriculum in practice was defined and delivered: first, as *areas or subjects* (mathematics, language, and so on); second, as *organizational strategies* (topic work, thematic enquiry, 'choosing', etc.); third, as *generic activities* (reading, writing, collaboration, construction, drawing/painting etc.); fourth, as a combination of two or more of these. We found the idea of *generic activities* to be particularly potent as a tool for describing and evaluating curriculum practice. Regardless of subject labels, children's curriculum experiences tended to be dominated by writing, with reading, using task-specific apparatus, and listening to the teacher also prominent; collaborative activity and talking – with the teacher or with other pupils – were a long way behind. Some of these discrepancies were related to children's age, gender and perceived ability. This alternative analysis reveals a pervasive imbalance in children's curriculum experiences and conflicts sharply with primary rhetoric.

In this and other respects, the principle of the 'broadly-based curriculum' appeared not to be reflected in practice. At each level of the system we found claims to breadth and balance undermined by countervailing policies and practices: by Authority special projects favouring some areas at the expense of others; in central INSET provision; in PNP development fund allocations; in the distribution of posts of responsibility in schools; in school-based INSET; in the status of postholders and the time they had to undertake their curriculum leadership responsibilities; in the areas of the curriculum subjected to review and development; in teacher expertise; and above all in the quality of children's classroom experiences. In the end, curriculum breadth and balance are less about time allocation than the diversity and challenge of what the child encounters. Moreover, if the goals of breadth and balance are to be achieved in the classroom they must be pursued at every other level of the system as well.

We undertook a comparative study of five areas of the curriculum – English, mathematics, science, humanities/environmental studies and art – and while acknowledging the many examples of stimulating and challenging practice, noted problems of imbalance in each of them. The National Curriculum may introduce a greater degree of consistency in respect of subject content, but quality in the way such content is treated will only be achieved if the anomalies at the various levels – LEA support, school curriculum management and development, classroom provision – are attended to.

The case of English, on which we assembled data relating to talking, listening and reading, was particularly disturbing. Classroom talk, despite the apparent conversational liveliness of many classrooms, could be shown on closer examination to be somewhat impoverished and unchallenging, with a general tendency to discourage children from asking their own questions and thinking things out for themselves, and a lack of informative feedback. Our analysis of reading scores at 7+ and 9+ from 1983–91 showed no evidence that the injection of extra staff and money into Leeds primary schools, especially those in the inner city, had had a positive impact on children's reading ability, at least as measured by the Authority's tests. On the contrary, scores showed a very slight decline towards the end of the evaluation period, especially in the inner-city schools where PNP resources were concentrated. However, the situation in Leeds needs to be looked at in a national as well as in a local context.

We have recommended that the Authority continues to monitor reading standards across the city but that the screening function of its traditional tests be taken over by National Curriculum Assessment at the end of Key Stage One. It is also clear that reading must be accorded high priority in inner-city schools and that teachers in those schools need support in this endeavour. However, we have also stressed that any decline in reading standards in the inner city must be set firmly within the context of the political and economic circumstances which lead to poverty and social dislocation. Teachers and schools, however well resourced and staffed, can only do so much to counter the effects of social disadvantage, and it is too easy to use them as scapegoats for the failure of political and economic policy.

Nevertheless, the reading scores analysis does raise important questions about the PNP strategy in general. It seems probable that if the programme had addressed the curriculum in a more direct and sharply focused way, concentrating attention and resources on particular curriculum areas at a time, then the impact on the quality of children's curriculum experiences, and hence on their learning, would have been much greater. In any event, though teachers continued to give reading their attention throughout the PNP period, it received very little attention in the Authority's INSET and support programmes.

The PRINDEP evaluation highlighted the primary curriculum as an area needing attention at three levels: Authority policy, school management and classroom practice. The National Curriculum will undoubtedly change matters to some degree at each of these levels, and indeed the situation in 1991 is already very different from that of 1985–9, but the National Curriculum cannot of itself provide the understanding, skills and commitments which are needed to prevent the weaknesses and inconsistencies we have identified from reappearing in another guise. In place of vague ideological statements and piecemeal policies the primary sector now needs a substantial programme of professional development and support aimed at enhancing the curriculum expertise of all its primary staff, and targeted in the first instance on those aspects of the curriculum where studies like this have identified the greatest problems.

TEACHING STRATEGIES

The Authority rightly identified teachers' classroom practice as a critical factor in children's learning and gave it considerable prominence in documents, courses and the day-to-day work of its advisory staff in schools. The messages thus transmitted were more precise and sharply focused than those on curriculum. The general conception of 'good primary practice' was a consistent one, with the generation of a 'quality learning environment' accorded high priority.

Given the strongly visual and organizational emphasis, the impact in classrooms was readily apparent, and the Authority and schools can take considerable credit for a general improvement in the physical circumstances in which primary children and teachers work.

However, we expressed certain reservations about the prevailing approach. Though ostensibly child-centred, it paid rather more attention to teachers and classrooms than to children's learning. It presumed that the particular classroom layouts and patterns of organization commended would promote children's learning more effectively than any others. It made much of 'flexibility' but in a way which implied that only certain versions of flexibility were permitted, and it failed to treat the notion of 'good practice' as the problematic issue it manifestly is.

That being so, teachers felt themselves to be under pressure to adopt practices whose efficacy we have shown to be debatable. The most notable examples were grouping, the practice of having a multiple curriculum focus in teaching sessions, with different groups working in different curriculum areas, and the kinds of teacher–pupil interaction associated with a commitment to discovery learning. The complex patterns of classroom organization associated with the versions of good practice commended in Leeds require considerable skill on the part of the teacher. They make adequate monitoring of children's learning a particularly demanding task and children themselves may find that such arrangements reduce their opportunities for the quiet, concentrated study required by the reading and writing activities which dominate their curriculum. School and advisory staff need to look very closely at the balance of benefits and costs, for both children and teachers, in the teaching strategies and patterns of classroom organization which have been so strongly promoted in recent years.

We found the issue of *time* to be revealing and important. While children were spending time on task and on different curriculum areas in similar proportions to those identified in other studies, it was also clear that such figures are by no means inevitable or appropriate. Although the time a child spends on task relates to many factors, including some beyond the teacher's control, the organizational complexity obtaining in many primary classsrooms would seem to play a significant part. This underlines our sense that it is a grave mistake to pursue the notion of teaching strategies as somehow disconnected from children's learning on the one hand, and from teachers' intentions and attributes on the other. There are important issues here.

Similarly, our analysis of how time was used across the curriculum provoked further challenges to conventional assumptions: that the way to do a subject justice is to give it more time; and that 'balance' is about the proportions of time given to the various subjects. We found it far more instructive to analyse balance in terms of the cross-curricular 'generic activities' of reading, writing, listening, drawing/painting, collaboration and so on which are a universal feature of primary classroom life, regardless of the curriculum labels used. We identified, and questioned, the apparent imbalance in such generic activities. We argued for much greater prominence to be given to the potential of genuine pupil–pupil collaboration, and less to low-level writing, reading and drawing tasks. We noted the mismatch between the mainly solitary activities children were undertaking and the gregarious settings in which they were often expected to undertake them. It would seem to be a basic condition of effective classroom practice that the setting in which children work should be consistent with and supportive of the particular learning tasks they are given.

The quantitative and qualitative analyses of teacher–pupil interaction showed how vital a part it can play in children's learning, yet how easy it is to waste the very limited time teachers have to interact with each child. We argued for a more discriminating balance of questions, statements and instructions; for fewer pseudo-questions and more questions of a kind which encourage children to reason and speculate; for more opportunities for children themselves to ask their own questions and have these addressed; for oral feedback to children which without being negative is more exact and informative than mere praise; for both questioning and feedback to strike a balance between the *retrospective* function of assessing and responding to what has been learned so far, and the *prospective* function of taking the child's learning forward; and for much more use to be made of structured pupil–pupil interaction both as a learning tool and as a means of helping teachers to function in a more considered manner and therefore more effectively.

It is essential that all these issues be addressed openly, free from ideology and rhetoric and from the sense, powerfully conveyed by respondents, that peda-gogical orthodoxies must not be challenged. The questions are clear: what kinds of learning should primary schools seek to promote, and what are the most effective ways of achieving them? It is here – with learning and educational outcomes rather than the 'learning environment' – that policy and planning for classroom practice should start.

Enhanced staffing under PNP enabled schools to break away from the tradi-tion of one teacher per class and experiment with various forms of classroom-based professional collaboration. This proved to be one of the most significant aspects of PNP, and one which had, and has, considerable potential. We identified four essential dimensions of such collaborations, which we – and subsequently others – termed TTT (teachers teaching together): purposes, par-ticipants, collaborative style and pupil organization. Applied to the practices emerging in the period 1985–9, this framework yielded a variety of ways in which TTT can help both children and teachers, and a diversity of forms that such collaborations can take.

However, we also identified problems that needed to be resolved: purposes have to be crystal clear; matters of status, leadership and the division of responsi-bility have to be negotiated; and all such collaborations have to be jointly planned. We therefore cautioned against seeing TTT as a panacea. If not properly thought through and implemented, it can be disruptive, disorganized and fraught with tensions between the teachers concerned – and therefore considerably less beneficial to children than the solo teaching it replaces.

Since teachers were the main resource in PNP, it is teaching – and hence learning – which should have benefited most from the Council's initiatives. There is little doubt that changes in teaching took place. However, the possibilities and limits of improvement were determined by a number of factors: existing classroom expertise, individual school and classroom circumstances, professional attitudes and commitments; and, framing all of these, the quality of the thinking which informed the appraisal of existing practice and the exploration of alternatives. In these respects, too, there was much variation between schools.

However, the lead given by the Authority in this regard was not a strong one. In an LEA where schools are encouraged to resolve these matters for themselves and in their own ways, the character of official thinking about classroom practice is not particularly important. But Leeds neither was nor is such an LEA, at least where its primary schools are concerned. The models of teaching it commended were expected to be influential, and the Authority saw itself as having a duty to provide a clear lead on the direction and character of primary classroom practice.

We have identified both strengths and achievements where classroom practice is concerned, particularly in the transformation of the physical settings in which teaching and learning take place, and the exploitation of the potential of classroom-based professional collaboration. However, if the Authority is to continue to seek to influence day-to-day classroom practice to this degree (and this itself is a proposition which must now be questioned) then certain fundamental changes are called for.

Thus, 'good primary practice' must cease to be presented as an uncontentious absolute. Good practice is conceptually and empirically problematic, and ought to be treated as such. It is inappropriate to act as though consensus exists (or should exist) over good practice, and doubly inappropriate to expect conformity to a particular version of it.

Much more account should be taken of the individual teacher in discussing classroom practice; the notion that a 'practice' can exist independently of the practitioner and can be imposed without regard for the individual's personality, intentions and preferences is both professionally demeaning and impractical.

Teaching needs to be discussed in a much more rounded and comprehensive way, with far less emphasis on surface aspects like display and resources; far more emphasis should be placed on the character of the minute-to-minute encounters which children have with teachers and each other, on the precise nature and purposes of the tasks they are given and the activities they undertake, and on the relationship of these and other aspects of the practice of teaching to learning.

Classroom organization and teaching strategies need to be seen as a means to an an end, not as ends in themselves, and to allow this shift the ends or purposes need to be discussed and clarified. The dilemmas and compromises which are inherent to the task of teaching need to be honestly identified and openly confronted.

Above all, the notion that the LEA can be the sole definer, arbiter and guardian of good classroom practice must be abandoned. Expertise in such matters is as likely to be found in schools as in the LEA; but in any event good practice is defined and achieved dialectically and empirically, not by decree.

LINKS WITH PARENTS AND THE COMMUNITY

Although the fostering of links between schools, parents and the community was one of the main aims of PNP, it received notably less attention than the other three. There was no clear policy on this matter, only a series of apparently unrelated initiatives. By the end of PNP, despite PRINDEP findings and recommendations on this matter, policy was still awaited.

We found the lack of apparent commitment to this aim at Authority level reflected in the deployment of PNP resources. There was virtually no INSET, and schools felt that PNP resourcing had very little impact on what they did in the home–school area.

Nevertheless, our surveys showed schools undertaking a wide range of activities in pursuit of home–school rapport and cooperation, particularly where younger children were concerned, and many schools went well beyond the obvious activities like information exchange, open days and social events to pursue more adventurous and long-term programmes.

By the end of PNP, parent–teacher liaison had a higher profile, but this was mainly due to the need to meet the requirements of the 1988 Education Act and to undertake consultations over school reorganization.

There were three specific initiatives: home–school liaison officers, Portage, and the Early Education Support Agency. Of these, only the first was part of PNP and it proved to be the most problematic, partly for administrative reasons and partly because of the delicacy of the issues of culture and status which it raised. In any case, the HSLO initiative was on a very small scale. Nevertheless, in so far as it addressed the complex issue of home–school relationships in multi-ethnic contexts, it was an important initiative which deserves to be extended in some form.

The absence of policy and the paucity of central support and initiatives meant that the majority of schools devised their own home–school policies, strategies and roles. Some exploited PNP resources, especially enhanced staffing, for this purpose. But how they acted, and with what effect, depended mainly on the attitudes and commitments of heads. This is not to say that practice was unsatisfactory: rather that it was highly variable and that it mostly had little to do with PNP, despite the Authority's intentions and despite its being written into the job specifications of PNP appointees.

We have to conclude that home–school links was the forgotten PNP aim. Yet, paradoxically, the quality and character of the relationships which are forged between a school, its parents and its immediate community seem a much more appropriate focus for LEA policy than, say, the fine detail of classroom practice. The whole structure and ambience of local government are community-centred: the electoral ward system produces elected community representatives on councils; elected members seek to respond to community needs and views and to safeguard community interests; and councils have a generous array of other policies which engage directly with the quality of life which communities experience. Schools, and especially primary schools, have always been regarded as essential to a concept of a complete community, and many schools have taken their responsibilities and opportunities in this regard very seriously.

It might also be argued that despite recent legislation (some would say because of it) parent–teacher relations are still too often fraught with fear, suspicion and misunderstanding; that there is still too much teacher stereotyping of 'good' and 'bad' homes and parents; and that many parents still lack power in relation to their parental rights and responsibilities. The Authority missed the opportunity to use PNP resources to bring about change here: it needs now to explore other avenues. As with classroom practice, it can learn much by attending to the best of what is taking place in its schools.

MANAGING PNP IN THE SCHOOL

The Authority recognized that the effective management of PNP ideas and resources within each school was critical to the Programme's success. Its main lever for change was enhanced staffing, and in particular the role of PNP coordinator.

The phase disparities in enhanced staffing were deliberate – the Programme was one of positive discrimination in favour of children and schools with the greatest needs. However, the low enhancement in Phase 3 raised the more general question of minimum effective levels. Though any help is better than none, it is only when the enhancement is one extra teacher or more that schools really acquire the flexibility in staffing that they need if they are to carry through major reforms in curriculum and classroom practice. Most Phase 3 schools received enhancement well below this level. Moreover, the lack of seniority of most Phase 3 appointees further reduced their potential to generate change. At the other end of the scale, some Phase 1 schools were flooded with PNP staff yet scarcely knew how to employ them.

It may well have been a more sensible policy, therefore, to make the Phase 1/3 disparity less extreme, and to use the resources to ensure that *all* schools were staffed on the 1986 Select Committee recommended basis of *n* registration groups plus one, with further pro rata adjustments for school size and specific challenges like those of the inner city. The current LMS formula should be kept under review with these issues in mind.

We identified a wide range of roles undertaken by PNP Scale 1/MPG staff, with releasing class teachers and TTT most prominent. Because class size has always been a cause for complaint in primary schools, some heads used their staffing enhancement to create smaller classes. Such reductions might be marginal and therefore the enhancement tended to have less impact than when it was used for cross-school initiatives. However, many staff deployed in the latter way encountered problems in working with colleagues. The Authority appeared to have underestimated these in its programme of INSET and support. Nevertheless, in many schools enhanced staffing stirred up traditional structures and assumptions to produce a more open and reflective professional climate.

The key role of PNP coordinator was applied to a variety of tasks, of which staff development, curriculum development and special needs were pre-eminent over the evaluation period as a whole. The initially strong emphasis on special educational needs (and the attendant confusion over whether PNP was a special or general needs programme) gave way to a concentration on curriculum development, mainly in response to the shifting national agenda.

Coordinators were initially expected to do far too much. Their success depended on a sensible and achievable role being negotiated with their heads, on heads' support, staff attitudes and their own skills. They were sometimes denied the authority necessary for the fulfilment of their expected role, and it was critically important that they were seen as part of a school's management team rather than being relegated to the position of mere facilitator. Thus empowered, they could achieve a great deal, particularly in the areas of curriculum development and staff support.

Though LMS is widely felt to have reduced the scope for staffing enhancement in primary schools, we believe it to be essential that schools retain the broader managerial repertoire which PNP has encouraged. Under PNP, schools have been able to break away from the traditional conception of primary school professional life centring on just two roles: those of head and class teacher. Although one person may not be able to combine the range of roles and tasks in the way that some coordinators have, it is perfectly possible to spread these across the staff as a whole and thus maintain the momentum of innovation and support. The PNP coordinator idea, whatever its problems and imperfections in practice, represents a vision of professional collaboration, development and decision-making which primary schools can ill-afford to abandon, least of all in the era of the National Curriculum.

New staff roles dictate new management structures. We identified six main types or clusters, and noted the way that recent changes under PNP and ERA have encouraged a shift, particularly in larger schools, towards three-tier and matrix management structures. While each school must evolve its own way of working, it is clear that the traditional two-tier model has limited capacity to cope with change on the scale now being experienced.

The role of deputy head was all too often a marginal one. All deputy heads need a clear job specification and a place in school development and decision-making commensurate with their experience and seniority.

Change challenges a school's capacities for receiving ideas, reviewing practices, and making decisions. During the PNP period, many Leeds primary schools acquired greater sophistication in such matters, and both understood and exploited delegated responsibilities and collegial action. Initially, they found their way by trial and error, as LEA support was concentrated elsewhere. Subsequently, the level of Authority investment in management training expanded considerably.

However, it is important to note and counter the limitations of mainstream approaches to management training, with their top–down assumptions, their tendency to exclude all but the head and senior staff, and their focus on strategies at the expense of educational purposes. Management has become an whole-school process, entailing that every member of staff has a managerial role of some kind, and it should be approached as such in any INSET or support programmes.

The exclusion of many heads from the development of PNP, and the attempt to use PNP coordinators to carry the Authority's versions of good practice directly from Merrion House to the classroom, had unfortunate consequences for both the success of the programme and school–LEA relationships.

Heads responded to advisory views of good practice in different ways, ranging from unthinking conformity to outright rejection. Such variation reflects as much on the Authority's style and the quality of its thinking as it does on the heads, and there is a clear need for much greater dialogue between the two levels. However, it is encouraging to note the recent evidence of greater consultation between school and Authority staff and the increased participation of teachers in Authority working parties.

Equally important was dialogue on matters of purpose and policy *within* each school, especially between head and staff. Without such dialogue, and the associated openness in management and decision-making, there could be a substantial gap between a school's espoused philosophy and its classroom practice. Heads' realization of the headship role tended to fall into four main types. The more successful heads were those who remained in close touch with classroom realities and teachers' everyday concerns, who valued and developed individual staff potential, and encouraged collective decision-making.

However, while current challenges facing primary schools demand greater delegation and role specialization than hitherto, it is essential that schools avoid the trap of over-bureaucratization, and that they seek to retain and nurture the close informal collaboration which has always been an essential ingredient in effective school management.

We expressed concern about the poor quality of head–staff relationships in some schools, admittedly not always the fault of the head but often a consequence of an indefensible degree of autocratic behaviour. Equally, we noted some heads' resistance to developing their own professional understanding and their failure to engage with current educational issues. Such characteristics could have a corrosive and debilitating effect on the entire staff of a school to the obvious detriment of children as well as teachers. In such circumstances, the currently fashionable notion of 'closed-circuit' school-led INSET has certain limitations. The Authority needs to retain a significant stake in INSET run by itself and other institutions in order to prevent schools from simply recycling and reinforcing their own inadequacies.

SUPPORTING REFORM: THE ROLE OF THE LEA

PNP was an ambitious programme of reform, conceived on a large scale. The LEA's role in the Programme was an interventionist rather than a facilitating one: it devised PNP's goals and strategy, and sought closely to influence and control the Programme's implementation. The success of PNP at school and classroom level, therefore, is closely related to the role adopted by the LEA.

It would seem that in some respects the Programme, and indeed wider aspects of the Authority's approach to primary education, were centralized to an excessive degree and that this generated reactions from heads and teachers which were both powerful and counterproductive. Much of their concern centred on what they saw as the imposition from above of particular versions of 'good primary practice' and the relationship between teachers' allegiance to these and their career prospects.

The matter is a complex and delicate one, yet of all the findings from this evaluation it is one of the most pervasive and consistent, recurring in questionnaire responses and interviews, and validated by extensive observation. It also has serious implications for the professional health of the Authority and its schools, since the belief that getting on is merely a matter of saying and doing what significant others wish to hear and see produces not just disaffection and cynicism but also unthinking conformity and the loss of the professional analysis and debate which are essential to educational progress.

PNP policy was embedded in the broader framework of Authority-thinking about children's needs, the curriculum, teaching strategies, classroom practice, school management and home–school relationships. These ideas had, and were intended to have, considerable influence at school and classroom levels. Because of this, they needed to be firmly grounded in careful analysis of the issues, and justified in terms of a coherent value-position, argument and evidence. These basic requirements were not often met, and teachers were confronted with, and expected to adopt, ideas which might be little more than expressions of officially endorsed belief.

Those constructing future policies and principles should strive to make them exemplary in this regard, not least because of the encouragement this will give to schools to be rigorous in their own thinking. The particular themes of PNP – needs, curriculum, teaching strategies, home and school – remain areas of central concern, and about each of them there is now a substantial body of conceptual and empirical material to be tapped, some of it in the twelve PRINDEP reports.

In any event, the experience of PNP raises important questions about the proper focus of an LEA's policies. We showed how in certain areas – for example home–school links, the curriculum, and whole-school management – clear policies can be appropriate and helpful; and how in other areas – notably classroom practice – advisory staff seemed eager to prescribe in some detail how teachers should organize their classrooms and manage their teaching, a focus for policy and action at that level which seemed rather less appropriate. It would seem more apposite for the Authority to concentrate on identifying the goals and aspirations of the service, on raising teachers' educational sights and their expectations of children as high as possible, and on providing the opportunities and facilities for teachers to explore, debate and develop their own ways of achieving such goals, aspirations and expectations.

In the devising and implementing of PNP the Authority's advisory service was pivotal; it did much to raise the profile of primary education in Leeds, and to secure development on a number of significant fronts. Collectively, however, the service was not well regarded in the schools since it was seen to be enact many of the tendencies referred to earlier. Yet individually, advisers and advisory teachers earned considerable respect for the extent and quality of support they provided. The workloads of advisory staff, and the physical circumstances in which they work at Merrion House, are unsatisfactory and should be reviewed.

The Authority's administrative services at Merrion House acquired a poor reputation, and efforts should be made to make them more accessible and responsive.

The Authority mounted a substantial in-service programme in support of PNP, which later merged with its general primary INSET programme. The range in content and style of these courses was considerable, and over the PNP period they focused on many aspects of the curriculum, on social issues, professional roles, classroom management, curriculum development and school management, and on specific areas of child need. This report has analysed the programme of courses mounted at the Primary Schools Centre, and the teacher-days spent on them. The Centre, developed as part of PNP, made a significant and welcome contribution to professional development in the Authority. Other INSET initiatives, particularly school-led INSET and management training, were being developed towards the end of the evaluation period but they were beyond the reach of PRINDEP's time and resources.

The success of these courses in influencing the quality of school and classroom practice depended on a number of factors, some of them – like the receptiveness of teachers attending them and the willingness of schools to encourage and accommodate change – beyond the control of the course providers. At the same time, there were two recurrent factors within providers' control: the clarity and appropriateness of the messages being conveyed, and the appropriateness of the methods used to convey them. Unfortunately, certain courses were characterized by diffuse or ambiguous messages, or by the tendency to unsubstantiated assertion and prescription referred to earlier.

Our study raised wider questions about INSET, and about professional development in general. We argued that the critical requirements in an INSET programme are that the very diverse needs of different teachers be recognized and addressed, that teachers themselves be central to the process of defining their needs, and that diverse needs be met by diverse provision, in respect of not just content and level but also style and venue. The move to school-led INSET, in Leeds as elsewhere, has the potential to meet the first two of these requirements, but not necessarily the third. Accordingly, and referring to earlier anxieties about 'closed-circuit' professional development, we expressed certain reservations about the tendency of LEAs, with government encouragement, to put all their eggs in the basket of school-led INSET. Our analysis of the professional climate and management structures of primary schools suggests that such an approach would do more harm than good in some schools, and that it is therefore essential that a mixed economy for INSET be maintained, a minimum combination being provided by the school, the LEA, and independent agencies.

The Authority devised a number of strategies for implementing PNP at both school and LEA levels. The key components were, at LEA level, the work of advisory staff, centralized INSET, and central administrative support; and at school level, enhanced staffing, the coordinator role, extra capitation and re-furbishment. It is clear that enhanced staffing proved to be the single most potent strategy in the Programme, though it was not without its problems, and the potential of some PNP appointments was frustrated by attitudes and decisions at the school level.

Two other points are also clear however: first that heads ought also to have featured explicitly in the strategy from the outset, since their role proved to be critical; second, that there was a serious lack of *linkage* between the strategy's various components, particularly where advisory staff, heads, PNP coordinators and class teachers were concerned. By treating each of these as a separate constituency, rather than as a team, the Authority exacerbated the problems of communication, understanding and relationship referred to earlier, and reduced the Programme's impact.

Although we have raised questions about the Authority's role in PNP, nothing can detract from the vision of increased educational opportunity and improved practice which PNP represented. However, because the success of a policy depends so heavily on the way it is devised and implemented, and because the experience of PNP raises such serious questions about the Authority's role in this regard, it is clear that a review of Authority practices and procedures, as they affect primary education in the city, is now merited. The current restructuring of the advisory service provides a timely opportunity to address some of these issues.

9   The Primary Needs Programme: conclusions and recommendations

The summary of findings in the previous chapter has identified the main characteristics, gains and problems of the Primary Needs Programme, taking each of its aims in turn and then considering the framework of school management and LEA policy and action in which these aims were set. In this chapter we offer judgements of a more global kind before setting out some fifty-five specific recommendations to inform future policy, planning and practice in classrooms, schools and the LEA.

THE STRENGTHS OF THE PRIMARY NEEDS PROGRAMME

It is clear that the Primary Needs Programme had many positive and productive features. We would summarize these as follows.

1 The Authority's reversal of years of neglect and under-resourcing by investing in primary education.
2 The commitment to positive discrimination in favour of children and schools having the greatest social and educational needs.
3 The focus of PNP policy on four central aspects of the educational endeavour: children's needs, the curriculum, teaching strategies and links between school, home and community.
4 The generally equitable formula for distributing resources to those schools having most need of them.
5 The comprehensive programme for identifying, diagnosing and providing for children with special educational needs, and the related in-service support programme.
6 The initiatives taken to meet the needs of children from ethnic minority groups, and the effective, though small-scale, programmes aimed at combating racism and increasing multicultural understanding.
7 The attempt to tackle issues of equal opportunity and gender at every level of the system, from Council staffing policies down to classroom practice.
8 The attention given to improving the physical quality of the environment in which socially and materially disadvantaged children are educated.

9 The abandoning of the 'ring fence' staffing policy and the introduction to Leeds schools of primary teachers from other parts of the country.

10 The use made of enhanced staffing to promote curriculum review and development at whole-school level through curriculum leadership.

11 The use made of enhanced staffing at classroom level to promote curriculum support and improvement through teachers teaching together (TTT).

12 The impact of TTT on special needs provision and professional development.

13 The use of increased capitation to extend schools' resources for teaching and learning.

14 The positive impact on classrooms of the Authority's concern with the physical environment of learning.

15 The use of enhanced staffing in some schools to foster and improve home–school–community relations.

16 The opening up, as a result of enhanced staffing, of new ways for teachers to work together in the classroom and the school.

17 The innovative and often influential role of PNP coordinator.

18 The move to more collaborative and collegial approaches to policy formulation and decision-making in some schools as a result of enhanced staffing in general and coordinator activity in particular.

19 The rationalization of curriculum-related roles, the increased delegation of curriculum responsibilities, and the attention given to curriculum leadership.

20 The provision of much extended advisory and support teams for primary education.

21 The establishment of the Primary Schools Centre as a major venue for INSET and curriculum development.

22 The extensive and diverse programme of centralized INSET made available to primary teachers.

THE LESSONS OF THE PRIMARY NEEDS PROGRAMME: ALTERNATIVE STRATEGIES

The list above represents a substantial and undeniable achievement. At Authority level, policies were subjected to review, firm commitments were made, and substantial resources were allocated. At school level, the resources, at best, were used to the considerable advantage of both children and teachers.

On the basis of our evidence and analysis, therefore, we can conclude with confidence that PNP was an initiative well worth the Authority's investment.

Yet our analysis also shows that in conception and practice PNP was something of a curate's egg. Thus, if it were to be asked – as it needs to be – whether the £13.75 million was well spent, the answer would have to be that a different strategy might have given better value for money.

To those who will seek to capitalize on this judgement and on the problems which we have identified, we would point out that with a programme of such novelty and complexity the outcome could hardly be otherwise. The important thing is to learn from this experience. The extent to which those involved are prepared to do so is perhaps the most important test of the seriousness of their commitment to the long-term improvement of primary education.

In our view the Primary Needs Programme would have been considerably more effective if the following conditions had been met.

1 The programme should have had a considered and meaningful rationale, grounded in careful analysis of the issues and with close attention being given to the national research evidence in respect of the various problems to be tackled.
2 If the dominant concern was to be inner-city education, there should have been a full and radical re-assessment, before the programme started, of the needs of the children in question, having particular regard to the kinds of curriculum which would be most likely to both counter the adverse effects of disadvantage and maximize these children's educational prospects.
3 The extra resources should have been distributed to the city's primary schools in a way which responded to the particular needs and challenges identified, yet also acknowledged the historical under-staffing of *all* primary schools, avoided the extremes of Phases 1 and 3 and ensured that every school had a staffing complement which permitted viable cross-school initiatives. In our view, the minimum enhancement should have been one extra teacher per school.
4 To achieve and maintain sharpness of purpose the programme should have concentrated on a succession of carefully targeted aspects of learning, curriculum, teaching and management, putting the combined resources of staffing, capitation and in-service support behind each of these in turn.
5 There should have been close consultation and cooperation between class teachers, PNP appointees, heads and advisory staff at every stage and on every aspect of the programme, so as to nurture a professional culture which was collaborative and negotiative rather than coercive, to ensure unity of purpose and the most economic use of resources, and to maximize teachers' sense of ownership of the process of reform.
6 The LEA should have encouraged a style of engagement with the issues which was open and analytical, and which sought to develop teachers' and heads' professional knowledge, raise their expectations of their pupils, and extend their repertoire of ways of tackling the problems identified.
7 The situations and dilemmas of practitioners – both heads and class teachers – should have been acknowledged, and efforts should have been made to enable these to be articulated and addressed.

THE LESSONS OF THE PRIMARY NEEDS PROGRAMME: RECOMMENDATIONS

Looking ahead now, there are a number of ways in which Leeds LEA and its schools can build upon the gains of the Primary Needs Programme and learn from its problems. These are set out as recommendations.

1 The Authority should maintain its commitment to addressing the needs of specific groups of children in primary schools, but should extend the range of needs so addressed to include other groups.

2 The Authority should continue to seek ways of integrating its primary and special needs support activities and services.

3 The adequacy of school staffing to meet the needs of SEN and statemented children in the context of LMS should be carefully monitored during and beyond the transitional period leading to full budgetary delegation.

4 An even greater investment than hitherto should be made in improving teachers' knowledge and understanding in the fields of multicultural education and gender.

5 More attention should be given to identifying appropriate day-to-day curriculum provision and classroom practice in the areas of multicultural education, equal opportunities and gender, and the experience of successful teachers should be more fully exploited.

6 Schools should ensure that they avoid management strategies which convey gender-specific messages about the curriculum.

7 The Authority should continue to acknowledge and meet the particular resource needs of inner-city schools as far as this is possible within the constraints of LMS. At the same time, it should move, and help schools to move, from a *resource*-dominated attack on the problem to a *curriculum*-dominated one.

8 Without reducing the quality of care and concern manifested for children experiencing social and/or material disadvantage, schools should strive to maximize the educational prospects of these children through the expectations teachers hold of them and the curricular experiences they provide.

9 The particular needs of very able children should be acknowledged and systematically addressed.

10 Every effort should be made, at both LEA and school levels, to raise teachers' expectations of what children can achieve. Without diminishing in any way their commitment to supporting children with specific needs and problems, the Authority and schools should now act to focus much more attention on children's *potential*.

11 Teachers should be helped to extend their skills of diagnosis and assessment in relation to all children.

12 The diversity of strategies for curriculum review and development which emerged during PNP should become part of the basic management repertoire of every school. Particular note should be made of the range of cross-school and classroom-based roles undertaken by the more successful PNP coordinators.

13 The skills required for curriculum leadership and development, and in particular those of working with colleagues and conducting and participating in meetings, should feature prominently in INSET.

14 Great care should be taken to ensure that the processes of curriculum review and development are applied to *all* areas of the curriculum, not just to the National Curriculum core subjects.

15 Care should also be taken to secure similar comprehensiveness and balance in the allocation of human and material resources to the various curriculum areas, at both LEA and school levels.

16 Schools should look carefully at the way time is used in the curriculum, adjusting the balance by achieving greater efficiency in the subjects allocated most time, and avoiding the strategy of using certain curriculum areas as time-fillers.

17 In reviewing the quality and balance of the curriculum, schools should also look at the range and balance of *generic activities* which their children experience in the classroom. Overall, it needs to be more clearly understood that curriculum balance is a multi-layered problem involving resources, INSET, management, planning, timetabling, classroom organization and pupil–teacher interaction, and that to define and attempt to address the problem in terms of time allocations alone is inadequate.

18 The Authority should continue to monitor reading standards across the city, replacing current tests by ones which are more comprehensive in their focus; the screening function of existing Authority tests should be taken over by National Curriculum assessment.

19 While the concern with curriculum breadth and balance is of central importance, the Authority should target future curriculum initiatives more precisely and systematically, grounding their prioritization in a careful analysis of need. Immediate priorities should include reading and spoken language.

20 The Authority's policies on the curriculum should be thoroughly reviewed, and attention should be given to enhancing the expertise of all staff with curricular responsibilities.

21 Without denying the importance of display, layout, resources and organization, the emphasis in discussion of classroom practice in the Authority and its schools should now shift from these to *learning*: to its purposes and content; to strategies for diagnosis and assessment; and to extending the professional repertoire of strategies, tasks and activities for making learning happen.

22 The potential of collaborative group work and pupil–pupil discussion should be more fully explored and exploited.

23 The common practice, endorsed in Leeds and elsewhere, of multiple curriculum focus teaching, should be reviewed against two main criteria: its capacity to maximize children's learning and progress; and teachers' ability to manage such strategies successfully without reducing their opportunities for proper monitoring, diagnosis and assessment. Where multiple curriculum focus teaching falls short on any of these counts, teachers should be encouraged and supported in the adoption of alternative strategies.

24 Attention should be given to ways of improving the quality of classroom talk and using it to stimulate and challenge children's thinking. In particular, more discriminating use should be made of questioning as a classroom strategy.

25 Teachers should maintain their commitment to giving pupils praise and en-

couragement. However, they should avoid devaluing these by indiscriminate use and should always seek to provide feedback to children which is precise and informative.

26 Teachers should look carefully at the way they invest their time in the classroom, ensuring that it is fairly and appropriately allocated in respect of all their pupils and each area of the curriculum. The 'unequal investment' strategy of neglecting certain pupils and certain curriculum areas in order to concentrate on others should be weighed against the entitlement of all pupils to appropriate attention and a curriculum of consistent quality.

27 Teachers should strive for match between the nature of the learning task and the context in which children undertake it. This is particularly important where solo tasks requiring quiet and concentration are concerned, given the near-universal adoption of group work and an ideology in which physical and verbal 'busyness' are deemed to be among the hallmarks of good practice.

28 The above points notwithstanding, the practice of making specific aspects of teaching and classroom organization the subject of Authority policy or prescription should be abandoned, as should the Authority's model class-room. However, the amount of attention given to classroom practice in Authority and school INSET and advisory activity should not be reduced; rather, its emphasis and style should change radically. There should be more open discussion, analysis and weighing of evidence; more emphasis on the development of professional understanding and skill. Where a need appears to exist, as in the cases exemplified in the preceding paragraphs, the concern should be to help teachers explore and understand the nature of the problem and hence work out the most appropriate solution, rather than to present them with ready-made solutions to problems left undefined.

29 Though the process may take time (the problem being a historical and national one), all parties should strive to divest discussion of primary curriculum and classroom practice of its ideological and rhetorical baggage, consciously seeking out a more open and analytical mode of discourse.

30 The Authority should abandon its role of definer, arbiter and keeper of 'good primary practice', opening the issue up to the alternative processes defined above, and placing classroom teachers at the centre of the debate. Class teachers should no longer be expected to conform to particular models of good practice, but should be encouraged and enabled instead to review alternatives, and the arguments and evidence for and against these, before making their own decisions. Good practice should henceforth be treated as problematic, rather than as an uncontentious absolute.

31 The potential of classroom-based professional collaboration (TTT) should continue to be exploited. Particular attention should be given to resolving the division of responsibility in classroom collaborations, to establishing clear agreement about purposes, and to joint planning.

32 Links between school, home and the community are a proper and necessary area for Authority policies, and these should be developed without delay.

33 In addition to the Home–School Liaison Officer experiment, the Authority should identify other roles and strategies to improve the quality of home–school cooperation.

34 The Authority's LMS formula should preserve weightings to support inner-city schools in their particular tasks, but the staffing discrepancies between these and other schools should be kept under close review to ensure that the extra resources are well used, and that other schools are not thereby prevented from undertaking their own developmental and support work.

35 The principle of staffing all but very small primary schools on the basis of one teacher for each registration group plus at least one extra should be pursued, notwithstanding the constraints of LMS.

36 Schools should seek to retain the *range* of managerial roles and strategies made possible by the introduction of PNP coordinators. In the absence of staffing on the PNP scale, such roles and strategies should be spread across the staff as a whole, rather than confined to one or two people.

37 Schools should adopt management structures consistent with the range of tasks they now, in the 1990s, have to undertake, and existing structures, together with roles, responsibilities and procedures, should be reviewed with the new agenda in mind.

38 All deputy heads should have a job specification and a place in school management and development commensurate with their experience and seniority.

39 The management needs of *all* staff, not just heads and senior staff, should be addressed in management INSET. Management should be tackled as a whole-school issue, entailing participation by all staff. Though effective management strategies are needed and must therefore feature prominently in INSET, they should be balanced by, and embedded in, a full exploration of the educational tasks which they exist to promote.

40 The Authority should ensure that it fully involves heads in the development of all future policies for primary education in the city.

41 Heads should likewise ensure that they involve all staff in the development of any school policies which affect their day-to-day work.

42 The Authority should give continued and substantial attention to the professional development of heads, especially those experiencing problems in professional relationships and those out of touch with or resistant to current educational thinking.

43 The Authority should act to improve relationships with its primary schools.

44 In its approach to future policy-making the Authority should adopt and exemplify the approach it commends for schools: proper consultation, careful analysis of the issues, and full consideration of evidence from a variety of sources.

45 The Authority should provide resources and opportunities to meet the professional development needs of advisory staff as well as staff in schools.

46 Advisory staff should be properly accommodated and serviced, and their administrative burden should be reduced so that they can concentrate more on professional support.

47 The Authority should make its administration more accessible and responsive to the needs of schools.

48 The Authority and school governing bodies should act to maximize teachers' confidence in the processes of appointment and promotion.

49 A mixed economy of school-centred, LEA-provided and independent agency-provided INSET should be achieved. The Authority should ensure that it is always able to ensure externally based forms of INSET in the case of schools without the professional capacity adequately to generate their own.

50 At the same time, teachers and schools should as far as possible be involved in identifying their own development needs.

51 Future strategies for school improvement should ensure that there is effective linkage and commonality of purpose among the various individuals and bodies concerned.

52 The Authority should take steps to ensure that it has full, up-to-date and readily accessible records on the factual and logistical bases of primary schooling, so as to aid policy-making and facilitate longer-term monitoring of the effectiveness of such policies.

53 Officers of the Authority and heads of all schools should seek to encourage a climate of professional discourse in respect of primary education which is more reflective, analytical and open to new ideas, less doctrinaire and dependent on ideology. The discourse should encompass the entire professional community, teachers being treated as partners in the enterprise rather than as subservient.

54 The Authority should review its roles and responsibilities in respect of children, curriculum, teaching, school management and professional development in primary education. In doing so it should identify those aspects of school life in which it is appropriate for it to invest and intervene, and those aspects which are more properly the concern of individual schools, noting our general conclusions that the current balance is neither appropriate nor conducive to school and staff development and that radical adjustment towards a much greater degree of school self-determination is therefore needed.

55 The 1991 review of advisory structures and roles should be extended to include the issues raised here.

Part II
Local initiative and national agenda

10 Policy, politics, and culture in primary education

FROM THE PARTICULAR TO THE GENERAL

We now move from the particular case of Leeds to the condition of primary education nationally; in so doing, we also shift from the collective style of a report grounded in data gathered by a research team to the more individual perspective of the present author.

The changes of focus and tone beg one immediate and important question: how far is our material generalizable beyond Leeds? The press coverage of the Leeds report, to which I refer below, tended to assume not only that the material was nationally generalizable but also – in the case of several newspapers – that it constituted a national study.

There is no doubt that much of the Leeds data accords with that gathered elsewhere, especially in respect of important findings like, for example, the incidence of teacher under-expectation, the apportioning of curriculum time, and the balance and character of classroom action and interaction. Such correspondences are indicated in the text, and some are of a quantitative as well as a qualitative kind. Indeed, it is the powerful sense of the way the evaluation confirms and consolidates a significant tradition of empirical enquiry in primary education which prompts the confidence of many of our conclusions and recommendations, particularly in relation to classroom practice.

More pervasively, it is evident that the report managed to touch a chord in readers elsewhere. For all that it was concerned with just one LEA, the report seems to have identified issues, tendencies and problems which teachers and parents in other parts of the country had no difficulty in recognising. I suspect that this shock of recognition – for many correspondents portrayed it thus – owed much to the way the findings and analysis were contextualized. Unlike much educational research in which for very good reasons anonymity is essential, this did not describe classrooms and schools which by being anywhere might as well have been nowhere; instead it presented a complete and identifiable local system of primary education, from LEA to school and classroom, and this allowed connections and influences to be uncovered, cause and effect to be indicated, and – most important of all – implications for policy and action to be explored.

It is thus all the more necessary that at this point we enter a caveat about generalizability. While the *issues* would seem to be nationally generalizable the research makes no such claims for the specific *findings*, nor, given its scope and methodology, is it in a position to do so. This is particularly important when commentators move beyond a concern with these issues to assert or assume that all primary classrooms are like some of the Leeds classrooms, or all LEAs are like Leeds LEA. The national system has its commonalities, but it also has considerable diversity.

THE REPORT AND THE MEDIA

Over four months elapsed between my presenting Leeds LEA with the final draft of the report and its appearance in print. Much of this time was spent on detailed paragraph-by-paragraph negotiation of the final wording and on re-drafting (despite some of the local protestations of alarm, the report was essentially a negotiated document, and in this process the LEA's officers played a prominent part). It has to be said, too, that the LEA's chosen publication date of 30 July 1991 was seen by some to coincide happily with the start of the press 'silly season' and thus to make it likely that the report would quietly emerge before disappearing without trace.

In the event, the report received extensive media coverage. These headlines give some of its flavour:

PROGRESSIVE TEACHING IN SCHOOLS WAS £14M FAILURE . . . Advisers said children should sit on the floor (*Daily Telegraph*, 2.8.91).

LEEDS £14M PROJECT FAILS TO IMPROVE TEACHING (*Guardian*, 3.8.91).

GOOD PRACTICE UNDER SIEGE . . . A GRAND BUT FLAWED VISION . . . £14 MILLION PROJECT FAILS TO FOCUS ON PUPIL NEEDS . . . GOOD PRACTICE THAT DOES NOT MAKE PERFECT . . . THE PITFALLS OF THE PRIMARY NEEDS MODEL (*Times Educational Supplement*, 2.8.91).

READING STANDARDS FALL AT CITY SCHOOLS . . . Row brews as report pins blame on poverty (*Yorkshire Evening Post*, 2.8.91).

VERY PECULIAR PRACTICE FOR STATE SCHOOLS . . . Found out at last (*Mail on Sunday* 4.8.91.)

METHODS OF PRIMARY CONCERN . . . Conflicts between traditional and modern teaching methods in primary schools (*Yorkshire Post*, 9.9.91).

DOOMED BY THE EXPERTS (*Daily Telegraph*, 12.9.91).

A GENERATION OF WASTED TIME . . . The education of millions of primary school children has been blighted in the name of an anarchic ideology, says a new study (*Daily Telegraph*, 19.9.91).

The headline emphases are instructive, the ensuing pieces even more so. The articles sought in the main to portray the Leeds initiative as an extravagant failure. Few mentioned the report's main conclusion that 'PNP was an initiative well worth the Authority's investment' or the list of twenty-two 'positive and productive features' which preceded it. The recurrent themes in the stories, often reduced to caricature, were the same throughout: declining educational standards as indicated by reading scores; the pervasiveness of 'trendy' progressive teaching methods; the baleful influence of a (Labour) LEA and its advisers, and, more generally, of an 'educational establishment' of inspectors, advisers, teacher-trainers and assorted theorists.

Thus, a complex and carefully qualified analysis was reduced to a simple pathology. The cure for the condition thus identified was equally straightforward: return to chalk and talk methods, introduce subject teaching, abolish inspectors, advisers and teacher-trainers, and train all teachers in the classroom. The two glaring contradictions in this supposed solution to the problems of primary education – that the new generation of teachers who would put things right were to be trained by the very people whose practice was deemed so deficient, and that the evidence against the theory-bound educational establishment was itself a prime example of 'establishment' research and theorizing – were never addressed.

THE POLITICAL CONTEXT

It is important to remind ourselves of the political climate into which the Leeds report was launched. A Conservative administration was approaching a general election after an unbroken spell in office of twelve years but with rather less confidence than it had displayed at equivalent junctures in 1983 and 1987. The government had recently experienced a traumatic change of leadership and the eruption of ideological differences which had been kept very much on a leash during the Thatcher years. In contrast, the main opposition party was displaying unprecedented unity of purpose.

During this period education had featured prominently on the political agenda. In 1988 the government had used its impregnable majority to force through the Education Reform Act, the most radical piece of educational legislation since the Butler Act of 1944. After decades of *laissez-faire*, control of curriculum content was placed firmly in the hands of central government: a National Curriculum of ten subjects (nine at the primary stage), together with religious education, was introduced progressively from September 1989. School accountability to both parents and government was assured through a number of measures heralded in the 1988 Act and consolidated in the 1991 Parents' Charter: open enrolment, or the right of parents to send their child to the school of their choice; a national system of assessment at ages 7, 11, 14 and 16; mandatory annual reports on each child's progress; regular and public reports on every school; and area school performance tables. School self-determination was increased through the delegation of budgetary control from LEAs to individual schools, through a parallel delegation of INSET budgets, and through the right of schools to seek Grant Maintained Status or to 'opt out'.

As part of this process the 'educational establishment' was subjected to considerable pressure. LEA power was diminished, though as agents of quality assurance LEA advisers and inspectors retained far greater influence than many of their opponents had hoped. Initial teacher-training institutions were subjected to an intense barrage of criticism, including an unprecedentedly vitriolic attack from the prime minister himself, about the supposed inadequacy and irrelevance of their courses, which did not always square with the rather more positive reports and surveys on initial training provided by HMI. But the days of the latter, too, appeared to be numbered. After a brief internal enquiry, the government announced in 1991 that the inspectorate would be cut from 480 to 175 and the central inspection function which it had fulfilled for over 150 years would be taken over by teams of inspectors appointed locally.

At the time of going to press many of these changes had been enacted; others required further legislation, and this would obviously depend on the timing and outcome of the 1992 general election. However, a highly partisan press saw to it that the agenda remained prominent, that educational issues were consistently defined as party political issues, and therefore that they were presented in terms which were at the same time simple and starkly adversarial. Against this background the Leeds report was a media gift, as we have seen.

Yet for those with reasonably good memories much of the press coverage conveyed a sense of *déjà vu*. Though controversy about reading standards, progressive primary teaching, and the relevance or otherwise of theory have been a familiar part of the educational scene for several decades, the last time the controversy peaked in the way it did over the Leeds report was in the 1970s. Then the initiative was seized by a group of commentators who were portrayed as uniformly right-wing but who in fact held fairly diverse views. In a series of four 'Black Papers' published between 1969 and 1975 they mounted a sustained attack on two targets: the egalitarian principles embodied in the then relatively new comprehensive schools; and progressivism, particularly in primary education. The initiatives which had prompted the developments of which the Black Paper authors were so critical were the Labour government's 1965 circular requiring LEAs to submit plans for replacing selection at age 11 by a comprehensive system, and the 1967 publication of the Plowden Report.

Within the second theme, progressivism, the concerns were very similar to those voiced in the wake of the Leeds report. Thus, evidence was cited (Cox and Boyson 1975) for a decline in reading standards; complaints were made about the 'lottery' which allowed one child to experience a broad curriculum, another a curriculum which barely extended beyond the 'basics'; and about 'the progressive shibboleths of reading readiness, free expression, team teaching and integrated days'.

The solutions, too, look familiar. Thus, presaging the 1990s advocacy of school-based teacher-training:

Teachers do not need longer training . . . . They want both a spell as a pupil–teacher apprentice to a skilled teacher and to be taught the techniques of teaching and a body of subject knowledge which they can pass on to their pupils.'

(Cox and Boyson 1975: 4)

And, foreshadowing key elements in the 1988 legislation:

National standards . . . could be laid down for the 7, 11 and 14 year old and should be the minimum standards for all pupils of over 70 IQ . . . . The 7+ examination should cover literacy and numeracy and pupils should be expected to pass such a test before they pass to junior school. The 11+ and 14+ tests should also cover a body of minimum geographical, historical, scientific and literary knowledge. Teachers could teach beyond these basic syllabuses and could introduce other subjects; but such syllabuses would ensure that all schools offered a reasonable education, which is not now the case . . . . The enforcement of the 7+, 11+ and 14+ national tests . . . would ensure standards.

(Cox and Boyson 1975: 4)

Evidence which could be used to support such criticisms and recommendations emerged with increasing frequency over the next decade or so: the William Tyndale primary school affair in 1975 which was billed as indissolubly coupling extreme progressivism with wilful or incompetent management and leftist politics; Neville Bennett's apparent rebuttal of progressive methods (Bennett 1976); the 1978 HMI primary survey (DES 1978b) which for the first time charted the extent of curriculum inconsistency claimed by commentators like those cited above, and similarly targeted follow-up surveys of first and middle schools; the important sequence of primary school and classroom studies of the 1980s from Galton, Bennett, Mortimore, Tizard and others, to which we have already referred at several points and which gave to the debate about primary teaching methods a precision which the earlier rhetoric had lacked; and the exposure by a number of commentators, including the present author, of the doctrinaire character and conceptual inadequacy of the ideas and values by which some of the observed school and classroom practice was sustained.

Yet, despite this, the story of post-war primary education has been one of remarkable continuity and consistency. Each new *cause célèbre* has produced discomfort which though acute has usually been short-lived. It was this persistence in the face of apparently incontrovertible evidence which fuelled the frustrations of those seeking radical change, and their belief that such change was being blocked by an educational establishment which was far more committed to protecting its members' interests than to educating children.

Hence, with the publication of the Leeds report, the charges most characteristically expressed in the *Daily Telegraph*:

A generation of wasted time . . . . The education of millions of primary school children has been blighted in the name of an anarchic ideology . . . . The 'progressive' theories that have dominated primary school education for the 'progressive' theories that have dominated primary school education for the past 25 years have been exposed as a fraud . . . . This anarchic regime was rigorously imposed from the top. Teachers believed that if they did not toe the line they would not be promoted . . . . Equivalent in educational terms to the breaching of the Berlin Wall and the dismantling of the Soviet Empire, the report should pave the way for a long-awaited return to classroom sanity . . . . it is clear that it will become a significant landmark in the history of primary education . . .

(Clare 1991)

Can one change educational practice by railing against it? Probably not: such attacks engender solidarity rather than self-awareness, defensiveness rather than appraisal. As politicians have increasingly come to understand, professions are extremely slow to change of their own volition, and tend particularly to resist change which rides on the back of charges of incompetence or self-interest. Even the more judiciously couched appeals to professional goodwill and expertise may achieve little in a climate of suspicion and antagonism. That being so, a government's more effective strategy is legislation. If change cannot be achieved by consent then it must be mandated. The adversarial encounters then serve a different, softening-up purpose: of marshalling and manipulating public opinion, isolating the professions in question, and creating the climate in which draconian measures seem to offer the only solution.

The National Curriculum is a particularly good example of this process at work, the more so as the evidence for the need for legislated change seemed so convincing. Witness, for example, the long-running and not particularly successful attempts by central government between 1977 and 1988 to persuade LEAs to take seriously their statutory obligation to have coherent policies on the curriculum (Leeds, as we have seen, being one of the LEAs displaying deficiency in this area).

The National Curriculum is an important example in another respect: its assumption being that to effect genuine change what is mandated needs to penetrate to the deeper levels of educational *structures* – in this case, the character and scope of the subjects of which the new curriculum is constituted. However, the government initially failed to realize what in this book we have constantly emphasized, that content and pedagogy are indissolubly linked. By late 1991 – possibly aided by the Leeds report – they had come to recognize that the key to the transformation of curriculum content was the transformation of pedagogy. Yet the 1988 Act and subsequent ministerial pronouncements had explicitly stated – as we ourselves have done in relation to the Leeds initiative – that the important decisions about pedagogy are those taken by teachers at the level of the classroom, and it is therefore with teachers that responsibility for pedagogy should rest. Opening up, therefore, was a vision of the government's commitment to raising educational standards through its reforms of curriculum and assessment being frustrated by primary teachers' continued control of classroom practice.

As this book goes to press, we await a promised ministerial statement on the 'outlawing' progressive methods will be followed up, and indeed whether the government will go back on its earlier assurances and start legislating for particular kinds of pedagogy. That would constitute a change even more devastating for primary teachers than the National Curriculum, because it is pedagogy rather than content which constitutes the most basic reality of teaching. On the other hand, it would at last represent a recognition that pedagogy is important – we have never taken it particularly seriously in this country. Moreover, it would spell the end to the gradualism which the mismatch of curriculum and pedagogy have always produced. The progressive revolution – which was centrally about pedagogy – was frustrated in part by the persistence of nineteenth-century assumptions about curriculum content; the National Curriculum was domesticated by pressing it as far as possible into the Plowden mould. Thus does a culture protect itself.

THE CULTURE OF PRIMARY EDUCATION

The Leeds research provided powerful confirmation of the pervasiveness of the culture of primary education. In an earlier book (Alexander 1984) I have explored this culture in some depth, analysing its origins, beliefs and concerns and exemplifying its distinctive language (see also Alexander 1988, 1989).

It is the distinctiveness of these beliefs and values, and of the language through which they are expressed, which provides the most striking evidence of the nature of the primary professional world-view, and which gives most support to the proposition that here we do indeed have something which is sufficiently coherent as to merit the term 'culture'. Others besides myself have, in different ways, explored the various manifestations of primary cultural identity (Blyth 1965; Sharp and Green 1975; King 1978, 1989; Pollard 1985; Cunningham 1988; Nias 1989) and have shown how it pervades not only teachers' assumptions and actions in the classroom but also how they relate to each other and to outside agencies.

I do not propose to repeat the analysis, only to note that one of its most obvious manifestations is the ideological package concerning children, childhood, the curriculum and classroom practice which was fostered in Leeds during the period under review. Ideology – a group's array of central ideas, values and beliefs – is a key element in any culture because it serves to define, justify and control a culture's members. That too was a prominent element in the Leeds experience: the sense that properly to belong one needed to accept and enact the ideology, and that mechanisms existed to encourage such acceptance; and the tendency for members to acquiesce in the hierachy and dependency which cultural continuity required. Of course, as we saw, such acquiescence could not be guaranteed, and there were many heads and teachers who thought things out for themselves and made their own decisions; indeed, this divergence needs to be strongly emphasized in view of the media tendency, in the wake of the publication of the Leeds report, to portray the primary world as uniformly and unthinkingly 'progressive' in outlook and practice.

The vital thing to understand about the primary culture – especially if one is interested in how primary education might in fundamental ways realign itself to address the agenda of the 1990s – is the strength and longevity of its historical and structural roots.

As I showed in my earlier analysis (Alexander 1984), today's primary schools are the direct descendants of the nineteenth-century elementary schools which were set up to provide a minimal basic education for the working classes. In two significant ways, the elementary legacy has persisted unchanged and indeed unchallenged for over a century. First, in respect of the prevailing view of a curriculum for young children divided into two distinct categories, the high-status basics (now redesignated the 'core' subjects and numbering three rather than two) and the lower-status residue. Second, in respect of the means for delivering that curriculum: the class-teacher system whereby one teacher is given a class for a year and teaches them everything.

Despite the progressive reaction against the minimalist and regimented elementary curriculum, the subject hierarchy was firmly maintained, and the system for delivering it remained unchallenged. Thus, as HMI found in 1978 (DES 1978b), primary schools consistently gave high priority to language and mathematics, but the rest of the curriculum was characterized by considerable unevenness and inconsistency (a trait we noted over a decade later in Leeds). Thus, too, in seeking to devise ways to improve the situation, HMI argued for class teachers to combine a generalist role with a cross-school specialist brief for curriculum support and development, but did not contest the assumption that the class-teacher system was the most appropriate way for primary schools to be staffed.

For as long as the primary curriculum remained minimal, and parts of it (what I call 'Curriculum II' or the area beyond the basics) were effectively regarded as optional, the class-teacher system seemed adequate for the purpose. However, once, from the late 1970s onwards, the spotlight shifted to the curriculum as a whole, to its scope and balance, to consistency, continuity and progression, and to the place of subjects like science, the efficacy of the class-teacher system was increasingly open to question.

Yet still, few bothered – or dared – to challenge it. There are two reasons for this. First, those having an eye on educational budgets would be unlikely to question a staffing strategy which was relatively cheap and whose replacement would incur considerable additional expenditure. Second, within the primary profession itself the class-teacher system was fundamental to the point of impregnability. It was so central a part of the structure of primary schools, so basic to the primary teacher's sense of what being a teacher was all about, that to question it was unthinkable: it would strike at the primary teacher's very identity. The almost hysterical reaction to the November 1991 discussions about the role of specialist teachers in primary schools illustrates the extreme sensitivity of the issue.

Moreover, the ideology which has developed in conjunction with the emergence of primary schools, was in part concerned – as ideologies are – with sustaining the structure that primary teachers had inherited. Hence, for the generalist, the need to assert strenuously that subjects and subject knowledge are not significant – 'child not curriculum . . . children not subjects'. Hence, too, the strong advocacy of the seamless or integrated curriculum and thematic enquiry: to allow anything else was to confront the possibility that one's curriculum knowledge might be insufficient to the task. Hence the emphasis on process rather than content, 'how' rather than 'what', learning how to learn rather than learning something – a collection of tautologies which begged questions about the content of learning and the expertise of the teacher which by constant repetition of the slogan could be avoided. Hence, in the classroom, the prevalence of unfocused questions, legitimated as 'discovery' but prompting the suspicion that anything more sharply focused required a depth of subject knowledge which was not necessarily available; hence, too, topics justified as reflecting children's interests but quite commonly reflecting those of the teacher.

It is important to insert here two qualifying statements. First, the ideology was not universally espoused, still less universally reflected in practice. Second, as a theory of education it enshrined many important principles which deserved – and still deserve – to be taken seriously, especially when seen as a corrective to the drabness and narrowness of elementary and some post-war primary education. Thus, the ideology arose in part for entirely praiseworthy and appropriate reasons, as a positive theory of primary education at the heart of which, as the Plowden Report famously asserted, was the child. In Leeds, we came across many heads and teachers who enacted this theory with conviction and success. They did so, it must be added, not because they had been told to, but because their professional intelligence and independence had led them to this position.

At the same time, it is hard to avoid the impression that despite its packaging as a positive philosophy, this ideology had a strongly defensive element. Indeed it is possible to interpret much recent primary thinking on curriculum and classroom practice as a way of coping with the ever-widening gap between what primary education needs to offer, and what the generalist class teacher system is able to provide. Thus, the more the public debate has highlighted the curriculum, the more it has exposed the problem of curriculum expertise in primary schools, and the more strenuously, therefore, the anti-subject ideology has had to be defended.

THE INTERDEPENDENCE OF IDEAS AND STRUCTURE

I have introduced this level of detail – and shall be returning in the final chapter to the central question of the future of the class teacher system – in order to drive home a point of some importance: that in any culture, and certainly in the culture of primary education, there is an inescapable relationship between ideas and structure. They do not exist independently of each other. Ideas generate structures; but structures also generate ideas in order to explain and sustain the structures. In conjunction, ideas and structures secure collective cohesion and continuity, and confer identity and security on the individual. In primary education, the ideological package with which we are now all familiar has derived much of its force and staying power from the way primary schools have been staffed and managed, and from the way primary teachers, as generalists, have been trained.

Thus, when in 1991 the Secretary of State for Education and Science attacked 'barmy theory' and argued that a system of school-based training would eliminate it (Clarke 1991), he missed two basic points. First, that all practice is informed by theories – ideas, values and assumptions – of some kind, and the notion of theory-free classroom practice is essentially a contradiction, since practice, of course, is no more and no less than ideas in action. Second, that for as long as the primary school culture persisted, the theory too would persist because it constituted not so much a random set of ideas as a professional cosmology. Thus, far from eliminating whatever the Secretary of State meant by 'barmy theory', a school-based model of training would guarantee its preservation.

The issue, then, is not the abolition of theory in teaching, but its improvement. Teachers need not no theory but the best theory: carefully thought-out, grounded in clear and defensible views of children's development and learning, of curriculum and pedagogy, informed by an articulated and justified vision of what it is to be educated, and consonant with classroom circumstances. The means of achieving such a transformation of professional theory lie as much in the schools themselves as in initial training.

This discussion leads us to a dual agenda, therefore: the need to attend to the policy frameworks and structures within which primary education is located, and the parallel need to open up debate about the core ideas of which primary practice is constituted. Both agenda items are necessary. In arguing the interdependence of ideas and structure I do not wish to seem to imply that if structures are changed then ideas will automatically change too. Though this is to some extent likely, for reasons I have already discussed, there still remains the question of whether in themselves the ideas are appropriate, valid and educationally defensible, whether in fact the new ideas will be better than those they replace. Moreover, to institute policy one must have reasons for doing so, and this takes us back to ideas. Ideas, then, also have a life of their own, and need to be tackled in their own right; they, rather than structures, should be our starting point.

The Leeds study pinpointed specific areas in which discussion of ideas, values and assumptions is required: how we perceive children and define their needs (Chapter 2); how we conceive of a broad and balanced curriculum (Chapter 3); how we deliver that curriculum in the classroom (Chapter 4); how we forge meaningful and productive relationships between home and school (Chapter 5); how schools might manage themselves and most appropriately deploy their human and material resources (Chapter 6); how LEAs might best support and sustain schools in their work (Chapter 7).

Overriding and to some extent encompassing all these is the central idea of 'good primary practice': that to which all teachers naturally aspire but about which there is remarkably little debate. The reasons for the absence of debate are complex, and some of them have been considered in previous chapters; but among them is this chapter's hypothesis that the ideas least likely to be exposed to proper debate are those on which a culture most heavily depends for its identity and survival. Such ideas become the standard around which the troops will rally in the face of assault and which they will at all costs defend. The *Times Educational Supplement* headline 'good practice under siege' was in this sense more apt than its author can have realized. If 'good primary practice' crumbles, so does much else besides, because it connotes much, much more than teaching methods.

For these reasons, if for none other, the pivotal notion of good primary practice now demands to be explored and de-mystified.

11 The problem of good primary practice

THE QUEST: PRACTITIONER VIEWS

What is 'good primary practice'? Is it really as elusive and problematic as we claimed on the basis of the Leeds evidence?
The words of practioners themselves provide one obvious starting point for our quest. Consider, for example:

- *Why do we do it this way? Well, it's good primary practice, isn't it?*

Here, immediately, we encounter one of the most prominent features of the discourse: the easy assumption of consensus, which pre-empts any further discussion. If one does pursue it, however:

- *In this school we adopt best practice and approach the National Curriculum thematically. We don't adopt the old-fashioned method of keeping it in little boxes. It's unnnatural – children don't see the world that way, so why should we impose our adult views on them?*

Thus, good practice *is* definable, but strictly in terms of certain canons. Where do these come from?

- *By dividing the curriculum into subjects the government is sabotaging all the good practice established by primary schools since Plowden.*
- *I have no problem about good practice: Plowden is still my Bible, whatever the government or any airy-fairy academics say. They are not the practitioners – I am!*

So the centre of gravity would seem to be the Plowden Report of 1967 or at least those ideas and practices which can claim descent from this famous document. Note next the characteristic use of buzzwords, slogans and shibboleths:

- *The curriculum isn't subjects: it's a walk through autumn leaves.*
- *We apply all the basic principles of good practice here – a stimulating environment with high quality display and plenty of material for first hand exploration; a flexible day in which children can move freely from one activity to the next without the artificial barriers of subjects; plenty of individual and group work.*
- *We encourage freedom, flexibility, spontaneity, discovery. These are the watchwords of good primary practice.*

With this is frequently combined a tendency to set up simple – and usually false – dichotomies, with no middle ground deemed possible or admissable:

- *We don't believe in teaching here. The job of the teacher is to create the environment in which children can find things out for themselves, not to tell them what they should know.*
- *It isn't what the children learn that matters, but how.*

To be fair, this is a tactic used by the opposition too:

- *Forget the trendy Sixties. The child cannot find it all out for himself. He needs to be told, he needs to be taught.*

Note in the antepenultimate quotation above, the reference to *belief* as the basis for action, still more graphically put in the earlier assertion that 'Plowden is my Bible' and frequently illustrated in job advertisements:

- *The successful candidate will be familiar with good primary practice. A belief in a child-centred approach is essential.*
- *Candidates should be committed to a child-centred approach to learning via first-hand experience.*
- *We are looking for committed, enthusiastic child-centred teachers who believe in activity, a cross-curricular approach and enquiry-based learning.*

Conviction, of course, can frequently breed intolerance of alternative viewpoints, including (and perhaps especially, because they are more threatening) those which are grounded in evidence of some kind:

- *Plowden is still my Bible, whatever the government or any airy-fairy academics say. They are not the practitioners – I am!*
- *Six-year olds can't understand the past, so what's the government playing at bringing in history at Key Stage One? It just shows how out of touch they are.*
- *I don't care what the ILEA research shows: the integrated day is right for me and right for my children.*

But then, as the previous chapter's account of press coverage of the Leeds report showed, dismissiveness and intolerance are deployed at least as frequently by the counter-culture. Thus, Prime Minister John Major in October 1991:

- *I will fight for my belief, and my belief is a return to basics in education. The progressive theorists have had their say.*

By this stage in our analysis, however, other cracks are beginning to show, as the old seeks to accommodate itself to the new:

- *Don't worry about the National Curriculum – if you look at the attainment targets and programmes of study you'll find that we do all that already. In fact they just confirm good primary practice.*
- *The SATs will be cross-curricular and activity-based so as to be in line with good primary practice.*
- *I have terrible problems planning, because we're all supposed to use topic webs and show them to the head, and I'm not very good at them, and find them impossible to use, especially as now I have to add all the attainment targets. So what I do is a topic web to satisfy the head, and my own planning for me.*

This brings us squarely to the context of power, and perhaps even patronage, within which the good primary practice issue is sometimes located (the first quotation below nicely capturing the authoritarianism with which, somewhat paradoxically, child-centredness is sometimes associated):

- *When I go into one of my classrooms I don't expect to see all my children sitting down. I expect movement. I expect them to be busy. A quiet classroom is a dull classroom.*
- *If it's Authority policy to do it this way, you have to do it, at least when the advisers are around.*
- *I won't get this job, because the adviser thinks my practice is too formal. Actually, she only came in once, and even then didn't see me teach.*
- *I give my children the occasional spelling test, but I daren't tell the head.*
- *If you don't have drapes and triple mounting, you won't get on here.*

This in turn can present the teacher (or in these two examples, the student teacher) with considerable dilemmas:

- *On my first teaching practice I wasn't allowed to class teach – everything had to be done in groups, and I found it very difficult, especially when there were things that could most sensibly be discussed with the class as a whole and I had to repeat them six times.*
- *My class teacher tells me that good practice is a topic-based curriculum with lots of group and individual work. That's all very well – she's experienced enough to make it work. But I'm not. Anyway, my tutor says there's no one right way, and good practice is finding what works best for me, so who do I believe, and if I want to pass this teaching practice what on earth am I to do?*

THE QUEST: THE APPEAL TO AUTHORITY

Clearly, while statements such as those above begin to uncover the scope of the problem, they do not take us very far in what should be an open debate, a quest in which we ought to be able to follow any path which might seem promising. Are there other starting points?

A second possibility is to go not to practitioners but to those official documents which purport to define the characteristics of good practice in an authoritative way and which are free, one assumes, of particular foibles, preferences or prejudices.

In 1967, the Plowden Report adopted the device of describing rather than prescribing. They portrayed three schools 'run successfully on modern lines', whose characteristics tellingly endorse some of the assumptions we encountered and questioned in the Leeds research, as these extracts show:

> The children . . . spread into the hall, the corridors and the playground. The nursery class has its own quarters and the children are playing with sand, water, paint, clay, dolls, rocking horses and big push toys under the supervision of their teacher. This is how they learn . . . . Learning is going on all the time, but there is not much direct teaching . . . . The class of sevens to nines had spread into the corridor and were engaged in a variety of occupations. One group were gathered round their teacher for some extra reading practice, another was at work on an extraordinary structure of wood and metal which

they said was a sputnik, a third was collecting a number of objects and testing them to find out which could be picked up by a magnet and two boys were at work on an immense painting of St Michael defeating Satan. They seemed to be working harmoniously according to an unfolding rather than a pre-conceived plan . . . . As he leaves the school and turns into the grubby and unlovely street onto which it abuts, the visitor passes a class who, seated in a quiet, sunny corner, are listening to their teacher telling them the story of Rumpelstiltskin.

(CACE 1967: 103–5)

Twenty years later, the agenda had changed somewhat, though its antecedents were still discernible, as the following extracts from HMI's direct encounter with the good practice problem show.

First impressions were of an informality which typifies many primary class-rooms. Closer investigation revealed that the freedoms were not there merely by chance . . . . The children were keenly interested in their work. Their commitment to what they were doing extended beyond the more obviously enjoyable aspects of their practical activities . . . . The children were being taught to listen carefully and speak clearly and articulately . . . . Their written work caused them to use a variety of styles . . . . The high quality of teaching was the strongest feature common to all the examples . . . there were variations in the teaching styles reflecting the needs of the situation and the personality of individual teachers . . . . Teachers had a sound knowledge of their pupils' social and cultural backgrounds . . . . A dominant factor in the achievement of high standards was the strength of commitment on the part of the teachers to ensure that pupils were making progress . . . . Challenges were set so that the work was neither too difficult not too easy . . . . The overriding characteristic is that of agreed, clear aims and purposeful teaching.

(DES 1987: 32–4)

Thus, the appearance might be that of a Plowden classroom, but the teacher had by now become considerably more prominent, and – crucially – the organic model of an unfolding sequence of intrinsically educative experiences had been replaced by a firm emphasis upon detailed prior planning. This theme was also taken up at school level, underscoring the way that serendipity was to be replaced by management, and individualism by collective endeavour:

In each school the head and staff had agreed aims . . . a shared sense of purpose . . . curricular guidelines which had been carefully thought out . . . . These guidelines had been written after staff discussions . . . . Schools were exploring ways of deploying the staff so that more effective use was made of their abilities and curricular strengths . . . . Schools were making positive efforts to strike the delicate balance which is involved in making the best use of the curricular expertise of a primary school staff as a combined teaching unit.

(DES 1987: 31–2)

Two years later, the Plowden–HMI synthesis was reasserted by the National Curriculum Council, but expanded to leave no ambiguity about the re-emergence of traditional values:

> The aims of the National Curriculum are more likely to be achieved where . . . pupils are properly equipped with the basic tools of learning. In particular, where numeracy, literacy and oracy are given highest priority by teachers and are soundly taught. These skills form the basis of a proper and rigorous education to the highest standards which parents and public expect . . . . Due recognition is given to the importance of first-hand experience and practical tasks . . . . Pupils are led to ask questions and seek answers . . . . Teachers' expectations of what pupils are capable of achieving are high and pupils' learning is structured, relevant and stimulating . . . . Pupils are encouraged to become self-confident, self-disciplined and courteous.
>
> (NCC 1989: 2)

Yet the key assumptions of the Plowden era in respect of classroom practice remained intact. In 1990, the School Examinations and Assessment Council's guidance to teachers about to embark on Key Stage One assessment offered a check list which appeared to presume both grouping and multiple-curriculum focus teaching as discussed in Chapters 3 and 4:

> Is the classroom organised to enable children to work independently or in groups without disturbing others? . . . . Is there a balance in the activities you have planned so that all children will not need all your attention at the same time?
>
> (SEAC 1991)

THE INVISIBLE CRITERION PROBLEM

A notion of good practice presupposes criteria for judgement. While the 1987 HMI and 1989 NCC extracts make criteria explicit, they remain tacit or only partly explicated in the Plowden extract, and in some of the quotations from practising teachers there is even an assumption that criteria are not needed at all – either because good practice is about belief rather than justification, or because the (pseudo) consensus makes their explication unnecessary.

In general, good primary practice discourse is strong on assertion and weak on justification. As a result, the necessary task of defining and defending criteria is frequently neglected. Regrettably, this is a tendency to which even HMI – who have probably been more influential than any other group in shifting primary discourse away from purely 'process' preoccupations to matters of curriculum content and management – are not wholly immune. Thus, for example, the Senior Chief Inspector's annual report:

> 33% of the work was judged to be good to very good, about 36% satisfactory and about 30% poor . . . . About 70% of English lessons were judged satisfactory or better with examples of good practice again occurring in the

early years .... About 75% of mathematics lessons were satisfactory or better, but work of any distinction was rare ...

(DES 1991a: 6)

THE NOTION OF GOOD PRACTICE: WHAT DO WE MEAN BY 'GOOD'?

Our brief reference to the problem of criteria in good practice statements takes us from our initial desire to discover the characteristics of those classroom practices defined as good, to the much more fundamental question of what the notion of 'good practice' actually means. This, then, after consideration of the views of teachers and official sources, is the third possible starting point for our quest. It is qualitatively different from the other two in that it is concerned with a meta-level of analysis.

When we say of something we do, see or wish to commend 'this is good educational practice', what are we *really* asserting? There seem to be four possibilities:

1 *This is the practice which I like, and which accords with my personal philosophy of education.*
2 *This is the practice which works for me, and which I feel most comfortable with.*
3 *This is the practice which I can prove is effective in enabling children to learn.*
4 *This is the practice which I (or others) expect to see, and it should therefore be adopted.*

The status of each of these statements is significantly different:

Statement 1 is a statement of *value* or *belief*.
Statement 2 is a *pragmatic* statement.
Statement 3 is an *empirical* statement.
Statement 4 is a *political* statement.

If we now return to the teacher views with which the chapter started, we see that they can fairly readily be classified. However, it will also be noted that the statements cited are mostly statements of value or belief (what the teacher believes is right) or political statements (what the teacher is obliged by others to do). Many of them combine both attributes, being expressions of belief which one group imposes on another. For a profession generally much preoccupied with the 'nitty-gritty' or practical, surprisingly few of the statements are concerned with what works (pragmatic), or with what can be shown to be educationally effective (empirical). On the contrary, some (for example those from teachers teaching in ways to which they are not committed but to which they feel themselves compelled to conform) show how pragmatic considerations are over-ruled by power and belief; and others touch on empirical issues (the reference to academics and the ILEA research) but only to dismiss such sources as of no account.

So we appear to have a situation – strongly reinforced in the Leeds data – in which the 'good' in 'good primary practice' tends to be asserted but seldom demonstrated; where educational justifications for practice may be tacit rather than articulated; where those with power may assume the right to impose their preferred versions of good practice on those without; and where the front of consensus has to be maintained at all costs in order that the whole edifice does not come crashing down.

Good practice, then, becomes a matter more for decree than discussion. The climate of debate about good practice then becomes partisan and adversarial, rather than open, considered and reasoned. The discourse becomes tautologous: we do it this way because we do it this way.

THE NOTION OF 'GOOD PRACTICE': WHAT DO WE MEAN BY 'PRACTICE'?

There is a further difficulty. So far, we have considered one word in the phrase 'good practice' – the epithet 'good'. What of the other one, the notion of 'practice' itself? Is it reasonable to assume that when we speak of good primary practice we are all talking of the same phenomena, and the only problem concerns the basis on which we rate them as good, bad or indifferent?

To answer this we need to return once again to the earlier quotations. The Plowden extract, and that report's discussion of teaching in general, was preoccupied with the following:

* the use of time;
* the use of space;
* relationships;
* children's motivation, attitude and behaviour;
* the school and classroom context;
* pedagogic processes;
* the whole rather than the parts;
* evolution rather than structure;
* the needs of the child, defined developmentally and motivationally.

In contrast, the HMI extracts, and the many HMI documents since the seminal 1978 survey, imply a very different agenda:

* aims;
* planning;
* curriculum content;
* staff expertise and deployment;
* challenge in learning experiences;
* diagnosis and assessment;
* matching child and curriculum task;
* structure, progression and continuity;

- the parts as well as the whole;
- the needs of the child, defined in relation to societal realities and expectations.

If we place alongside these fairly dramatic differences of emphasis the teacher views with which the chapter started, we find a recurrent concern with:

- the whole rather than the parts;
- flexibility rather than structure;
- the visual impact of the classroom;
- curriculum integration;
- organizational principles rather than strategies.

In general, the quotations suggest a stronger sense of affiliation with Plowden than HMI, and this was certainly the case in the Leeds data referred to in earlier chapters. There, we suggested, there was a general tendency to highlight the visible features of practice like display and grouping, to focus on the environment of learning rather than learning itself, and to imply that securing the former would guarantee the latter.

The issue here, however, is not the reiteration of our earlier critique of certain aspects of the view of good primary practice which prevailed in Leeds during the period of our research – we have already undertaken this in considerable detail in previous chapters – but to point out the more general *conceptual* problem raised by every single account of good practice discussed thus far: namely that they are all, in one respect or another, incomplete.

Consider, for example, the following statement from a recent HMI report on an initial teacher-training institution:

> The college declares publicly its philosophy of good primary practice. This is stated in all substantial course documents. The philosophy has several key elements. These are stated to include:
> - the recognition of the uniqueness of the individual child
> - the importance of first-hand experience
> - the value of an attractive and stimulating learning environment.
>
> (DES 1991f: 1)

The problem here is not so much the *substance* as the *scope* of this statement. Few would dissent from the three principles thus enunciated, and many would applaud them. But as a *philosophy* of good primary practice this is surely woefully deficient. It is rather like a play with scenery but no actors or text, or a concert with orchestra but no music, or the National Gallery's Sainsbury Wing bereft of its pictures. It provides the context for education and gently hints at its conduct, but it indicates nothing of its purposes, scope, content or outcomes.

The problem with many accounts of good practice is that not only do they leave vital questions of value and evidence unexplored, and not only do they sometimes tend towards the authoritarian, but they also focus in a frequently arbitrary way upon particular aspects of practice which are then elevated to the status of a complete and coherent 'philosophy'. More often than not they are merely philosophical fragments or preliminary clearings of the throat.

In its everyday usage, therefore, the phrase 'good primary practice' is deeply flawed, both ethically and conceptually. Some who use the phrase are intuitively aware that this is so, and in writing adopt the apologetic device of placing the words in inverted commas, providing the digital equivalent in conversation. This is rarely more than a tic, since having made this passing acknowledgement that the phrase is problematic they invariably go on to treat it as though it were not.

A FRAMEWORK FOR CONCEPTUALIZING PRACTICE

In order to judge the adequacy of a good practice claim, therefore, we need not only to test the criterial and evidential basis on which practice is judged, but also to be clear about which aspects of practice are defined in this way and which aspects are ignored. There is of course no reason why a good practice statement should not be selective and sharply focused, and indeed every reason why sharpness of focus is desirable: it is difficult to talk meaningfully about teaching unless we engage with its specifics. The problem comes when over time, or within a statement purporting to stand as a complete educational rationale, some aspects of practice are consistently emphasized while other aspects are consistently ignored. The underlying message of selectivity in this context is that *what is emphasized is all that matters*. That, essentially, was the problem in Leeds.

How can we begin to draw up a map of the vast territory of educational practice? In absolute terms it is an impossible enterprise. However, there may be a level at which such a map is not only possible but might also serve as a useful prompt to those involved in the examination, execution and judgement of practice.

My own shot at such a framework starts, as did the Leeds model, with what one encounters on entering a classroom: a *context* comprising first the physical and organizational features of furniture, resources and participants, and second the relationships observable as existing among and between these participants. This, then, is the setting.

Looking closer, one notes that most of the relationships and interactions are not random, but are framed by *pedagogic process*: teachers adopt particular strategies, particular combinations of class, group and individual work, particular patterns of interaction; and pupils are organized so as to facilitiate these.

Next, we note that these processes are focused upon specific tasks and the acquisition of specific knowledge, skill, understanding or attribute: the *content* of teaching and learning.

Finally, we recognize that what we see and what the participants experience is subject to the teacher's *management*: it is planned, implemented and evaluated.

Thus far, we are dealing with what can be observed. However, to make sense of what we see we need to encounter the educational ideas and assumptions in which the observable practice is grounded. Without them practice is mindless, purposeless and random. It is reasonable to assume that although we may not necessarily agree with such ideas as an explanation and justification of what a teacher does, ideas of some kind are the basis for all observable practice. Talking with teachers about their practice in the context of the Leeds research and an earlier study of professional thinking (Alexander 1989) and in my day-to-day work in initial teacher-training (ITT) and INSET, I find I can group such ideas under three broad headings.

The first concerns *children*. Most teaching rests on assumptions about what they can or cannot do, what they need, how they develop, how they learn, how best they can be motivated and encouraged.

The second collection of ideas concerns *society*. Teachers usually have some sense of the demands and expectations which emanate from outside the school, of the needs of society or particular sections of it, and of the needs of the individual in relation to that society. Reconciling and balancing these is one of the central challenges of every teacher and every school, and many primary teachers have a powerful sense of having moved from the era of Plowden in which the needs of the individual were paramount to one in which these are made subservient to, or are redefined in terms of, economic and political imperatives.

Finally, all teaching rests upon ideas about the nature of *knowledge*: its structure, its character, its source (whether newly created by each individual and culturally evolved or handed on from one generation to the next), and its content.

It will probably be apparent that at this point I have telescoped a line of analysis which deserves to be greatly extended, and indeed it derives from a conceptual framework which I have developed for a higher degree course on primary education which I run at Leeds University. However, for present purposes the intention is not to provide in fine detail a fully comprehensive framework for analysing and exploring classroom practice, but simply to illustrate that some such framework is perfectly feasible.

Thus my own framework has two main dimensions and seven main components, as shown in Figure 11.1 below. The categories are of course not discrete, but are simply presented as such for analytical purposes. More important, the two dimensions, here presented as a sequential list, interact: each aspect of practice is to a greater or lesser extent informed by one, two or all of the areas of ideas, values and beliefs.

These seem to constitute not so much the totality as the minimum: whatever else classroom practice encompasses, it contains these elements.

Armed with such a framework we can return to any good practice statement, test its emphasis and scope, and examine the thrust of the ideas and justifications, if any, in which it is rooted. The model, incidentally, has its parallel version at whole-school level. There the *observable practice* components include *context*, *management*, and *external relations*, but because the focus of this discussion is the classroom I am not elaborating that part of the framework in the same way.

Applying such a framework to the various examples given earlier, and to the wider contexts of the Leeds research and the emergence of the National Curriculum, we can venture some basic propositions. Plowden, for example,

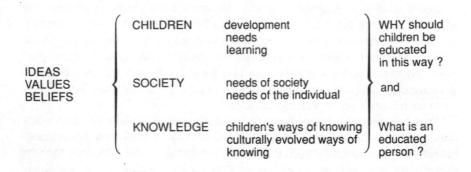

Figure 11.1 Educational practice: a conceptual framework

tended to fixate on *context* and *pedagogy* and neglect *content* and *management*. Its vision was firmly grounded in views of *the child*, especially the child's development and learning. About *society* and its needs it had little to say; while its view of *knowledge* was an extension of its view of the child.

In contrast, from 1978 HMI developed a view of practice which dealt with all four elements, but focused particularly on *content* and *management*, with a relatively subsidiary interest in *pedagogy*. The justificatory basis had less to do with children's development than with their entitlement to breadth, balance and challenge in the curriculum, and was firmly guided by a sense of *knowledge* as cultural artefact, handed on from one generation to the next and providing an essential tool for the individual to make sense of, participate in, and act upon *society* and to respond to its needs.

The National Curriculum is even more distant from Plowden. The emphasis here (at least until the interventionist rumblings of late 1991) is almost exclusively on *content* and *management* – or rather those aspects of management which are concerned with delivery of content and proof of such delivery, *planning* and *assessment*. (The postal nuances of the language of the National Curriculum are startingly pervasive, and have built remorselessly on former Secretary of State Keith Joseph's initial concept of the curriculum as educational package). The justificatory basis is unambiguously societal, or rather economic.

The Leeds model was nearer to Plowden than to HMI. It focused on *context* and *pedagogy*, and only began to attend to content and management when this was dictated by the arrival of the National Curriculum. The justificatory basis was tacitly Plowdenesque, though in fact, as we have seen, as a model it tended to be particularly deficient in the area of ideas and justifications, albeit fairly strong on values.

Analysed in this way, we can see the extent of the gulf, or culture clash, between the established view of primary education and the new regime; between the ideology of progressivism and the 1980s/90s emphasis on economic imperatives; between the mainstream culture of primary education as we explored it in the previous chapter and the new, tougher and much more instrumental educational culture legitimated by the 1988 Act. We can see, too, how at a time when the bedrock ideas and values of the education system were undergoing revolution, for an LEA to neglect ideas and concentrate on the external features of practice was particularly debilitating to its teaching force.

WHERE IS GOOD PRACTICE TO BE FOUND?

To take stock: 'good practice' statements come in different forms. Some are statements of *value or belief*; some are *pragmatic* statements; some are *empirical* statements; some are *political* statements; some combine more than one of these characteristics; and all presuppose a *concept* of practice itself.

Pursuing our quest for good primary practice in this way, therefore, we can see that while in a physical sense it resides in primary schools and classrooms, to know what we are looking for and to begin to understand how we might define and judge it, we need to recognize that it lies, *conceptually*, at the intersection of the five considerations or dimensions which we have explored: value, pragmatic, empirical, political and conceptual. Figure 11.2 represents this relationship.

The quest for good primary practice, then, is as much a conceptual as a geographical one. Before we can ask an LEA or a head to show us schools or classrooms in which good practice is to be found we need to be clear what we, and they, mean by good primary practice, and whether there is sufficient agreement to make the journey worth while. 'What do we mean by good practice?' must precede 'Where is good practice to be found?'

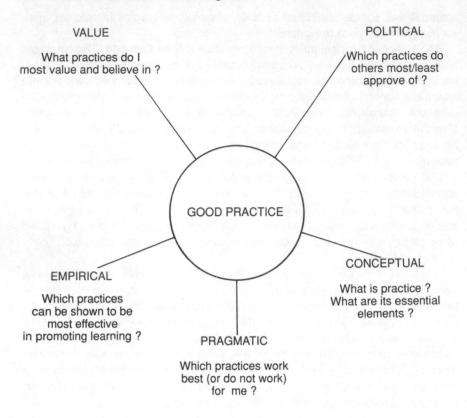

Figure 11.2 What is good practice? Reconciling competing imperatives

In other words, to provide a reasonably defensible view of good practice we need to be able to answer the following questions:

Conceptual. Am I clear what practice I am talking about? Is my version of practice as balanced and as comprehensive as it ought to be, or am I operating on the basis of a rather limited view of practice, missing out some aspects and over-emphasizing others?

Value. Why do I value or believe in this particular practice? Can I defend my value-position in terms of basic ideas and principles about what it is to be educated? Are these sustainable values or are they merely blinkered prejudices? Do I value this practice not so much because I have good reasons as because I've always done it this way – do I like what I know rather than know what I like?

Pragmatic. Does the practice work for me? Why? Is it reasonable to assume that it will work for others? If not, should I be commending it in this form? What are the necessary classroom conditions for making this practice practicable?

Empirical. Do I actually have evidence that the practice I am commending or adopting promotes learning? What kind of evidence? My own experience? Research findings? Am I prepared to allow for the possibility that there might be contrary evidence? Am I prepared to allow for the empirical perspective or am I going to press my view of good practice regardless?

Political. (a) Am I expecting people to adopt this practice not so much on its merits but because I say they should? Am I taking refuge in my authority because I haven't really thought through the arguments for the practices I am pressing for (or against)? Am I pressing for (or opposing) particular practices for other than educational reasons? Is this, in effect, an abuse of my power? (b) Does the view of good practice *x* is expecting me to adopt have good arguments and evidence to sustain it? Or if I am simply expected to adopt the practice because *x* says so, what can I do about it? Assuming *x* to be reasonable, am I prepared to argue the toss? How far am I prepared to compromise my own judgements in order to gain approval and advancement? When I achieve similar eminence how will I use the power I shall then have to influence the practice of others?

GOOD PRACTICE: THE PRIMACY OF VALUES AND EVIDENCE

It will be evident that in very few instances can we satisfy all of these conditions when determining classroom strategies. Our own values may lead us in one direction; alternative values in another; practical constraints may make neither course of action in its pure form possible without modification; we may know of evidence which makes us doubtful about the wisdom of adopting the compromise position to which we find ourselves being steered; our decisions may be further shaped by external pressures or expectations; and so on.

Primary practice – any educational practice – requires us to come to terms with and reconcile competing values, pressures and constraints. If this is so of practice in general, it must also be the case, *a fortiori*, with practice we wish to define as 'good'. Far from being an absolute, therefore, as it has been treated for decades, good primary practice requires us to compromise. Beliefs and actions are rarely congruent with each other.

However, there has to be a qualitative difference between practice and good practice if the latter notion is not to become redundant. Or is it the case that good practice is no more than the best we can do in the circumstances? Is our quest for educational quality to run into the morass of relativism?

I believe not. Though I have presented and discussed the five considerations or dimensions as if they have equal weight, the pursuit of good practice has to move beyond a mere balancing of competing imperatives. There have to be superordinate reasons for preferring one course of action to another, which enable education to rise above the level of the merely pragmatic.

The five considerations, therefore, are not in any sense equivalent. Each set of questions is wholly different from all the others. However, it is possible to order and group them.

Thus, the conceptual questions stand apart from all the rest as being concerned with the scope and comprehensiveness of our definition of practice: before we consider judgements of quality we must be clear what it is that we are talking about.

Next, the political and pragmatic questions remind us of the pressures and constraints of the circumstances in which practice takes place. Such pressures and constraints cannot be ignored, and they may yield practice which is as likely to be bad as good.

There remain the value and empirical dimensions. In the end, it seems to me, close attention to these two is what distinguishes *good* practice from *mere* practice. Education is inherently about values: it reflects a vision of the kind of world we want our children to inherit; a vision of the kinds of people we hope they will become; a vision of what it is to be an educated person. Values, then, are central: whatever the other ingredients of good practice may be, they should enable a coherent and sustainable value-position to be pursued.

Yet values alone are not enough. They provide no recipe for action, only the broad criteria by which we judge what we do is right. The methods we choose must also be *effective* as means to our chosen ends. We need, therefore, knowledge of a range of practical strategies together with evidence about their viability and effectiveness, and especially about their capacity to deliver learning of the kind which accords with the goals we have set or adopted.

Some go so far as to argue that the good practice problem is resolved at a stroke by talking of 'effective' practice (or the effective teacher/effective school) instead. This is mere sleight of hand: effective in relation to what? In relation, of course, to a notion of what it is to be educated. Good practice, then, is intrinsically educative as well as operationally effective. Effectiveness as a criterion existing on its own is meaningless.

Equally, some argue that value and belief alone should guide our action. Quite apart from the dangers of assuming that we have a right to impose our beliefs on the children we teach, I suspect that it is the excessively single-minded pursuit of belief in primary education which has made some of its professional community blind to the limitations of some of the methods they have commended and adopted. Yet how often does one hear practices justified by statements which begin 'We believe . . .'?

In any event, while beliefs and actions need to be consistent, they are not synonymous. Thus, a belief in cooperation and a distaste for competition might imply and seem to justify group work, but does the belief of itself make such a strategy effective as a tool for the acquisition of knowledge, understanding and skill? Or a belief in the unity of knowledge might imply and appear to justify an integrated curriculum, but does it follow that this is the most effective way for children to come to know? Or a belief in the importance of an enquiring mind might imply and justify asking questions but never providing answers, but does it follow that through this strategy children themselves will learn to question what they experience?

Classroom strategy can never be merely an enacting or an extension of educational belief. Yet this is exactly how good practice has frequently been defined in primary education. First work out your 'philosophy', then construct your practice to fit it: if the philosophy is right, the practice will be sound. In this version of good practice, faith alone provides the justification and evidence becomes irrelevant. As one of our earlier-quoted respondents retorted: 'I don't care what the ILEA research shows: the integrated day is right for me and right for my children.'

We are now in a position to sum up. Figure 11.2 represented good practice as existing at the intersection of the five considerations and as a matter of reconciling competing imperatives. I have now suggested that this approach does not take sufficient note of what the 'good' in 'good practice' might dictate, and that although all the considerations are important, they are not equivalent. The pursuit of good practice sets the considerations in a hierarchical relationship with ethical and empirical questions pre-eminent, and with both dependent on a prior conceptualization of the nature of educational practice itself. This alternative relationship is shown in Figure 11.3.

Using this framework, we can see fairly readily the extent to which the various protagonists in primary education may pursue very different versions of quality, each of them in their own way somewhat restricted. Indeed, it is instructive visually to locate on the framework typical prescriptive statements about what counts as quality in primary education from different sources – from, say, a politician, an administrator, an adviser, a teacher educator, a head, a teacher, a parent, a child – and note the different kinds of incompleteness which each reveals.

For some, especially at present, pragmatic considerations are all-important; but the proper concern with operational viability can become a distorting lens through which the whole educational enterprise is reduced to the question 'Does it work?' and the rest is dismissed as 'mere theory'. In a country notably unimpressed by intellectual endeavour, the stance has considerable popular appeal.

On the other hand, there are contexts in which the 'mere theory' charge is amply justified as the analysis of practice spirals upwards into the stratosphere of conceptual or ethical debate but never addresses pragmatic and empirical questions.

The pragmatic preoccupation tends to be shared by politicians, whose powerful value-orientations may be offered to a more or less gullible electorate as 'plain common sense'. The alliance of political and pragmatic calculations, however, yields a somewhat minimalist version of good practice; also a dangerous one, since the only partly explicated values can then be imposed on child, teacher and parent alike.

Or again, the researcher's proper preoccupation with the effectiveness of a teaching strategy in terms of learning outcomes may result in a counsel of perfection which no teacher can possibly expect to emulate because it takes so little account of the particular context of constraints and opportunities within which he or she has to work.

Finally, the prevailing culture of primary education, as we have seen, tends to demonstrate its particular bias towards a combination of no-nonsense pragmatism and high-sounding belief, with, necessarily, a weather eye open to two kinds of political pressure – from governments and from the professional hierarchy of primary education itself.

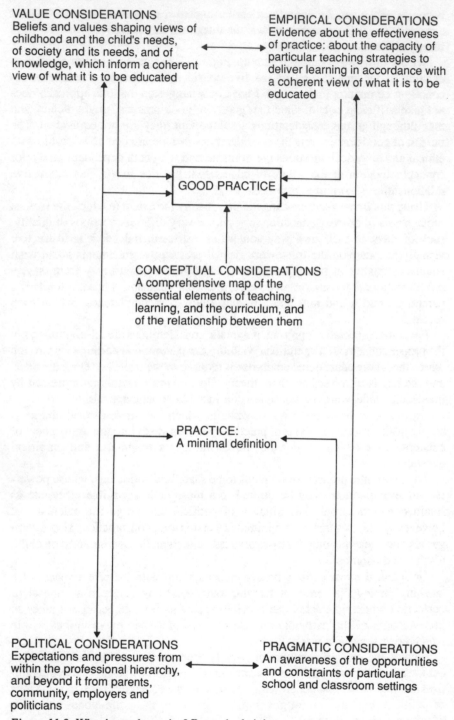

VALUE CONSIDERATIONS
Beliefs and values shaping views of
childhood and the child's needs,
of society and its needs, and of
knowledge, which inform a coherent
view of what it is to be educated

EMPIRICAL CONSIDERATIONS
Evidence about the effectiveness
of practice: about the capacity of
particular teaching strategies to
deliver learning in accordance with
a coherent view of what it is to be
educated

GOOD PRACTICE

CONCEPTUAL CONSIDERATIONS
A comprehensive map of the
essential elements of teaching,
learning, and the curriculum, and
of the relationship between them

PRACTICE:
A minimal definition

POLITICAL CONSIDERATIONS
Expectations and pressures from
within the professional hierarchy,
and beyond it from parents,
community, employers and
politicians

PRAGMATIC CONSIDERATIONS
An awareness of the opportunities
and constraints of particular
school and classroom settings

Figure 11.3 What is good practice? Beyond relativism

Similarly, we can apply the analysis not just to constituencies of opinion but to the practices themselves, and show how challenging the reconciliation of the various considerations becomes.

Consider, for example, the laudable commitment to individualized learning, never easily reconciled with the reality of large classes, and so often frustrating the very diagnosis it claims to promote by forcing the teacher into a crisis management mode.

Or consider curriculum integration and the tensions between powerful holistic and anti-subject values, the legal requirement that subjects be delivered in the classroom, the empirical evidence that, covertly or otherwise, they are there anyway, yet the pragmatic problem that without some degree of integration the National Curriculum (in its early days at least) is undeliverable in the time available.

Or consider the collaborative ethic, its manifestation in group work, the empirical evidence that such group work is not particularly collaborative and may well frustrate the individual learning tasks of which much primary teaching is constituted, the organizational challenges it poses, yet at the same time the pragmatic counter-argument that the only way a teacher stands a chance of delivering a whole curriculum to a large class is through group work.

Or take the curiously contradictory notion of the integrated day, in which the fact that different areas of the curriculum are pursued simultaneously is taken to demonstrate that they are integrated, which self-evidently they are not, and in which the holistic intentions can give way to a much more serious fragmentation of teacher-time, energy and attention.

Good primary practice, like education itself, is as much an aspiration as an achievement; but at least we can try to become clearer about what it is we aspire to, and why; and in confronting the various considerations which bear upon classroom practice we can inject a greater degree of honesty and realism into professional discourse and thereby make the gap between achievement and aspiration a diminishing one. Moreover, thus armed we may be able to counter the journalistic and political hijacking of the debate about pedagogy rather more convincingly than we have hitherto.

12 Improving primary education: reform or revolution?

AT THE CROSSROADS

Since the 1960s, primary schools have had to accommodate to many changes and pressures: the disappearance of the apparatus of streaming and 11-plus selection and the need to find an alternative rationale and structure for the 7–11 phase; Plowden's celebration of child-centredness and the still continuing counter-revolution; the less inspirational but no less significant recommendations of Bullock, Taylor, Warnock, Rampton, Swann and Cockcroft; HMI surveys and commentaries on the system as a whole, often more sharply critical than their cautious tone suggests; HMI individual school reports, since 1983 open to public scrutiny; falling pupil rolls; salary and professional restructurings; changes in initial training – the move from certificate to B.Ed., the growing importance of the PGCE, and the centralization of course content and accreditation; the rationalization of INSET; the growing pressure to transform the primary curriculum from a cottage industry into something properly managed and of consistent quality; the unprecedented shake-up of curriculum, assessment, finance and management heralded by the 1988 Education Reform Act; the increasing need to work closely and in different ways with parents and governors; the ever more dazzling glare of the spotlight as governments, researchers and the media have decided that this hitherto unregarded phase of education was important; and the costs as well as benefits of such exposure.

The sheer volume of initiatives alone might suggest that primary schools are now vastly different places from those 1960s schools which launched themselves into the great Plowden adventure, let alone those sober and hard-working establishments of the 1950s preparing their oldest pupils for the 11-plus. Educational change, however, is a curious phenomenon: it is a slower process than many would care to acknowledge; it galvanizes some but leaves others untouched; and it can modify actions without affecting beliefs and values – and occasionally vice versa – when these need to be in tandem for change to be meaningful.

The evidence from this period, therefore, tends to show, first, a fairly patchy and uneven response to external initiatives, and, second, the persistence of many of the same *problems* first identified years ago: low expectation, underachievement, curriculum imbalance and inconsistency, for example.

In explaining this, it is worth noting the time-scale. Thus, HMI's 1978 nudge in the direction of properly conceived science teaching, less randomness and circularity in topic work, and consultant-led whole-school curriculum planning, only began to be felt in the mid-1980s as schools finished putting their mathematics and language policies in order and moved to other areas. Similarly, the reforms of initial teacher-training heralded by DES Circular 3/84 and the setting up of the Council for the Accreditation of Teacher Education (CATE) only began to yield results at the end of the decade: courses had to be planned, inspected and approved, and the majority route for primary teachers, the B.Ed., did not produce its first post-CATE graduates until 1989.

Both sets of changes were in any case overtaken by the 1988 Act. This fractured the gradualism of the previous decade and insisted on change now, the scope of which the government was forced by 1991 to reduce, at least in respect of the science and mathematics attainment targets and assessment (DES 1991g, 1991h, 1991i). This fairly rapid retreat is in itself highly instructive in that it suggests a belated acknowledgement that the pace of change can be forced only up to a point.

It is also worth asking what – in addition to the problems – has *not* changed in primary education, because this might provide the clue to the puzzle of why the catalogue of events listed in the first paragraph does not, or does not yet, add up to a revolution.

The answer is deceptively simple. There have been two fundamental continuities, one at the level of ideas and the other at the level of structures. The dominant ideology of primary education is alive and well, having shown remarkable resilience in the face of considerable provocation; and the structural foundation of primary education, the class teacher system, is intact, having been no more than superficially adjusted in order to accommodate curriculum consultancy.

These two continuities must be addressed and indeed challenged if the system is to deliver the vision of improved quality and higher standards to which both Plowden and the 1988 Act in their different ways subscribed. For just as the surveys and research studies of the 1970s and 1980s revealed a 'myth of progressivism', so the studies of the 1990s and 2000s may well reveal a 'myth of radical reform'. The Plowden revolution was constrained by the persistence of the elementary tradition's minimalism: a curriculum dominated by the basics, taught in ways which were fundamentally didactic though they may have pretended to be something else. In its turn, the 1988 curriculum revolution, being in part a restatement of the centrality of the basics, may well turn out to have been frustrated by the ideology and trappings of progressivism (a possibility which, by autumn 1991, central government had at last detected).

It is of course early days. Yet it is also clear that neither of the two ostensibly revolutionary prescriptions – Plowden or the National Curriculum – included more than a cursory look at the basic structural fact of primary education – the class-teacher system – and both made the very questionable assumption that a revolution in thinking could be achieved without a change in structure.

Thus, both revolutions were expected to be delivered by the same person, a generalist class teacher responsible for the child's full range of curriculum experiences. Both initiatives presumed that this same generalist class teacher would be operating on the basis of minimal or no non-contact time. Yet, both made very substantial demands on the class teacher's curriculum expertise – the 1988 Act in an obvious way, Plowden to an extent which most people since 1967 have managed to understate, with (as Chapters 2, 3 and 4 of this book show) damaging consequences for children's learning.

Both revolutions, then, presumed that one person could accomplish the task and be trained to do so; and when this proved impossible everybody preferred to blame the teacher trainers rather than ask whether the expectations held of class teachers were realistic.

The late-twentieth-century visions of primary education and the late-nineteenth-century structure for delivering them have become increasingly incongruent. This, at least, can be offered as a hypothesis to be borne in mind as we consider in more detail the general agenda for reform implied by the Leeds report.

LIBERATING THE PROFESSIONAL CULTURE OF PRIMARY EDUCATION

The *sine qua non* of reform is a transformation of the professional culture of primary education. The prevailing ideology – frequently constraining and oppressive while ostensibly libertarian – must give way to the kind of open debate about educational purposes and classroom practices which the current climate needs. It is an ideology grounded in the best of intentions which for many has lost its early intellectual excitement and has become a mere shell of slogans and procedures, sometimes adopted for no other reason than the desire or need to conform. The ideology attends to but a small part of the educational enterprise. It is highly defensive, deliberately and successfully preventing the exposure of precisely those problems in curriculum and pedagogy which the generalist class-teacher system creates.

All the sacred cows and shibboleths – the resistance to subjects, integration, thematic work, topics, enquiry methods, group work and so on – must be subjected to clear-headed scrutiny in the light of the kinds of consideration we looked at in the previous chapter: conceptual, empirical, ethical, pragmatic and political. Among these, the conceptual and empirical tests should be applied the most stringently.

Ideology breeds counter-ideology, and this in turn should be countered. The Leeds report has been interpreted by both its supporters and detractors as a call for basics and regimented classrooms, which, manifestly, it is not. The 'traditionalists' in this bizarrely polarized debate see themselves as ideologically untainted, the apostles of common sense. In fact, they are no less ideologically blinkered than other protagonists: as often as not, 'common sense' means 'my sense', my way of looking at the world, my values, my policies – and my power to impose them.

The problem here, as we discussed in Chapter 11, is that all education is necessarily underpinned by values. What has made their exploration particularly difficult since the 1960s, and especially since the early 1980s, is the political hijacking of certain key value-positions on curriculum and pedagogy, and the reduction of conceptual and empirical questions about knowledge and class-room practice to the simple adversarialism of progressive (= left) and traditional (= right).

Without denying the inevitability of ideological debate or the need for edu-cational decisions to be ethically grounded, we now need to stake out the high and low ground of ideological conflict more carefully. Questions about educational purposes or ends will by their nature always provoke value dilemmas and confrontations. Though means and ends cannot readily be separated, classroom practice being a *manifestation* of values as well as a route to achieving them, it ought to be possible to make questions about curriculum structure, classroom organization and teaching strategy much less ideologically fraught, and thereby to remove them as far as possible away from the political arena.

THE EDUCATIONAL AGENDA: IDENTIFYING ITEMS

As a test of the bid for relative value-neutrality, we might consider the list of fifty-five recommendations to Leeds City Council contained in Chapter 9. Though some are of only local interest, the larger proportion resonate with other surveys and research studies. Of the latter, we can highlight the following as examples of what might feature on a reform agenda.

- Raising teacher expectations of all children.
- Eliminating stereotyping.
- Focusing on the needs of the very able as well as other groups.
- Looking at children's potential as well as their problems.
- Sharpening the professional skills of diagnosis and assessment.
- Adopting classroom strategies which maximize teachers' time to exercise such skills.
- Shifting the thrust of debate about teaching strategies more towards learning processes and outcomes.
- Rethinking group work.
- Rethinking multiple curriculum focus teaching.
- Maximizing opportunities for productive teacher–pupil and pupil–pupil inter-action.
- Making teacher–pupil talk more focused and challenging.
- Balancing encouragement with informative feedback.
- Managing time in the classroom as effectively as possible.
- Matching learning task to child.
- Matching classroom context to learning task.
- Rethinking the problem of curriculum balance by addressing it at every level of the system, from DES, NCC and LEA to school and classroom.

- Examining curriculum balance in the classroom in terms of *generic activities* as well as subject labels.
- Ensuring that consistent quality is achieved in all curriculum areas, regardless of their level of priority.
- Developing and fully exploiting the specialist and managerial expertise of every teacher.
- Extending and facilitating the cross-school roles of teaching staff, particularly in respect of curriculum support, review and development.
- Delegating responsibilities and securing participative decision-making.
- Addressing management as a whole-school rather than a hierarchical issue.
- Making questions of managerial strategy contingent on prior questions of educational purpose, process and outcome.
- Developing teacher–parent relationships which reconcile the rhetoric of partnership with the distinct responsibilities of each party.

Notwithstanding the way that some of these issues have acquired a strong ideological gloss in recent years, it should be perceived that most if not all of them are amenable to treatment as, in the main, conceptual, empirical and pragmatic questions. Put another way, few people would disagree with the proposition that whatever one's educational beliefs, items like those listed above require attention in each and every educational context.

SUPPORTING REFORM: POLICY ISSUES

The other point to make about the list is that while many of the items concern those who make policy and provide resources, all of them are not only of direct concern to teachers and heads but can also be addressed by them, regardless of policy.

However, the extent to which schools make headway on issues such as these depends partly on the resolution of certain broader questions.

The role of the LEA

The Leeds study does not sustain an argument for abolishing LEAs. On the contrary, the findings reinforce the case for LEAs continuing to undertake strategic planning and resource distribution in the forms which are possible only with detailed local knowledge. The study also underlines the need for LEAs to provide the kinds of professional support which must always supplement even the most effective school-led INSET, and to retain the power of intervention in weak schools. How such roles are undertaken, however, is another matter, and the Leeds experience suggests the need for a careful review and delineation of those aspects of a school's work which are properly the subject of LEA policy and involvement, and those aspects which schools themselves should determine. There are also questions about the particular concepts of 'vision' to which many LEAs are committed and which they have been explicitly encouraged to adopt by bodies like the Audit Commission (1989a). Necessarily a vision or policy expresses values. Whose values should be thus expressed, and on what aspects of the educational enterprise should they focus? Is there a conflict between devolution and diversity on the one hand and a centrally determined vision for the system as a whole on the other?

Inspection and quality assurance

In showing how an entire local system of primary education can be informed in its judgements of quality by a particular package of beliefs, values and preferred practices, the Leeds study raises important questions about both the agents and processes of inspection and quality control.

At the time of going to press, the precise future of LEA advisers/inspectors and HMI is unclear, following the government's publication of *The Parents' Charter: You and Your Child's Education* (DES 1991j) which envisages the introduction of new inspection procedures from September 1993.

However, whether inspection is undertaken by accredited inspection teams, as envisaged in *The Parents' Charter*, or as at the time of writing by HMI and LEA advisers/inspectors, there is a more general and perennial question about procedures. In Leeds, as we have seen, inspection and advice tended to be framed by a powerful set of values and assumptions, and to be somewhat selective in the aspects of school and classroom practice deemed appropriate for scrutiny and comment. This raises the wider question of the proper focus of inspection – under any model – and of the particular skills which inspection requires. What should inspectors be looking at and for? Surface or substance? The enacting of prescribed or preferred values and practices, or evidence of learning, regardless of the practices adopted? What procedures will yield whatever evidence is required? Brief visits? Talking to the teacher? Talking to the children? Looking at children's work? Checking test results and individual records? Observation? Are these activities straightforward, or are they complex and demanding of specific skill? If so, what kinds of skill and how can they be acquired?

These are simple and obvious questions, but they indicate the need for a full debate on the *criteria* and *methods* of school inspection, and for inspectors, like the teachers they inspect, to be rigorously trained. Making a professional judgement about a teacher is no less demanding of expertise than making a judgement about a child. Whatever the future of HMI, this body undoubtedly possesses an unrivalled fund of experience and knowledge on these matters.

It is also evident that there are significant spin-offs for inspection methodology from recent school and classroom research. For example, by fitting teachers with radio microphones and recording everything they and their pupils said for later transcription and analysis, we found ourselves in the Leeds research gaining access to pupil–teacher discourse at levels which are impossible to the ordinary observer. Without going so far as to argue that this technology should become part of the basic fabric of inspection, I would suggest that it could be invaluable in the training process.

The example also prompts the need for extreme caution in the whole area of evidence-gathering. If, as is inevitably the case in this kind of exercise, evidence is partial or suspect, should it not be open to challenge in contexts where it is used to inform judgements of quality which are made public or which in other ways affect individual and institutional prospects?

Research

Though many argue their essential difference, inspection and research seem to lie on the same continuum. Both are processes of enquiry, both involve the gathering, analysis and interpretation of evidence, both involve the drawing and presenting of conclusions. Yet research is able to adopt a specificity of focus and methodology which is impossible in a national or local system of inspection, where exactly the opposite imperative applies: the need to use standardized procedures and criteria across the system as a whole so that comparisons between schools – one of the purposes of the inspection process – are demonstrably valid and fair. Moreover, inspection is inextricably linked to policy and the political agenda which informs it. Research has an interest in policy, and policy in areas like education can benefit from being informed by research, but the two fields are contingent rather than interdependent, and research is able to be value-neutral to an extent which inspection is not.

That being so, the reform of primary education needs to be attended by a properly focused research agenda. Four contenders for inclusion on the agenda are: children's learning, especially in the context of the curriculum as now redefined and restructured; economy and effectiveness in teaching strategies; the harnessing of individual staff strengths in the interests of effective school management; and – as discussed below – comparative study of different ways of staffing primary schools and deploying primary teachers in the context of the generalist/specialist debate.

In-service education and training

During the 1980s, schools were given an increasing level of control of INSET. In 1987, the central pool of funds, contributed to by all LEAs, was abolished and replaced by Grant-Related In-service Training (GRIST) which gave LEAs direct control of INSET budgets and effectively eliminated full-time and many part-time advanced courses provided by higher education institutions. In parallel with GRIST, the government introduced a programme of Educational Support Grants (ESG) through which funds were targeted on areas of national priority. GRIST was replaced in 1988 by the LEA Training Grant Scheme (LEATGS) much of the funding for which many LEAs devolved to school level; in turn this and ESG were merged into Grants for Education, Support and Training (GEST). At the same time, the scheme for the Local Management of Schools (LMS), introduced under the 1988 Act, considerably reduced the proportion of centrally provided funds available for LEA discretionary purposes.

The net result of this feast of acronyms has been to reduce both the LEA and higher education stake in INSET, to increase considerably the direct in-service role of individual schools, and to enable central government to earmark funds for training in specific areas of national priority such as National Curriculum subjects, assessment and management.

The question raised by the Leeds study is how far this process of devolution should go. We have highlighted the dangers of 'closed-circuit' INSET in which a weak school reinforces its inadequacies and an ideologically driven school remains firmly blinkered. We have argued for the retention of a mixed economy of school-led, LEA-provided and HE-provided INSET. This is essential not merely to provide a safety net in the case of the two kinds of school just mentioned, but for more fundamental reasons of expertise and perspective.

A school staff ought to be able to identify their needs with some precision. Needs-identification, however, is a complex process, requiring the will to look critically at collective and individual practices, open-mindedness, a commitment to collective debate, and an awareness of alternatives. Not all schools have these attributes. Nor, necessarily, do all LEAs or higher education institutions, despite their much larger size. The bringing to bear of multiple perspectives upon the tasks and needs of schools makes it more likely that the needs-identification process will be a comprehensive and honest one.

Similarly, having determined needs, a school needs a vocabulary or repertoire of alternative kinds of INSET provision on which to draw. It is still not uncommon to find that this vocabulary contains just one item: the visiting speaker. In contrast, a full analysis of the scope of notions of school-based INSET can yield a large number and variety of kinds of activity. For example, my own analysis suggested over 400 permutations of the four main INSET dimensions of *focus, control, location* and *mode* (Alexander 1980).

Then there is the question of provider expertise. The self-help model of curriculum consultancy has been significant and influential, but our analysis indicates that the National Curriculum has highlighted the limits to this model in respect of the kinds of expertise normally found in primary schools. In any event, as many schools realize, the motivational power of self-generated professional development needs to be balanced by the ability to stand apart from one's particular values and practices and the need for an awareness of a range of alternative ways of thinking and acting.

For all these reasons, and especially at a time of change, the mixed INSET economy is essential.

Initial teacher-training

At the time of going to press, the Council for the Accreditation of Teacher Education (CATE) is preparing proposals for the Secretary of State in response to his declared intention to make initial teacher-training more 'school-based'. In this intention he is supported by a wide spectrum of opinion ranging from the out-and-out advocates of a full apprenticeship model from which higher education is excluded, through an educational version of the teaching hospital principle used in medical training, to a more cautious advocacy of an equal school and higher education partnership. Like the idea of a national curriculum, the principle of school-based training has broad cross-party support.

The rationale for this shift is the supposed failure of mainstream initial training to produce teachers at the level of skill and knowledge required. This is coupled with the accusation that the ideology we have had cause to refer to so frequently in this volume originates in the teacher-training institutions and is peddled by them to trainees who, thus brainwashed, enter a professional world which is imbued with value-neutrality and plain common sense.

Like much of the discourse surrounding recent primary education, that on primary teacher-training indulges heavily in simple dichotomizing and caricature. There is little doubt that the heyday of the former training colleges (the 1960s and early 1970s), which coincided with the appearance and maximum influence of the thinking enshrined in the Plowden report, was characterized by a tendency to missionary zeal, some of which persists, especially where early years teaching is concerned. By the 1980s the position had changed considerably. From having a monopoly of primary teacher-training, those colleges which survived the cuts of the 1970s were in competition with polytechnics and universities, each bringing a much tougher outlook to the task -- the one grounded in a strong tradition of vocationalism, and the other in intellectual rigour. Indeed, the ideological centre of gravity had by then shifted to the schools themselves and to LEAs, as the products of the most ideologically loaded courses moved into positions of professional power and influence, with consequences exemplified in the Leeds study.

Whatever the merits of the right-wing attack on the educational establishment, it seems fated to be flawed by poor chronology. In the 1960s, Black Paper authors blamed Plowden for the 1968 student unrest (the rioting students had in fact attended the traditional primary schools of the 1950s, and most beneficiaries of Plowden were still unborn or at best in their prams). In the early 1990s, in contrast, the right-wing attack on teacher education was aimed at a model of teacher-training which had all but disappeared some ten years earlier.

There is of course a much more serious case to be made for extending and institutionalizing the role of teachers and schools in teacher-training which has to do partly with arguments about the way professional skill is most effectively acquired, and partly with concern that the standing of a profession is necessarily bound up with the degree of control it exercises over the training and induction of its members. The second point seems incontrovertible; the first is more debatable.

However, this is not the place to start a detailed discussion of the process of teacher-training. Rather, I wish to pick up certain issues which relate directly to the matters under review in this book.

Without prejudice to the outcome of CATE's deliberations, which in any case will be known by the time this book is published, I would suggest the need to address two basic questions in the light of this book's particular concern with primary education. First, how school-based can primary initial training realistically become? Second, what kind of primary teacher should we be training anyway?

We have seen that curriculum knowledge is an essential and substantial element in any teacher's expertise – primary no less than secondary, reception no less than sixth form – even though the precise nature of that knowledge will need to differ according to the context of its application. We have also seen that the persistence of the class-teacher system has made primary teachers increasingly vulnerable in respect of the range and depth of the curriculum knowledge they are expected to possess, and that this vulnerability reveals itself not just at the level of issues like curriculum continuity and progression emphasized by HMI in the late 1970s and early 1980s but also, and perhaps more critically for children's learning, in the fine detail of classroom interaction and the learning tasks teachers give to their pupils.

The vulnerability is not the fault of individual teachers; it is an inevitable consequence of the way primary schools are staffed and of the generalist class-teacher system itself. For as long as this system persists, the notion of a trainee teacher picking up curriculum knowledge apprentice-style from a class teacher is a non-starter. It is suspect in any event, not least for precisely the same reason that critics of child-centredness argue against discovery methods: there are some things which have deliberately and systematically to be taught. (The irony here is that the critics of discovery learning in primary schools are the same people who advocate a discovery approach to the training of primary teachers.)

There is a second fundamental respect in which the school-based model has drawbacks. As we showed in the Leeds study and in our discussion of good practice in the previous chapter, there is a pervasive tendency for debate about classroom practice to veer between belief and pragmatism, and sometimes to become extremely dogmatic and intolerant of alternatives. Values tend to be presented as given, and empirical evidence which does not sustain the values tends to be rejected.

This is hardly an appropriate context for acquiring the skills of teaching. A trainee teacher needs to encounter, try out and explore a variety of kinds of practice, and to do so in a context which is as ideologically neutral as possible so that he or she can raise questions about the justifications, possibilities and problems of any approach witnessed or tried, and have them addressed openly, honestly and analytically.

This requires access to several schools and classrooms (apprenticeship is generally restricted to one or two), and, more important, very particular dispositions on the part of the teachers with whom the trainee works so that apprenticeship becomes what at best it can be: critical dialogue rather than uncritical imitation.

Neither reservation – about curriculum knowledge or about classroom skill – damages the general principle of school-based training; but together they imply the need for extreme caution for as long as the primary professional climate combines vulnerability and ideology to the extent identified here.

I have argued that both the ideology and the vulnerability can be shown to stem in part from the demands of the class-teacher system. The question now begged, therefore, is what kind of a teacher we should be training. For over a century the model was that of generalist, though certificate and B.Ed. students have always had specialisms to turn to the advantage of themselves and their colleagues. From 1984, the development of a specialism alongside the acquisition of generalist capacities became mandatory. The result of this requirement was that primary training courses – in contrast to their rather more leisurely secondary counterparts – became increasingly heavily timetabled as training institutions strove to cram in more and more subjects. By 1989 the requirement for all primary courses was the nine National Curriculum subjects, religious education, a specialism for consultancy purposes, a substantial element of school experience, and a lengthy list of general professional skills and issues (DES 1989h). The pressures became most acute in the one-year primary Post Graduate Certificate in Education (PGCE).

At the time of writing, CATE is debating ways of tackling this problem, and there are certainly ways that it can be alleviated, if not solved, particularly if the induction of new teachers is strengthened and systematized so that certain aspects of training can be postponed until that point or even later. However, to date the problem has been defined solely as one of the structure and content of training: we may now have to acknowledge that the main reason why it is becoming increasingly difficult to train someone adequately for the class-teacher role is that the role itself has become an impossible one to train for.

The end of the class-teacher system?

Much of the earlier discussion has touched on this issue, and cumulatively our general consideration of ways of improving primary education leads us inexorably to the question of whether a system of teaching introduced in the nineteenth century on the grounds of cheapness can sustain the demands of primary education in the 1990s.

To recapitulate: primary schools are still staffed on the same basis as their predecessors, the elementary schools – one teacher covering the whole curriculum with his/her class. Moreover, primary classes are substantially larger than secondary – in 1990 an average size, nationally, of 22 compared with the secondary average of 15.25 (DES 1991n) – and primary schools are much more modestly resourced. Thus, the age-weightings built into each LEA's LMS formula under the 1988 Education Reform Act produces a differential in one fairly typical LEA of £632 for a 7-year old, and £1,740 for an 18-year old; since the weightings only start to rise at age 11 this means that primary schools operate on a shoe-string budget by comparison with secondary. They have hardly any room for manoeuvre, and certainly little opportunity to deploy their staff as other than class teachers, except by increasing class sizes. It was the impact of enhancement on flexibility in staff deployment which caused us to argue strongly in the Leeds report that all primary schools should be staffed on the basis of *n* registration groups plus one extra.

This model, also endorsed in the 1986 Select Committee report (House of Commons 1986), introduces flexibility, but only up to a point. It is premised on the class-teacher system as the norm, with back-up provided by curriculum consultants. Each primary teacher, however, is expected to combine both roles, and therefore the issue of whether a generalist role is possible is evaded: it can be done, the thinking seems to go, with a bit of help.

As I have suggested above, the weight of evidence against this proposition now seems overwhelming. For as long as the curriculum was minimalist – give high priority to the basics, do what you can with the rest – the class-teacher system worked quite well. The consultancy idea was a useful patching device as the curriculum expanded. HMI were able to report its having considerable impact on whole-school planning and coordination, though its influence on individual teacher competence and the quality of curriculum delivery in the classroom was less evident. Yet for as long as the only statutory requirements in respect of the primary curriculum were the 1944 Act's distinction between the religious and secular curriculum (the latter being left to LEAs and schools), the issue could remain fudged, even though by then some were aware of how serious the problem had become (Alexander 1984).

At the same time, professional ideology, as we have seen, effectively deflected attention from the problem. The extreme child-centred position managed to deny the validity of curriculum altogether, while even somewhat more moderate teachers ruled questions of curriculum expertise out of order by denying the validity of subjects. Integration begged the question, which was rarely addressed, of precisely what was being integrated. The focus of attention was more on the environment of learning than learning itself, on how the child learned rather than what. Assessment concentrated on progress and endeavour in relation to the moving and singular criterion of individual progress, rather than on definable achievement in relation to objective criteria specified in advance.

The 1988 Act dramatically highlights the problem. The 'basics' have now become the three core subjects; primary teachers have to teach these, a further six foundation subjects, religious education, and a range of cross-curricular themes, skills and dimensions. We now have to confront, finally, the question of whether the class-teacher system can deliver all this. My own view is that it cannot.

The evidence is cumulative as well as recent. It is provided by the HMI surveys of the late 1970s and 1980s, by the studies of National Curriculum implementation, and by the succession of other research studies we have referred to throughout this volume, as well as by the Leeds study.

Some argue that the problem occurs only where older children are concerned (years five and six). The matter is not that simple. Though the problem becomes more acute the older the child, it does not suddenly materialize during the summer holidays at the end of year four – any more than under current arrangements it occurs in the six-week gap marking the transfer from primary to secondary school. This is an administrator's analysis, denying the less tidy reality, ignoring the fact that evidence shows the problem to occur earlier, and failing to acknowledge that all primary teachers, not just those working with older children, have to teach nine National Curriculum subjects.

To seek to solve the problem by introducing specialization for years five and six – let alone by reintroducing streaming, as has also been proposed – would be premature and ill-conceived. The issue is a large and complex one. The resources required are likely to be substantial. It is imperative that they are properly deployed and that they address the problem in its entirety.

In the first instance we need to broaden our repertoire of possibilities. There are four possible versions of the primary teacher role:

- the *generalist* who teaches a class full-time;
- the *generalist/consultant* who teaches a class full-time but also has a specialism for cross-school consultancy;
- the *semi-specialist* who divides his or her time between specialist and generalist teaching;
- the *specialist* who teaches his or her subject all the time.

Primary schools are currently staffed for the first of these, but HMI/DES pressure and the Secretary of State's teacher-training criteria since 1984 have shifted them to the second, though still within the logistical assumptions of the first. Because of this mismatch between model and resources, consultancy does not have the impact it could.

How far do we proceed along the road to specialization? As I have said, monolithic suggestions like confining specialization to the last two years of the primary phase should be treated with caution; so too should proposals that primary schools be run like preparatory schools. The truth of the matter is that some generalist class teachers are extremely effective across the board, while some specialists are extremely ineffective even within the one professed subject. It is naïve in the extreme to see full specialization as a panacea – were this the case, there would be no problems in secondary schools.

There are questions to be asked, therefore, about each of the roles postulated, and about their combination in a school. If the job of generalist is excessively demanding, is not that of generalist/consultant likely to be even more so? Assuming that one person can combine generalist and specialist teaching, what is the best way of deploying him or her so that both tasks can be undertaken effectively? If consultancy has greatest impact in the classroom, how far can the model of the generalist teacher with time freed to provide classroom-based support be realized? What combinations of the different roles seem most apposite for primary schools of different sizes and for children of different ages? If there are four possible primary teaching roles, does this mean that there should be four distinct patterns of primary teacher-training? What are the logistical and recruitment implications of introducing specialists and semi-specialists? How many extra teachers would be needed? Where would the money come from?

A NEW ENQUIRY INTO PRIMARY EDUCATION?

At the time of going to press, there are signs of the issue of specialist teaching being given serious attention by DES, HMI and ministers. This is extremely encouraging. However, I would hope that a 'quick fix' response can be avoided, for reasons I have indicated. This has the makings of a radical and far-reaching reform. If handled well it could not only improve the quality of teaching and learning in primary schools but also meet the goal set out near the start of this chapter – that of liberating primary education from the shackles of ideology and opening up new avenues for professional thinking, action and enquiry. Yet all we have so far is a sense that the generalist model of primary school staffing has reached its limits: the alternatives are neither clear nor proven. Certainly, it would be a grave mistake to replace one monolithic model by another. In my own mind is a scenario in which primary schools are staffed sufficiently generously in terms of numbers and kinds of expertise to allow them to make their own combination of generalist and specialist teaching, according to need and circumstances.

In view of the uncharted nature of the terrain, the professional dislocation any change will inevitably produce, and the heavy cost likely to be involved, it seems essential to base new staffing and related initial training models on a formally constituted enquiry. This need not be lengthy or costly, but it would need to gather evidence, examine research findings and devise and cost alternatives before coming up with recommendations. It would not seek to encompass primary education in its entirety, but would be limited to the single issue of primary school staffing. At the same time, such an enquiry would be bound to consider contingent issues like primary teacher-training and INSET, and would need to be premised on a coherent analysis of the nature of primary education in the 1990s and 2000s.

In other words, though I am not envisaging the comprehensiveness of Plowden, the argument that primary education is at a crossroads, with which this chapter started, is an argument about rather more than staffing alone. In as far as culture is an amalgam of ideas and structure, it is the very *idea* of primary education as much as its structure which is now being called into question.

Appendix: the evaluation – themes, evidence and methods

THEMES

We identified six themes for the evaluation:

- Children's needs: definition, identification, diagnosis and provision.
- The curriculum: content, development, management and evaluation.
- Teaching strategies and classroom practice.
- Links between home, school and community.
- Staff roles and relationships, and the management context of PNP schools.
- Professional support and development, with particular reference to the LEA.

The first four themes related to the main aims of the Primary Needs Programme; the remaining two themes covered contingent aspects of the work of schools and the LEA. Chapters 2–7 in this book deal with the six themes in turn, following the sequence above.

KINDS OF EVIDENCE

To explore the themes we accessed the LEA and its schools at a number of levels.

First, through *annual surveys* we gathered information and opinion from total populations, without sampling: heads, PNP appointees, non-PNP appointees, advisory staff, other groups. These surveys covered the levels and kinds of PNP resourcing, the uses to which they had been put, and the successes and problems involved.

Second, we constructed a *representative sample of thirty primary schools*, ten from each PNP phase, to provide depth and a longitudinal element. From these we extended and enriched the picture of change and development over time provided by the survey data, and we undertook phase comparisons of the impact of particular policies, strategies and kinds of resourcing. This part of the study we called *Fieldwork B*, and it included an extensive programme of interviews and observation. It covered all six evaluation themes.

Third, through what we termed *Fieldwork A*, we undertook interviews and observation in a further sixty primary schools, selected as exemplifying interesting or significant practice which had emerged as a consequence of PNP.

Some of these schools were self-selected, others were recommended by advisory staff, and the rest were identified from information gathered by the project team. Fieldwork A focused on specific themes from those listed above.

Fourth, bridging Fieldworks A and B we undertook our *Study of Classroom Practice* in sixty schools. This was undertaken at three levels, progressively more detailed and sustained. At the first level we interviewed a teacher and observed his or her classroom practice on a single occasion in each of forty schools. At the second level, undertaken in ten of the Fieldwork B schools, we undertook more detailed observation, interviewed the teacher both before and after the teaching sesssions observed, and interviewed the head. The large body of other evidence by then available from these particular schools enabled us to prepare ten case studies of teachers at work and the influences to which they were subjected. At the third level, in a further ten schools, we undertook an intensive programme of observation and interviews for a fortnight, using two observers to target both teachers and their pupils, and with the aid of radio microphones tape recording all the sessions observed for subsequent analysis.

All sixty of the schools involved in the classroom practice study had been the subject of considerable PNP investment – extra staff, extra capitation and, in some cases, refurbishment – and all the teachers observed and interviewed had attended the LEA's pivotal PNP course on classroom organization.

Fifth, we observed and/or interviewed participants involved in a wide range of *contingent roles and/or activities*: staff and participants on twenty-five LEA PNP in-service courses; home–school liaison meetings, advisory and support staff concerned with specific areas like gender, special educational needs, multi-cultural education, second-language learning, home–school, and so on; and some of the advisers, officers and elected members most centrally involved in the setting up and running of PNP.

Sixth, we collected and analysed a large quantity of documentary material both from schools and the LEA.

Finally, we collected and analysed all 7+ and 9+ reading scores, covering the total population of schools and children, for the period 1983–9.

METHODS

We used four main methods of data collection: questionnaires, interviews, observation, and existing documentary and test material. Details of these now follow.

Questionnaires

1 All Phase 1 Scale 1 Appointees, 1986.
2 All Phase 1 Probationers, 1986.
3 Phase 1 Postholders, 1986.

These three preliminary questionnaires covered (a) general aspects of the first year of PNP and (b) the first stage of the PNP INSET programme. Together with the 1986 coordinators' and heads' questionnaires (4 and 13), their purpose was to identify issues and starting points for the evaluation.

4   All Phase 1 Coordinators, 1986.
5   All Phase 1 Coordinators, 1987.
6   All Phase 1 Coordinators, 1988.
7   All Phase 1 Coordinators, 1989.
8   All Phase 2 Coordinators, 1987.
9   All Phase 2 Coordinators, 1988.
10 All Phase 2 Coordinators, 1989.
11 All Phase 3 Coordinators, 1988.
12 All Phase 3 Coordinators, 1989.

Coordinators' questionnaires covered job specifications, roles, changes in roles, successes, problems, influences, INSET, support and resources. Their range of questions from one year to the next was consistent so as to permit longitudinal analysis of change and development between 1985 and 1989.

13 All Phase 1 Heads, 1986.
14 All Phase 1 Heads, 1987.
15 All Phase 1 Heads, 1988.
16 All Phase 1 Heads, 1989.
17 All Phase 2 Heads, 1987.
18 All Phase 2 Heads, 1988.
19 All Phase 2 Heads, 1989.
20 All Phase 3 Heads, 1988.
21 All Phase 3 Heads, 1989.
22 Heads of middle schools fed by Phase 1 primary schools, 1989.
23 Heads of 11–16 secondary schools fed by Phase 1 primary schools, 1989.

The 1986–8 PNP heads' questionnaires covered PNP resources, their use and impact, successes, problems, LEA INSET and support, and year-by year changes. Their range of questions from one year to the next was consistent so as to permit longitudinal analysis of change and development between 1985 and 1989. The 1989 heads' questionnaire was much more comprehensive and detailed than those in the previous three years: it focused on the implementation and success of each of the PNP aims and strategies in turn. The survey of middle and 11–16 heads gathered views on the impact of PNP from staff in the schools to which Phase 1 children had transferred.

24 Members of the Authority's advisory and support staff, 1989.

The advisory and support staff questionnaires covered the roles, responsibilities and experiences of these staff within the LEA and its schools. It also reviewed the whole PNP initiative, seeking respondents' views on the Programme's impact in terms of the four PNP aims, and inviting them to identify examples of good practice in respect of each.

25 Participants at 25 LEA INSET courses formally monitored during 1986–9.

Taking all these questionnaires together, we find a variable response rate. Those distributed during school and INSET fieldwork achieved a high response (95–100 per cent). Postal questionnaires to all schools achieved, inevitably, a lower average response rate (65 per cent). Responses from the representative sample (Fieldwork B) schools were rather higher (90 per cent).

Interviews

In Fieldwork B schools

1 Preliminary interviews with all heads, 1987.
2 Preliminary interviews with all PNP coordinators, 1987.
3 Preliminary interviews with selected non-PNP staff, 1987.

These preliminary interviews covered in turn each of the six themes of needs, curriculum, teaching, home–school, management and professional development, and in relation to each of them explored policy, support, priorities, management and emerging issues.

4 Heads' interviews on needs definition, identification, diagnosis and provision, in respect of each of the LEA's categories of need, 1987.
5 Coordinators' interviews on needs definition, identification, diagnosis and provision, in respect of each of the LEA's categories of need, 1987.
6 Heads' interviews on curriculum policy and management, 1987.
7 Coordinators' interviews on curriculum policy and management, 1987.
8 Postholders' interviews on curriculum policy and management, 1987.
9 Heads' interviews, 1988 (follow up to 1987 interviews, 4).
10 Coordinators' interviews, 1988 (follow-up to 1987 interviews, 5).
11 Heads' interviews, 1989 (follow-up to 9).
12 Coordinators' interviews, 1989 (follow-up to 10).
13 Deputy heads' interviews on roles and responsibilities, 1988.
14 Pre-observation interviews with ten teachers as part of Level Two of the classroom practice study, 1988.
15 Post-observation interviews with ten teachers as part of Level Two of the classroom practice study, 1988.

In Fieldwork A schools

16 Heads' interviews on home–school links, 1987.
17 Heads' follow-up interviews on home–school links, 1989 and 1990.
18 Interviews with home–school liaison officers, 1987 and 1989.
19 Interviews with class and support teachers in selected schools for the 1987 TTT study.
20 Interviews with class and support teachers in selected schools for the 1989 TTT follow-up study.

21 Pre-observation interviews with forty teachers as part of Level One of the classroom practice study, 1988.
22 Post-observation interviews with forty teachers as part of Level One of the classroom practice study, 1988.
23 Pre-observation interviews with ten teachers as part of Level Two of the classroom practice study, 1988.
24 Post-observation interviews with ten teachers as part of Level Two of the classroom practice study, 1988.
25 Interviews with heads in the same schools as part of Level Two of the classroom practice study, 1988.
26 Initial interviews, at the start of the two-week observation period, with heads in the ten schools at Level Three of the classroom practice study, 1989.
27 Initial interviews, at the start of the two-week observation period, with class and support teachers in the ten schools at Level Three in the classroom practice study, 1989.
28 Daily pre-observation interviews with class teachers throughout the two-week period of the Level Three classroom practice study, 1989.
29 Daily post-observation interviews with class teachers throughout the two-week period of the Level Three classroom practice study, 1989.
30 Final interviews with support teachers at the end of the Level Three classroom practice study, 1989.
31 Final interviews with class teachers at the end of the Level Three classroom practice study, 1989.
32 Final interviews with heads at the end of the Level Three classroom practice study, 1989.

Other interviews

33 Providers of twenty-five LEA INSET courses, 1987-89.
34 Teachers attending twenty-five INSET courses, 1987-89.
35 LEA advisory and support staff, including staff concerned with special educational needs, gender, multicultural education, the Primary Schools Centre, home–school links, the PNP schools refurbishment programme, ERA implementation, National Curriculum support and LMS, 1986–90.
36 The Director of Primary Education, Director of Special Services and other key LEA staff concerned with PNP and related Authority policy, 1986–90.

Observation

1 Observation of TTT collaborations in Fieldwork B schools, using semi-structured schedule, 1987.
2 Observation of TTT collaborations in selected Fieldwork A schools, using semi-structured schedule, 1987.
3 Follow-up observations of TTT collaborations in selected Fieldwork A schools, using semi-structured schedule, 1989.

4 Observation of PNP coordinators at work in Fieldwork B schools, using semi-structured schedule, 1987–9.

5 Observation of twenty-five INSET courses, using semi-structured schedule, 1987–90.

6 Observation of curriculum meetings in Fieldwork B schools, using semi-structured schedule, 1988.

7 Observation of forty Fieldwork A classrooms, using a structured observation schedule and one observer, as part of Level One of the classroom practice study, 1988.

8 Observation of teachers and children at work in ten Fieldwork B classrooms, using a more comprehensive structured observation schedule and one observer, as part of Level Two of the classroom practice study, 1988.

9 Systematic observation of teachers in ten Fieldwork A classrooms as part of Level Three of the classroom practice study, 1989. Using the PRINDEP Teacher Observation Schedule one of a pair of observers noted aspects of teacher–pupil interaction and classroom organization during each of two daily observation sessions over a two-week period. The data were then coded and computer-analysed.

10 Systematic observation of pupils in ten Fieldwork A classrooms as part of Level Three of the classroom practice study, 1989. Using the PRINDEP Pupil Observation Schedule, the second of a pair of observers noted aspects of the task-related behaviour and interactions of sixty target pupils during each of two daily observation sessions over a two-week period. The data were then coded and computer-analysed.

11 At the same time as the systematic observations of teachers and pupils at 9 and 10, all teacher–pupil interactions during each observation session over the two-week observation period were recorded, using radio microphones, for later qualititative analysis.

Existing documentary and test material

1 All LEA policy documents relating to PNP, 1985–9.

2 LEA policy documents on primary education, 1985–91.

3 Other LEA policy documents, 1985–91.

4 Relevant minutes and papers of the Council's Education Committee, the Primary Needs Monitoring and Evaluation Committee, and the Special Programmes Steering Group, 1985–90.

5 DES Form 7 from every Leeds primary school, 1985–9.

6 Staffing data, gathered by PRINDEP, on Fieldwork B schools, 1985–9.

7 PNP Development Fund bids, 1985–9.

8 HMI reports on PNP schools, 1985–90.

9 7+ and 9+ reading scores, from all primary schools, 1983–9.

10 Supplementary LEA reading test score data, 1990–1.

11 Course material presented at twenty-five LEA INSET courses 1987–9.

12 Lists of all courses and teacher attendances at the Primary Schools Centre, 1985–9.

13 Miscellaneous Fieldwork B school policy documents and guidelines on aspects of the curriculum, classroom practice, home–school relations, meeting specific pupil needs, etc., 1985–9.
14 LEA job specifications for PNP appointees, 1985–9.
15 Fieldwork B school job specifications for PNP appointees and other staff, 1985–9.

Bibliography

Adelman, C.M. and Alexander, R.J. (1982) *The Self-Evaluating Institution*, London: Methuen.

Alexander, R.J. (1980) 'Towards a conceptual framework for school-focused INSET', *British Journal of Inservice Education* 6 (3).

——(1984) *Primary Teaching*, London: Cassell.

——(1988) 'Garden or jungle? Teacher development and informal primary education', in W.A.L. Blyth (ed.), *Informal Primary Education Today: Essays and Studies*, London: Falmer Press.

——(1989) 'Core subjects and autumn leaves: the National Curriculum and the languages of primary education', *Education 3–13*, 17 (1).

——(1991) *Primary Education in Leeds: Twelfth and Final Report from the Primary Needs Independent Evaluation Project*, Leeds: University of Leeds.

——, Broadhead, P., Driver, R.H., Hannaford, P., Hodgson, J. and Squires, A. (1990) 'Understanding our world: towards a framework for curriculum planning in the primary school', Leeds: University of Leeds.

——and Willcocks, J. (1992) *Sixty Primary Classrooms*, Leeds: University of Leeds.

——, Willocks, J. and Kinder, K.M. (1989) *Changing Primary Practice*, London: Falmer Press.

Audit Commission (1989a) *Losing an Empire, Finding a Role: The LEA of the Future*, Occasional Paper No. 10, London: HMSO.

——(1989b) *Assuring Quality in Education: The Role of Local Education Authority Inspectors and Advisers*, London: HMSO.

——(1991) *Management Within Primary Schools*, London: HMSO.

Bennett, S.N. (1976) *Teaching Styles and Pupil Progress*, London: Open Books.

——(1978) 'Recent research on teaching: a dream, a belief and a model', *British Journal of Educational Psychology* 48.

——(1987) 'The search for the effective primary teacher', in S. Delamont (ed.) *The Primary School Teacher*, London: Falmer Press.

——(1991) *Managing Learning in the Primary School*, Association for the Study of Primary Education.

——Desforges, C., Cockburn, A. and Wilkinson, B. (1984) *The Quality of Pupil Learning Experiences*, Hove: Lawrence Erlbaum.

Berlak, A. and Berlak, H. (1981) *Dilemmas of Schooling: Teaching and Social Change*, London: Methuen.

Blyth, W.A.L. (1965) *English Primary Education: A Sociological Description*, London: Routledge & Kegan Paul.

Board of Education (1931) *Report of the Consultative Committee on the Primary School* (Hadow Report), London: HMSO.

Campbell, R.J. (1985) *Developing the Primary School Curriculum*, London: Cassell.

——Evans, L., Neill, S.St.J. and Packwood, A. (1991) *Workloads, Achievement and Stress: Two Follow-Up Studies of Teacher Time in Key Stage 1 Commissioned by the Assistant Masters and Mistresses Association*, Warwick: University of Warwick Department of Education.

——and Neill, S.St.J. (1990) *Thirteen Hundred and Thirty Days: Final Report of a Pilot Study of Teacher Time in Key Stage 1 Commissioned by the Assistant Masters and Mistresses Association*, Warwick: University of Warwick Department of Education.

Cato, V. and Whetton, C. (1990) *An Enquiry into LEA Evidence on Standards of Reading of Seven Year Old Children*, Slough: NFER.

Central Advisory Council for Education (England) (CACE) (1967) *Children and their Primary Schools* (Plowden Report), London: HMSO.

Clare, J. (1991) 'A generation of wasted time', *Daily Telegraph* 19.9.91.

Clark, C.M. and Yinger, P.J. (1987) 'Teacher planning', in J. Calderhead (ed.), *Exploring Teachers' Thinking*, London: Cassell.

Clarke, K. (1991) Speech to the Annual General Meeting of the Headmasters' Conference, 17.9.91.

Cox, B. and Boyson, R. (1975) 'Letter to MPs and parents', in B. Cox and R. Boyson (eds) *The Fight for Education: Black Paper 1975*, London: J.M. Dent.

Cunningham, P. (1988) *Curriculum Change in the Primary School Since 1945: Dissemination of the Progressive Ideal*, London: Falmer Press.

Dearden, R.F. (1968) *The Philosophy of Primary Education*, London: Routledge.

——(1976) *Problems in Primary Education*, London: Routledge.

Delamont, S. (ed.) (1987) *The Primary School Teacher*, London: Falmer Press.

Department Of Education and Science (DES) (1972) *Educational Priority: Volume 1. EPA Problems and Practices*, London: HMSO.

——(1977) *Ten Good Schools: A Secondary School Enquiry*, London: HMSO.

——(1978a) *Special Educational Needs: Report of the Committee of Enquiry into the Education of Handicapped Children* (Warnock Report), London: HMSO.

——(1978b) *Primary Education in England: A Survey by HM Inspectors of Schools*, London: HMSO.

——(1982) *Education 5–9: An Illustrative Survey of 80 First Schools in England*, London: HMSO.

——(1983) *9–13 Middle Schools: An Illustrative Survey*, London: HMSO.

——(1985) *Education 8–12 in Combined and Middle Schools: An HMI Survey*, London: HMSO.

——(1987) *Primary Schools: Some Aspects of Good Practice*, London: HMSO.

——(1988a) *Report by HMI on a Survey of Parent–School Liaison in Primary and Secondary Schools Serving Ethnically Diverse Areas Within Three LEAs*, London: DES.

——(1988b) *Education Reform Act: Local Management of Schools*, (Circular 7/88), London: HMSO.

——(1989a) *Report by HM Inspectorate on a Survey of Support Services for Special Educational Needs*, London: DES.

——(1989b) *Mathematics in the National Curriculum*, London: HMSO.

——(1989c) *Science in the National Curriculum*, London: HMSO.

——(1989d) *Aspects of Primary Education: The Teaching and Learning of Science*, London: HMSO.

——(1989e) *Aspects of Primary Education: The Teaching and Learning of Mathematics*, London: HMSO.

——(1989f) *Aspects of Primary Education: The Teaching and Learning of History and Geography*, London: HMSO.

——(1989g) *Standards in Education 1987: The Annual Report of the Senior Chief Inspector Based on the Work of HMI in England*, London: DES.

——(1989h) *Initial Teacher Training: Approval of Courses* (Circular 24/89), London: DES.

——(1990a) *English in the National Curriculum (No. 2)*, London: HMSO.

——(1990b) *Technology in the National Curriculum*, London: HMSO.

——(1990c) *The Teaching and Learning of Reading in Primary Schools: A Report by HMI*, London: DES.

——(1990d) *Aspects of Primary Education; the Teaching and Learning of Language and Literacy*, London: HMSO.

——(1990e) *Standards in Education 1988–9: The Annual Report of HM Senior Chief Inspector of Schools*, London: DES.

——(1990f) *Developing School Management: The Way Forward. A Report by the School Management Task Force*, London: HMSO.

——(1991a) *Standards in Education 1989–90: The Annual Report of HM Senior Chief Inspector of Schools*, London: HMSO.

——(1991b) *History in the National Curriculum*, London: HMSO.

——(1991c) *Geography in the National Curriculum*, London: HMSO.

——(1991d) *Local Management of Schools: Further Guidance* (Circular 7/91), London: HMSO.

——(1991e) *Department of Education and Science News 142/91*, London: DES.

——(1991f) *Bishop Grosseteste College: A Report by HMI*, London: DES.

——(1991g) *National Curriculum Science: Draft Statutory Order*, London: DES.

——(1991h) *National Curriculum Mathematics: Draft Statutory Order*, London: DES.

——(1991i) *Education (National Curriculum) (Assessment Arrangements for English, Mathematics and Science) (Key Stage 1) Order 1991*, London: DES.

——(1991j) *The Parents' Charter: You and Your Child's Education*, London: DES.

——(1991k) *Art for Ages 5–14: Proposals of the Secretary of State*, London; HMSO.

——(1991l) *Music for Ages 5–14: Proposals of the Secretary of State*, London: HMSO.

——(1991m) *Physical Education for Ages 5–16: Proposals of the Secretary of State*, London: HMSO.

——(1991n) *Statistical Bulletin 9/91*, London: HMSO.

—— and Department of Health and Social Security (DES/DHSS) (1983) *Assessments and Statements of Special Needs* (Circular 1/83), London: HMSO.

Entwistle, H. (1970) *Child Centred Education*, London: Methuen.

Galton, M. (1989) *Teaching in the Primary School*, London: David Fulton.

——and Simon, B. (eds) (1980) *Progress and Performance in the Primary Classroom*, London: Routledge.

——, Simon, B. and Croll, P. (1980) *Inside the Primary Classroom*, London: Routledge.

Gipps, C., Gross, H. and Goldstein, H. (1987) *Warnock's Eighteen Per Cent: Children with Special Needs in Primary Schools*, London: Falmer Press.

House, E.R. (ed.) (1973) *School Evaluation: The Politics and Process*, Berkeley: McCutchan.

House of Commons (1986) *Achievement in Primary Schools: Third Report from the Education, Science and Arts Select Committee*, London: HMSO.

Inner London Education Authority (1985) *Improving Primary Schools: Report of the Committee on Primary Education*, London: ILEA.

Kelly, A.V. (1990) *The National Curriculum: A Critical Review*, London: Paul Chapman.

King, R.A. (1978) *All Things Bright and Beautiful: A Sociological Study of Infants' Classrooms*, Chichester: John Wiley.

——(1989) *The Best of Primary Education? A Sociological Study of Junior Middle Schools*, London: Falmer Press.

Lake, M. (1991) 'Surveying all the factors: reading research', *Language and Learning* 6.

Lawler, S.M. (1988) *The Education Support Grant (Urban Primary Schools) Leeds Project: Interim Report*, Leeds: Leeds City Council.

Leeds City Council (1984a) *Submission to the Department of Education and Science for a Grant Under ESG Scheme F: Improving the Quality of Education Provided in Primary Schools in Urban Areas*, Leeds: Leeds City Council.

—— (1984b) *Special Educational Needs: A Handbook for Schools*, Leeds: Leeds City Council.

——(1985a) *Primary Needs Programme* (Education Committee Document), Leeds: Leeds City Council.

——(1985b) *Leeds Inservice for Special Educational Needs: Course Manual*, Leeds: Leeds City Council.

——(1985c) *PNP Coordinator: Job Specification*, Leeds: Leeds City Council.

——(1986) *Primary Needs Programme: Equal Opportunities for Girls*, Leeds: Leeds City Council.

——(1987a) *Anti-Racist Education: A Policy Statement*, Leeds: Leeds City Council.

——(1987b) *Early Education Support Agency: A Letter to Headteachers*, Leeds: Leeds City Council.

——(1987c) *Guidelines for Headteachers in the Use of PNP Staff*, Leeds: Leeds City Council.

——(1988) *Primary Education: A Policy Statement*, Leeds: Leeds City Council.

——(1989a) *PNP Conference Report*, Leeds: Leeds City Council.

——(1989b) *Early Education Support Agency: Report 5*, Leeds: Leeds City Council.

——(1989c) *The Leeds Scheme for Local Management of Schools*, Leeds: Leeds City Council.

——(1989d) *A Quality Learning Environment: Display*, Leeds: Leeds City Council.

——(1989e) *The Primary School: A Guide for Parents*, Leeds: Leeds City Council.

——(1989f) *Equal Opportunities: Guidelines for Primary Schools*, Leeds: Leeds City Council.

——(1990a) *The Curriculum 5–16: A Statement of Policy*, Leeds: Leeds City Council.

——(1990b) *Assessment, Recording and Reporting: A Support File*, Leeds: Leeds City Council.

——(1990c) *A Survey of Year 1 Pupils in Leeds Primary Schools*, Leeds: Leeds City Council.

——(1990d) *Primary Detail: Design and Technology*, Leeds: Leeds City Council.

——(1991a) *Towards a Coherent Management Policy: Leeds LEA*, Leeds: Leeds City Council.

——(1991b) *School Development Plan 1991–2*, Leeds: Leeds City Council.

——(1991c) *Advisory Division Review and Structure*, Leeds: Leeds City Council.

Lynch, J. (1983) *The Multicultural Curriculum*, Batsford.

McMahon, A., Bolam, R., Abbott, R. and Holly, P. (1984) *Guidelines for Internal Review and Development in Schools: Primary Schools Handbook*, London: Longman/Schools Council.

Maltby, F. (1984) *Gifted Children and Teachers in Primary Schools 5–12*, London: Falmer Press.

Mortimore, P., Sammons, P., Stoll, L., Lewis, D. and Ecob, R., (1988) *School Matters: The Junior Years*, London: Open Books.

Nash, R. (1976) *Teacher Expectations and Pupil Learning*, London: Routledge.

National Curriculum Council (NCC) (1989) *Curriculum Guidance 1: A Framework for the Primary Curriculum*, York: NCC.

——(1991) *Report on Monitoring the Implementation of the National Curriculum Core Subjects 1989–90*, York: NCC.

Nias, J. (1989) *Primary Teachers Talking: A Study of Teaching as Work*, London: Routledge.

——, Southworth, G. and Yeomans, R. (1989) *Staff Relationships in the Primary School: A Study of Organizational Cultures*, London: Cassell.

Peters, R.S. (ed.) (1969) *Perspectives on Plowden*, London: Routledge.

Pollard, A. (1985) *The Social World of the Primary School*, London: Cassell.

Primary Needs Independent Evaluation Project (PRINDEP) (1986a) *Reactions to the PNP Inservice Support Programme* (PRINDEP Report 1), Leeds: University of Leeds.

——(1986b) *One Year Into PNP: The View from Phase 1 Schools* (PRINDEP Report 2), Leeds: University of Leeds.

——(1987a) *Home–School Links: First Findings* (PRINDEP Report 3), Leeds: University of Leeds.

——(1987b) *Teachers Teaching Together: Emerging Issues* (PRINDEP Report 4), Leeds: University of Leeds.

——(1987c) *The PNP Coordinator: Opportunities and Ambiguities* (PRINDEP Report 5), Leeds: University of Leeds.

——(1987d) *PNP INSET: A Closer Look* (PRINDEP Report 6), Leeds: University of Leeds.

——(1988a) *Children in Primary Schools: Defining and Meeting Needs* (PRINDEP Report 7), Leeds: University of Leeds.

——(1988b) *The PNP Curriculum: Policy and Management* (PRINDEP Report 8), Leeds: University of Leeds.

——(1988c) *Reading Standards in PNP Schools* (PRINDEP Report 9), Leeds: University of Leeds.

——(1989) *Changing Classroom Practice: Decisions and Dilemmas* (PRINDEP Report 10), Leeds: University of Leeds.

——(1990) *Teachers and Children in PNP Classrooms* (PRINDEP Report 11), Leeds: University of Leeds.

Rogers, C. and Kutnick, P. (eds) (1990) *The Social Psychology of the Primary School*, London: Routledge.

Rutter, M., Maughan, B., Mortimore, P. and Ouston, J. (1979) *Fifteen Thousand Hours: Secondary Schools and Their Effects on Children*, London: Open Books.

School Examinations and Assessment Council (SEAC) (1991) *School Assessment Folder*, London: SEAC.

Sharp, P. and Green, A. (1975) *Education and Social Control: A Study in Progressive Primary Education*, London: Routledge.

Shipman, M.D. (1990) *In Search of Learning: a New Approach to School Management*, Oxford: Blackwell.

Simon, B. (1981) 'The primary school revolution; myth or reality?', in B. Simon and J. Willcocks, (eds), *Research and Practice in the Primary Classroom*, London: Routledge.

Taylor, P.H. (1986) *Expertise and the Primary School Teacher*, Windsor: NFER-NELSON.

Tizard, B., Blatchford, P., Burke, J, Farquahar, C. and Plewis, I. (1988) *Young Children at School in the Inner City*, Hove: Lawrence Erlbaum.

Turner, M. (1990) *Sponsored Reading Failure*, Warlingham: Education Unit.

Wolfendale, S. (1987) *Primary Schools and Special Needs: Policy, Planning and Provision*, London: Cassell.

Wragg, E.C. and Bennett, S.N. (1990) *Leverhulme Primary Project Occasional Paper, Spring 1990*, Exeter: University of Exeter School of Education.

Index